W9-CCG-114

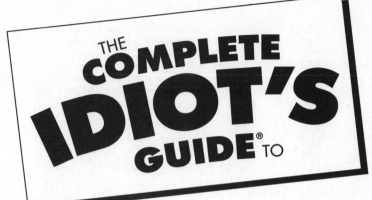

THE **COMPLETE** **IDIOT'S** **GUIDE®** TO

Getting Things Done

by Jeff Davidson, MBA, CMC

ALPHA

A member of Penguin Group (USA) Inc.

This book is dedicated to people I haven't cited before, who introduced critical thought, accomplished miraculous deeds, or simply made the world a better place—some of them known, some unknown, some close and some far, including Morgan Fox, Turner Walters, Lisa Kauffman, Ersell Lyles, Laura Hamilton, Jeff Stevens, Porter Witsell, M'Liss Dorrance, Carol Richards, Desiree Davism Jay Reeves, Dave Thaden, Michael Eisen, Ana Marie Chasseloup, Alison Porter, Ellen Pless Erb, Russell White, John Evans, Howard Schultz, Lynda Schultz, Jill Alexander, Lucas Hicks, Harold Taylor, Stacy Tetschner, Karis Wold, Ann Coulter, and whoever established the History Channel.

ALPHA BOOKS

Published by the Penguin Group

Penguin Group (USA) Inc., 375 Hudson Street, New York, New York 10014, U.S.A.

Penguin Group (Canada), 10 Alcorn Avenue, Toronto, Ontario, Canada M4V 3B2 (a division of Pearson Penguin Canada Inc.)

Penguin Books Ltd., 80 Strand, London WC2R 0RL, England

Penguin Ireland, 25 St Stephen's Green, Dublin 2, Ireland (a division of Penguin Books Ltd.)

Penguin Group (Australia), 250 Camberwell Road, Camberwell, Victoria 3124, Australia (a division of Pearson Australia Group Pty Ltd.)

Penguin Books India Pvt Ltd., 11 Community Centre, Panchsheel Park, New Delhi—110 017, India

Penguin Group (NZ), cnr Airborne and Rosedale Roads, Albany, Auckland 1310, New Zealand (a division of Pearson New Zealand Ltd.)

Penguin Books (South Africa) (Pty) Ltd., 24 Sturdee Avenue, Rosebank, Johannesburg 2196, South Africa

Penguin Books Ltd., Registered Offices: 80 Strand, London WC2R 0RL, England

Copyright © 2005 by Jeff Davidson

All rights reserved. No part of this book shall be reproduced, stored in a retrieval system, or transmitted by any means, electronic, mechanical, photocopying, recording, or otherwise, without written permission from the publisher. No patent liability is assumed with respect to the use of the information contained herein. Although every precaution has been taken in the preparation of this book, the publisher and author assume no responsibility for errors or omissions. Neither is any liability assumed for damages resulting from the use of information contained herein. For information, address Alpha Books, 800 East 96th Street, Indianapolis, IN 46240.

THE COMPLETE IDIOT'S GUIDE TO and Design are registered trademarks of Penguin Group (USA) Inc.

International Standard Book Number: 1-59257-421-1
Library of Congress Catalog Card Number: 2005930984

08   8 7 6 5 4

Interpretation of the printing code: The rightmost number of the first series of numbers is the year of the book's printing; the rightmost number of the second series of numbers is the number of the book's printing. For example, a printing code of 05-1 shows that the first printing occurred in 2005.

Printed in the United States of America

Note: This publication contains the opinions and ideas of its author. It is intended to provide helpful and informative material on the subject matter covered. It is sold with the understanding that the author and publisher are not engaged in rendering professional services in the book. If the reader requires personal assistance or advice, a competent professional should be consulted.

The author and publisher specifically disclaim any responsibility for any liability, loss, or risk, personal or otherwise, which is incurred as a consequence, directly or indirectly, of the use and application of any of the contents of this book.

Most Alpha books are available at special quantity discounts for bulk purchases for sales promotions, premiums, fundraising, or educational use. Special books, or book excerpts, can also be created to fit specific needs.

For details, write: Special Markets, Alpha Books, 375 Hudson Street, New York, NY 10014.

Publisher: *Marie Butler-Knight*
Editorial Director/Acquiring Editor: *Mike Sanders*
Senior Managing Editor: *Jennifer Bowles*
Development Editor: *Nancy D. Lewis*
Senior Production Editor: *Billy Fields*
Copy Editor: *Cari Luna*

Cartoonist: *Shannon Wheeler*
Cover/Book Designer: *Trina Wurst*
Indexer: *Tonya Heard*
Layout: *Ayanna Lacey*
Proofreading: *Donna Martin*

Contents at a Glance

Contents

Foreword

When Edwin Bliss first wrote his ground-breaking book, *Getting Things Done*, in 1976, the business world was relatively simple in comparison to today. Computers existed, but they were large, highly expensive, and required at least a Ph.D. in electrical engineering to operate.

The PC simply hadn't arrived and did not yet populate the desks of career professionals in the business world. Fax technology was available, but it was unwieldy, expensive, and used by few. The vast array of electronic devices that routinely adorn our desks, tabletops, cars, briefcases, pockets, and belts were not available. Information and communication was transmitted at a relatively slow and uniform pace. A person would catch the nightly news with Walter Cronkite, or Huntley & Brinkley, and feel reasonably satisfied with his understanding of the world.

Certainly people experienced office and work-related stress a generation ago. Even that was of a somewhat different nature, lesser in degree, and simpler to understand than the stress that plagues career professionals today.

Sometime between 1976 and today, the boundary that separated home and work began to blur. While the "man in the grey flannel suit" had always been taking work home, today the ability to get in touch with anyone, anywhere, at any time, has all but negated the notion of having a domestic sanctuary.

While Calvin Coolidge's insightful observation, "the business of America is business," was uttered in the 1920s, never was it more true than when the 1970s gave way to the 80s, that gave way to the 90s and today. Stand on a street corner, turn in any direction and the same relative scene appears: people walking hurriedly, with one ear adorned by a cell phone or an ear-piece, clutching a briefcase or folder, seeking to make their way along the same path as so many others at the same time.

Everyone wants to get things done, and in the long-term quest to do so, we adopt much of the same behavior, technology and equipment, many of the same techniques, and seemingly, the same mentality as everyone else. People strive to stay informed. They wire themselves so as to stay connected. They multi-task so as to be more efficient and concurrently they shortchange vital functions such as sleeping, resting, pausing, and reflecting.

Jeff Davidson will have none of that. In *The Complete Idiot's Guide to Getting Things Done*, from the first few chapters on, he lays down the proverbial law. Information and communication overload does not lead to greater clarity, understanding, depth, or focus. Multi-tasking is not all it's cracked up to be, hardly yields the intended benefits, and comes at too high of a mental, emotional, and physical cost.

Sleeping fewer hours than one's body requires does not indicate bravura and it does not make one more productive at work. It is utter foolishness. Similarly, shortchanging one's time to sleep, rest, pause, or reflect is prudent.

This is a book of amazing insight, laced with common sense, on top of proven techniques, adorned with fresh perspectives, with a touch of humor, all neatly interwoven with the style readers have come to know and enjoy in Jeff's books. You cannot help but become more productive after reading any section, chapter, or, indeed, any page of this book.

This is the seventh of his books in the *Complete Idiot's Guide* series, along with *The Complete Idiot's Guide to Managing Your Time*, *The Complete Idiot's Guide to Managing Stress*, *The Complete Idiot's Guide to Reaching Your Goals*, *The Complete Idiot's Guide to Managing Change*, *The Complete Idiot's Guide to Assertiveness*, and *The Complete Idiot's Guide to Reinventing Yourself*.

You picked up this book because there's a lot you want to get done, and time and resources are limited. Jeff respects that to the hilt and parcels out his meaty nuggets and vital insights in a highly enjoyable format. Speaking to you like a friend across the lunch table, Jeff offers the ins and outs of getting things done. He shares with you many of the habits and disciplines he's developed over the years on his way to 34 published books, translated in the aggregate 92 times, selected by 22 book clubs, with numerous reprints, revised editions, and conversion to other media.

The Complete Idiot's Guide to Getting Things Done represents the synthesis and the pinnacle of Jeff's business, career, and self-help–related advice. Read this book from cover to cover, or skip around between the chapters, and the benefits will accrue. Go to the index, find a key word, and approach the book on a topic-by-topic basis and the benefits will still accrue. *The Complete Idiot's Guide to Getting Things Done* is a book you'll want to hold on to, visit and revisit, discuss with your friends, give as gifts, and be glad that you happened upon it.

I am excited about the potential that this book holds for you, what you'll be able to get done, your long-term career outlook, and the quality of your life.

May yours be a wonderful journey.

Ronald L. Wagner
president, Citapei Communications

Introduction

Not too long ago, career professionals came to work, put in their 8 or 9 or 10 hours, left the workplace at the end of the day, and still managed to have a life. Before computers, cell phones and fax machines, the workplace, as well as society as a whole, resonated at a slower pace.

People worked hard. It took a sterling effort to rise to the top of the respective industry. Along the way, the populous seemed to be better off mentally and emotionally. The need to pop anxiety-relieving or stress-relieving pills was not so prevalent. The number of distractions in a given day was much less.

People remained in the same positions longer, worked with others familiar to them, reported to the same boss, perhaps even had the same parking space. The sameness in tasks and sequences of events that may seem kind of hum-drum today, nevertheless enabled the career professional of yesteryear to achieve some sense of balance, centeredness, and certainly identity.

Fast forward to today: living in the twenty-first century is overwhelming. We are tormented by the sheer number of tasks we face from the minute we begin our work day. Our careers are daunting, challenging, boring, repetitive, irritating, or, sometimes, overly exciting. There is a LOT of everything.

A study at Cornell University found that low-level noise both lowered job motivation and increased stress levels. It appears as well that an open-office type of environment can contribute to musculoskeletal problems such as a stiff back or tense neck and even heart disease due to increased levels of epinephrine, a stress hormone. In short, our environment inundates us and over-stimulates us. The result? We often feel overwhelmed and powerless.

You already know about the pressures you face at work, but what you may not realize is that nearly everyone is feeling the same way; we all seem to be people in a hurry. Is frantic any way to exist? Is it any way to run your career or your life?

The conditions we face have radically changed, even since the mid-1990s. Much of our day is consumed by activities that represent no more than "treading water," neither propelling us toward desired goals nor yielding any sense of balance.

We strive to pack more into each crevice of our already-overstuffed workday, aware that we will still be confronted with a new onslaught of stuff the next morning. There is always more to know and more to do. There is no end in sight. As such, *The Complete Idiot's Guide to Getting Things Done* addresses the all-embracing notion that you can complete most of what you want to get done at work and still stay sane.

Indeed, as the result of reading this book, it's my fond hope and entirely feasible that you'll be able to get more work done in a day. That, however, is gravy.

More likely, you will be able to do the same amount that you've been doing with greater ease and a greater peace of mind. Think of it, if you had a better sense of perspective and accomplishment of what you can and cannot do in a workday, wouldn't your days go better?

Once you understand the plethora of benefits that come with getting things done, versus the stress and anxiety that accrue with having things remain undone, you will more easily gravitate toward completions and avoid incompletions like the plague. May your days be cheery and bright and all your work days end before night.

How to Use This Book

To help you become a master at getting things done, I've broken this book into several large parts:

I believe that any book in this era of "getting things done" that does not first address the pervasive negative cultural developments and roadblocks to getting things done, impediments to information, and communication overload is not doing its job. In **Part 1, "The Challenge and Promise of Getting Things Done,"** we'll attack this and delve into issues related to getting organized, managing your time, and improving your efficiency … while becoming more effective.

Part 2, "Helpful Insights for Getting Things Done," contains three chapters, and each offers insights and perspectives to aid you on the path to getting things done. The first covers topics such as the importance of environment, why good ideas are like slippery fish, giving yourself the edge, and harnessing your passion. The next makes the bold assertion that whatever energizes you dramatically increases your ability to get things done, whereas whatever zaps your energy dramatically decreases your ability to get things done. The last discusses how what you do at home, and even how you arrive at work, can impact your ability to succeed.

Thus far, we've eased you into the get-it-done frame of mind. Now, in **Part 3, "Workplace Organizational Issues,"** come observations and suggestions that require a little more work on your part! To get things done, more often than not, you have to get your act together, and that means dealing with workplace organizational issues, including your desk, your office, the paperwork all around you, your computer, the web, and e-mail. All these arenas require some type of order so that you will be able to work comfortably, find things when you need them, and be in command of your resources.

Part 4, "Becoming More Efficient in the Workplace," contains four chapters that help you become more efficient in getting things done in both the short and long term, and in particular, stay in control on the bigger and more involved tasks and projects you face.

Part 5, "Efficiency Hazards and Sand Traps," can be summed up by the phrase "Thinking is the best way to travel." These chapters will guide you through the obstacles that block your path to getting more done.

In **Part 6, "Becoming More Effective at Work,"** we focus on how you can become more effective at work, which after all is one of the most important arenas of your life regarding getting things done. The four chapters included here are each compelling and illuminating.

The closing two chapters in **Part 7, "Keeping Your Career in Gear,"** provide you with the appropriate closure and inspiration you need to both finish the book and embark on that golden path to getting things done more easily.

Extras

Look for the little asides and comments I've added throughout the chapters to fill this book with the inside knowledge you need to succeed in getting things done.

Factoid _____
Useful, or at least interesting stuff, that embellishes your knowledge.

Word Power _____
Brief explanations of terminology for the employed.

Coming Undone _____
Pitfalls and sand traps to avoid while accomplishing more.

Dyna Moe

A hip career professional, who's been there, done that, and has some pithy insights worth considering.

Acknowledgments

Books don't write themselves. Non-fiction books in particular are a collaboration, first between author and acquisition editor, then between author and development editor, and finally between author and production editor. All the while, subject matter experts, interviewees, and authorities of all stripes play an important part in molding the perspectives and solutions an author has to offer.

As such, I would like to give a hearty thanks to Mike Sanders, my acquisition editor, who helped shape this book from top to bottom. I would also like to thank Nancy Lewis (development editor) and Billy Fields (senior production editor). A hearty thanks as well to all the other department heads and managers who make things hum. All are dedicated and highly competent employees of Alpha/Penguin who perform their magic under the watchful eye and guiding hand of Marie Butler-Knight, vice president and publisher, to whom ultimate praise must be accorded.

Thanks also to subject matter experts and authorities, past and present, including Earl Nightingale, Steve Allen, Mark McCormack, Aldous Huxley, Edwin Bliss, John Kenneth Galbraith, and Alfredo Pareto, and on a more contemporary footing, Robert Cialdini, Bert Decker, John Maxwell, Wayne McKinnon, David Lieberman, Paul Radde, Robert Fritz, Larry Rosen, Michelle Weil, Alvin Toffler, Rebecca Merrill, Bernie Seigal, Robert Fritz, Allen Lakein, Richard Chang, Deborah Benton, Soetsu Yanagi, Stephen Covey, David Meinz, and Robert Levasseur.

Thanks to Melissa Pinkerton for her lightning fast word-processing capability, editorial assistance, research, and copy editing, and to Cathryn Cummings for her assistance with final edits. Thanks to Valerie Davidson, age 15, for helping me to balance getting things done at work with having a life after work.

Trademarks

All terms mentioned in this book that are known to be or are suspected of being trademarks or service marks have been appropriately capitalized. Alpha Books and Penguin Group (USA) Inc. cannot attest to the accuracy of this information. Use of a term in this book should not be regarded as affecting the validity of any trademark or service mark.

Part 1 The Challenge and Promise of Getting Things Done

Modern man and his counterpart, modern woman, arguably face more challenges today than men and women of any previous generation. Unless one is a hermit in a cabin in Idaho, and even then, it's hard not to notice that society has gotten more complex. With that complexity comes a host of responsibilities and tasks for each of us. The two chapters in Part 1 lay the groundwork for the rest of the book.

Impediments to Getting Things Done at Work

In This Chapter

- ◆ Work distractions in all directions
- ◆ Information and communication overload
- ◆ More choices, more confusion
- ◆ Interruptions and productivity

Following World War II, and at least through the 1970s, it was widely held by time management specialists that the typical office worker earned a full day's pay for a 60 percent effort. In other words, over the course of an eight-hour workday, the typical worker actually performed job-related work for 60 percent of the time, or 4.8 hours.

The rest of the time, totaling 40 percent of the day, was frittered away on daydreams (most often thinking about sex), personal phone calls, coffee breaks, bathroom breaks, extraneous reading (not necessarily in the bathroom), and even crossword puzzles!

Some studies indicate that, despite all the demands and responsibilities they face, workers today still waste away a sizable chunk of most days. Concurrently, today's career professional faces more to do at work than his or her counterpart of, say, a generation ago. In this chapter, we will address the causes of information overload and the propagation of the human rat race.

Both Work Distractions and Productivity Are on the Rise

Without offering an involved and wearisome discussion about rising productivity levels, let me simply say that today's career professional, frittering and all, could beat the pants off of yesteryear's career professional in terms of getting things done. Today, workers in all types of organizations, including government, non-profit sector groups, health care, and education as well as private industry, devote a slightly higher percentage of their time to the tasks and responsibilities for which they actually were hired, and they have advanced tools that aid them in ways that the workforce ancestry could hardly imagine.

To be sure, intermittently many people goof off at the click of a mouse. Surveys show that non-job–related web-surfing and e-mail correspondence is rampant. Who doesn't make personal phone calls or attend to personal business during the workday?

Factoid

Surveys show that more than 60 percent of employers monitor employees' activities and at least 15 percent of employers observe employees via hidden camera.

Even with the latest diversions, most workers are making diligent efforts a decent percentage of the time. This may be because they're dedicated, goal-oriented, highly ethical, fearful of losing their jobs, or a combination of all the above. Or, it may be a result of improved workplace-monitoring techniques. An employer's ability to gauge actual performance levels of employees has never been greater than it is today. Local area networks rule. So do surveillance cameras. No fun.

In the typical office, before electric typewriters and certainly before PCs, getting 25 or 30 original business letters out the door in a day once represented an impressive achievement, all that an employer could expect from a worker in one day. Now, anyone, and I mean anyone, including some ten-year-olds, can generate 500 to 1,000 letters in a day if one chooses, and that wouldn't even be news. On any given day the aggregate of e-mails sent by individuals—and we're not talking about spam here—is 500 to 600 times greater than the entire aggregation of web pages accessible on the Internet.

The Unrelenting Information Generation

Enhanced communication technology spawns information overload. In 1905, the typical person generated only a tiny amount of information in his or her entire life. Whereas notable people wrote dozens and dozens of letters, the typical person wrote only a handful. Today, by some estimates, the written documents of career professionals account for 80 to 85 percent of all original documents.

One estimate holds that information doubles in the world every 72 days. The Library of Congress catalogues 7,000 additional items each day. More than 2,000 new websites go online each day. A minimum of two thousand books are published worldwide each day. In 1947, the first year *Books in Print* started collecting data, there were 85,000 titles in existence and 45 publishers listed. Fifty years later, there were almost 50,000 publishing houses in the United States alone.

Factoid

Researchers at the University of California at Berkeley in the Department of Information Sciences concluded that if the total amount of unique information annually generated in the world were to be parceled out to every man, woman, and child on earth, each person could be given a personal library equivalent to 250 books.

A few quotes and statistics shed revealing light on a pervasive challenge to getting things done these days: there is so much information available it often becomes a hindrance to productivity.

- The average business manager receives 190 messages per day. (Associated Press, May, 20, 1998)

- One third of managers are victims of "Information Fatigue Syndrome." 49 percent said they are unable to handle the vast amounts of information received. 33 percent of managers were suffering ill health as a direct result of information overload. 62 percent admitted their business and social relationships suffer. 66 percent reported tension with colleagues and diminished job satisfaction. 43 percent think that important decisions are delayed and their abilities to make decisions are affected as a result of having too much information. (Reuters's "Dying for Business" report)

- The web contains an estimated 3.2 billion pages of information. (NEC Research Institute, Princeton, NJ)

- A single super bookstore offers 150,000+ titles; stocks 2,500 domestic and foreign newspapers, periodicals, and magazines; and can order 200,000 more book titles from national distributors. The children's section includes 15,000 titles; the music section has 25,000 CDs and cassettes. (Barnes and Noble Booksellers)

◆ More information has been produced in the last 30 years than the previous 5,000. The total quantity of all printed material is doubling every five years, and accelerating. A weekday edition of any major newspaper contains more information than the seventeenth-century man or woman would have encountered in a lifetime. (Reuters Business Information)

◆ A typical computer-powered child's toy is approaching the computing power of yesterday's Cray Supercomputers.

◆ Analysis of e-mail traffic shows that spam as a percentage of total e-mail messages rose from 87 percent in January 2004 to 93 percent in January 2005. (Yahoo)

◆ By some estimates, the data-storage curve is rocketing upward at the rate of 800 percent per year. Organizations are collecting so much data they're overwhelmed. Families are no different; we have more things on disk, more photos, more items stored than we'll ever have to allocate time for. "Since Kodachrome made way for jpeg, pictures accumulate on hard drives like wet leaves in a gutter." (Jim Lewis, author of *The King Is Dead*)

◆ Largest U.S. Libraries: U.S. Library of Congress: 23,994,965 volumes; Harvard: 14,857,415; New York Public: 11,445,971; Yale: 9,932,080; Queens Public Library: 9,237,300; University of Illinois: 9,024,248. (*American Libraries* magazine)

Factoid

British author and psychologist David Lewis, Ph.D., says that "having too much information can be as dangerous as having too little. It can lead to a paralysis of analysis, making it harder to find the right solutions or make decisions."

No matter how competent, adept, organized, or clever one may otherwise be, virtually all career professionals today find themselves in a daily tidal wave of information, the likes of which are unprecedented in the history of the human race. And the unvoiced expectation is that you're supposed to be able to handle it all.

More Choices, More Complexity

Your everyday supermarket now carries roughly 40,000 items—twice as many as a decade ago. There are so many products, so many brands and sub-species of those brands, that no consumer is safe from the bombardment of choice overload.

A huge variety of product offering doesn't aid consumers. It is insanity. From the vast array of athletic shoes to bagels to portable CD players to bottled water, there quickly becomes a point at which mega-choices, like mega-information, do not serve the consumer; they abuse him.

It seems everywhere you turn, people seek to complicate things. Many of the devices that we buy could serve us simply, but do they? From TVs to answering machines to cell phones to copiers and everything in between, are our electronic gadgets getting easier to use? Where is the long-promised plug-in-and-play computer?

At the center of this information, communication, and technology glut, unquestionably, is the almighty microchip that plugs into the all-pervasive personal computer. Since 1971, when Intel invented the microprocessor, computers' labor-saving benefits have been widely touted. Computers provide us with the ability to accomplish a great deal of work in a relatively short amount of time, be it research, number crunching, document preparation, or communication.

While computers have contributed to productivity increases unlike any device that came before them, people everywhere continue to wrestle with how to use computers to their best advantage.

Computers thwart, contort, and befuddle us. We mess around with fonts, change screen backgrounds, slow down or increase mouse speed. We tweak and we piddle. We spend countless hours preparing PowerPoint slides that most people forget in seconds. We generate reports in duplicate and triplicate and then some that end up serving only one function for most of the recipients—to collect dust.

We sit in front of our keyboards and try to take control of our little corner of the world. We communicate with staff, impress our bosses, and do our best to stay on top of things, but at the same time, we visit our favorite blogs, comparison shop online, and pass jokes back and forth—not the essence of getting things done.

Management, with alarming irregularity, wants to know what we're typing, what we're looking at, with whom we're communicating, and what we're passing back and forth. The temptation that a PC in general, and the Internet in particular, provides can lure even the most diligent, loyal, and hardworking among us. Who has not strayed during the course of the day, sometimes for prolonged periods?

Who has not taken chunks of time here and there away from their employer, proceeding all the while as if no one will know the difference? Though the word is rarely used, such forays are actually a form of theft. You can rationalize your escapes as long as you get the job done, i.e., who cares if you take a couple of minutes here and there for your own interests? Besides, you're not on the clock, you're a salaried or commission-based employee. Still, if the tables were turned, you'd probably feel that you had a right to know when your employees were actually working versus not.

Hopefully, desirably, thankfully, you're not among the lot who strays for large blocks of time throughout the day. You have the ability to self-regulate. You recognize that we live in an information-overloaded society with too many websites, publications, and electronic media bidding for your attention.

Hacking Your Way Through an Information and Communication Jungle

You buck up and decide to get lean and mean. You're gonna hack your way through the tangle of information and communication overload. You strip away anything that smells of excess or encroaches upon your ability to stay on the straight and narrow path to high productivity.

> **CAUTION**
> **Coming Undone**
> When your brain is always engaged, when your neurons are always firing, when you find yourself in a continual mode of reacting and responding, instead of steering and directing, the best and brightest solutions that you are capable of producing rarely see the light of day.

You reflexively speed up your routine so that you can get through the day's deluge of e-mails, open the mail and address it, handle the memos, tend to the faxes, return the phone calls, and still come up smiling.

In deftly speeding through all that comes your way, however, a new kind of problem arises. In your quest to get one thing done after another, your creativity, spontaneity, and *joie de vive* diminish.

A No-Win Dilemma: To Accomplish More or To Have a Life?

You're firmly caught in a trap without realizing that you are. Like everyone else, you're adopting the same survival mechanisms, galloping along on the same treadmill, and defaulting into the same operational cycles.

If new insights or fresh perspectives spring forth, will you, can you, actually act upon them? Do you have any chance of thinking new thoughts or are you simply generating permeations of all your previous thoughts?

Since the 1980s, Attention Deficit Disorder (ADD) has been on the rise, not just among children, but now among the adult population as well.

The sudden rise of adult ADD, while it may have genetic components, certainly receives a major boost from our kinetic, hyper-speed, information-bombarded society. Victims of adult ADD are likely to initiate more tasks and projects than they'll ever finish, get bored easily, seek thrills readily, have a propensity to be late while loathing having to wait, and not be averse to taking foolish risks.

The typical fall fashion magazine compels readers to flip through 128 pages before finding the first feature article. In 1965, the typical news sound bite lasted 45 seconds. By the year 2,000 it had dropped to 8 seconds. Ad clutter has increased annually since 1985 and has now exceeded the overwhelming level for many viewers.

While the typical TV advertisement was 53 seconds in 1965, by 2000 it had dropped to 25 seconds with 15-second ads as well as 3-second ads peppering viewers at every turn. In 2002, every hour of daytime network TV offered nearly 21 minutes of commercials, up from 10 to 12 minutes decades before. Some cable networks feature 60 seconds of ads for every 140 seconds of programming, in other words, 30 percent of the total broadcast.

There is competition for every single moment you have to spare and for those you don't have to spare.

Never an Extra Moment

The "brave new world" is here. When you don't have, or feel you don't have, an extra moment to read philosophy, history, or science, when great literature, plays, and novels are as foreign to you as hieroglyphics, do you have any chance of seeing your work, career, or life in a new light? You might be doing well in the race, but it's the same race essentially down the same track with the same opponents that may prove to be less than sufficient in enabling you to get those kinds of things done that you want to have completed.

Even if you're among the rare few who recognize how crucial safeguarding your day and work time has become, the chances are highly likely that you are not immune to the call of the modern day sirens—the cell phones, pagers, and beepers.

> **CAUTION** **Coming Undone**
>
> "People never are alone now. ... We make them hate solitude, and we arrange their lives so that it's almost impossible for them ever to have it." —
> Aldous Huxley, *Brave New World* (Doubleday, 1932)

The All-Time Intruder

The results are in and the cell phone has become the most disruptive aspect of work and everyday life. With more than four fifths of the population sporting these little gadgets, it's now taken as a given that *any part of your day is subject to disruption.*

On a plane, in a meeting, during a presentation, at a business lunch, or yes, in the restroom, some probably well-meaning but otherwise totally boorish soul will whip out his cell phone and engage in public space cell yell. And the conversations, my goodness, are they inane. If everyone uses a cell phone in the restroom or a lunch or during a meeting and uses it at will, how long will it take before we all go mad?

I would be utterly embarrassed to have others around me hear my half of what can only be described as pedestrian. "Yes, the elevator has just pulled up to the 16th floor." Do these people have the ability to go, for say, an eight- or ten-minute stretch without being in contact with someone else? What are they afraid of? Confronting their own thoughts?

Factoid

The 2003 annual Lemelson-MIT invention index survey found that when asked to name the invention they hate the most but can't live without, 30 percent of respondents said the cell phone. Second to the cell phone were alarm clocks at 25 percent, followed by television at 23 percent, and razors at 14 percent.

It's not that you can't get things done with the use of a cell phone; indeed you can get a lot of things done. However, the nature of what you get done is highly skewed. Just as the man with only a hammer sees everything as nails, the incessant cell phone user accomplishes a variety of tasks, understandably enough, that accrue directly to having a cell phone.

Coming Undone

What kinds of new tasks and new responsibilities at work are you creating for yourself and others as a result of the constant communication and, need I say it, over-communication?

Sometimes this get-it-done kind of individual over-does this stay-in-touch aspect of what he's trying to accomplish. I mean, how many times can you call a client? How often *do* you need to stay in touch with your office? Would every 60 minutes do it, or would 45 minutes be better, or 30 better still?

Too many career professionals—gung-ho, get-ahead career types—are uncomfortable with solitude. Increasingly, this discomfort tolerates only shorter and shorter attention spans. To retreat into one's own mind, to pause, to reflect is now treated as if it were enemy territory.

As the world wide web and interactive media begin to purvey our lives at even higher levels than they do now through the myriad handheld and miniature devices as well as publicly pervasive audio/video displays, any career professional who wants a quiet, reflective moment is going to have to fight for it.

Work Distractions Feed Upon Themselves

Weirdly, oddly, sadly, the higher the level of distraction, as with information overload, the greater we tend to seek it. You can get things done with electronic gadgetry, but beware, the types of things you get done will be of a certain ilk. Whole other realms of accomplishments may be unknown or out of reach for you.

It is vital to regain or perhaps develop for the first time the ability to take quiet reflection. In doing so, at first you will feel as if you've been left out of the party, but was it a party you wanted to attend in the first place? And even if you wanted to attend, did you want to attend all the time at that decibel level with no breaks?

Long-term types of accomplishment, grand achievements in your career—the big stuff—may require going where you haven't gone before, to that place and frame of mind where the best of your thoughts can emerge. Soetsu Yanagi, in the *Unknown Craftsman*, writes, "Man is most free when his tools are proportionate to his needs." For example, for optimal productivity, a carpenter needs woodworking tools and an environment conducive to his work, not a steam shovel or army tank.

When you learn to value quiet reflection over frenetic activity, the breadth and scope of what you can get done improves remarkably. Silence can be golden, but only if you respect it, know how to harness it, and recognize the gift that it has always provided.

Let's turn now to Chapter 2 to see what the notion of getting things done is all about.

The Least You Need to Know

- Information and communication overload is among the most insidious obstacles to getting things done.
- Once taken off one task without completing the transaction, the mind continues to seek closure. Fight to stay focused on the task at hand.
- When your brain is always engaged, your best and brightest solutions are not likely to emerge.

◆ Over-communication at work can create a new level of tasks and responsibilities.

◆ Long-term types of accomplishment often require a frame of mind where the best of your thoughts can emerge.

The Four Components of Getting Things Done

In This Chapter

- ◆ Oh, to be organized
- ◆ An inside time management secret
- ◆ Efficiency matters
- ◆ Effectiveness is critical

Long before the era of information and communication overload, and long after it, people looked for and will continue to look for ways to get things done. Getting things done, however, can mean different things to different people. The terminology, to put it mildly, is nebulous. As used throughout this book, getting things done will refer to *one's ability to draw upon four components for success* at work including: becoming organized, managing your time better, improving efficiency, and increasing effectiveness.

This chapter will examine each of these components in detail so that you have a firm understanding and foundation of this concept of "getting things done."

Becoming Organized

The phrase "to get organized" as in "I've *got* to get organized!" serves as a rallying cry for some and invokes dread in others. The legions of career professionals whom I've met at more than 750 speeches I've given and more than 250 companies I've consulted for, seem to fall into one of two camps. They either:

1. Embrace getting and remaining organized and have reasonable skills in doing so, or

2. Are not good at getting and remaining organized and even if they have the skills, nobody can figure out when they're using them.

It's vital to acknowledge that there's no moral judgment attached to "getting organized." If you're perpetually disorganized, you're still a good person, unless of course, you forget to feed the cat, and then you're an ogre. Some of the greatest geniuses throughout history have had relatively poor organizational skills and most were not considered ogres. Being organized in and of itself doesn't necessarily add up to a hill of beans in terms of getting specific things done.

More often than not, however, those who are proficient at getting things done also have organizational skills. Think of a political campaign where there is little coordination, construction of a new building where work schedules are unpredictable, or a hospital where the admitting procedure is unstructured. That candidate will lose, the bridge will be over-budget (if ever finished), and the hospital admittance office … well, don't go there; literally.

On a personal level, disorganization can cost one time, money, and even respect of one's peers (who might have otherwise been willing to be of assistance). If personal organization has been a continuing problem, perhaps what I offer here will make a huge difference in your career.

Organizing Is Fundamental

You wouldn't drive your car and expect to cruise for 300 miles on a few gallons of gas in your tank. Likewise, your range of professional capabilities will be limited if you're low on one of the key components that keeps your getting-things-done vehicle operating smoothly. It's time to view organizing as a fundamental component to getting things done.

Generally, people aren't born with organizing skills; they are acquired along the way. When you seek to become organized, do you quit after a short time, believing it's hopeless? The key to getting and staying organized is making the effort. For many, it is a minor relief to learn how long it will take. It depends on how long your work space has been disorganized, but for most career professionals, allocating the equivalent of three full weekends should suffice.

> **Dyna Moe**
>
> Getting organized requires effort and thought, while saving time and offering peace of mind. The minor paradox is that you spend time to save time. If it's helpful, think of getting organized as preparation to respond to challenges.

Being neat and being organized are not the same thing. Not everything needs to be in its place as long as you know where items are and can access them freely. Why do some people shun getting organized? For whatever reason, they approach it with fear and trepidation. Like natives who believe that a photograph of them captures their soul, some people proceed as if getting organized will strip them of their inner essence. They become anxious about doing nothing but getting organized.

Many traps to getting started may await even when you know it makes sense to "clean house." Here are some major excuses for failing to get started:

1. "I have been meaning to." If this proves to be a familiar self-lament, then make getting personally and completely organized a high-ranking item in your life.

2. "I have never been good at organizing." Okay, no matter, all is forgiven! The difference between people "who are good at organizing" and "not good" is that organized individuals understand the level of effort required to maintain the organization. Those who are "not so good" at organizing believe that items somehow "get out of order" or "get lost."

3. "I don't know how to get started." Keep reading.

4. "I have so many other things to do." Of course, you do; you will for the rest of your career. After becoming organized, the other things "you have to do" will more directly support what you want to get done and you'll have a clearer understanding that they do.

5. "Organizing will take too much time." Initially, it takes the equivalent of about three weekends. Also, consider how much time disorganization has cost you.

6. "I don't see any value in organizing." Many aspects of your career are already organized. Now you're going to extend the procedures to enhance your ability to get things done.

7. "It makes me anxious; I don't feel that I am accomplishing that much." Tossing unnecessary files and papers to create more space in itself can accomplish a great deal.

Sometimes, people use getting organized as a stalling technique, but in general, being organized greatly enhances your ability to manage your time thereafter.

Don't Equate Organizing Time with Wasted Time

Sometimes it seems as if the energy and effort you expend in getting organized will be a waste. After all, if you're already feeling behind and have much to accomplish, wouldn't good time management necessitate simply jumping in and handling those things that beg for your attention? Not exactly …. Often, you have to slow down in order to speed up.

By slowing down, you give yourself a chance to collect your thoughts, form a more coherent plan, perhaps take a deep breath or get a glass of water, and then tackle the project anew.

Knowing where items are located on a file or disk puts you in charge, and provides freedom to concentrate on creative, fulfilling, or necessary tasks and not the clutter that surrounds you. Part 2 of this book offers many tips on getting organized.

Managing Your Time

Managing your time better at work is the second of four components that contribute to your ability to getting things done. You've read a lot about time management before you ever picked up this book. The great secret to time management, and perhaps you were the last on your block to be told, is that to speed up—operate at a productive pace and get a lot of the things done—often you first need to simply slow down and take a look at how to best proceed.

Minutes Add Up to Years

Have you ever considered how much time you have in your whole life, and how much time you've spent on various activities?

Suppose you graduated from college at the age of 22, and in the course of your life expect to work about 48 years, bringing you to age 70. In a 48-year career, on any

given day, too often it seems we don't value or perhaps recognize how small amounts of time add up. Hence, we do not sufficiently value our time. As I explain in *The Complete Idiot's Guide to Managing Your Time*, any activity in which you engage for only 30 minutes a day in the course of your 48-year productive work life will take one solid year of your life!

Dyna Moe

In this world, minutes and even seconds count. Money is not the key currency of life anymore, it's time.

If you read junk mail, on average, for 30 minutes a day, then in the course of 48 years you've spent the equivalent of one solid year, nonstop, reading junk mail. What a waste that would feel like!

The time in your career is being drained by frivolous activity; the cumulative impact of engaging in meaningless minutia is monumental; your precious years are being consumed. This is time the universe will not hand back to you.

What things do you know you need to stop doing because they are taking up valuable time in your life? Here are some suggestions:

♦ Reading junk mail because it's addressed to you. Reading unsolicited e-mail messages, jokes, and crazy schemes zapped over to you.

♦ Allowing drop-in visitors with no useful agenda.

♦ Handling tasks that should be delegated or outsourced.

♦ Not saying "no."

Plaguing Time Wasters

The top time wasters for career professionals on a daily, weekly, and monthly basis, year after year, change little. Lack of direction, shifting objectives, and inadequate planning that leads to crisis management is certainly high on the list. Equally troubling these days, as we've discussed, is the frequency of interruptions via the telephone, cell phone, pager, beeper, and other electronic gadgetry. As one person commented to me, "I can't tell you how often I've had a conversation interrupted because someone's Blackberry had buzzed with an incoming e-mail, which the person then stopped our conversation in order to reply to. People seem compelled to be reachable at all times."

Some people are plagued with the inability to say "no" and otherwise show lack of discipline in approaching vital tasks that they wish to get done. Certainly the lack of organization has manifested in cluttered desks and cabinets, in piles growing around the room, and misplaced items.

Some people are ineffective in delegating and are steeped in the "Promethean" urge to take care of everything by themselves. Attempting to tackle a great deal may be admirable, but seeking to do too much all the time is simply foolish. It leads to more errors, frustration, and the inappropriate allocation of resources. Fortunately for you, prudent time management principles are presented throughout this book.

The Difference Between Efficiency and Effectiveness

Let's focus on the other components of getting things done: improving *efficiency* and becoming more *effective*. First, we need to differentiate between the two.

Word Power

Think of **efficiency** as taking the right approach to a job, doing it quickly with few or no errors, generating results with little or no wasted effort. **Effectiveness** by contrast, means undertaking the right task, with the goal of producing a desired, worthwhile effect.

Efficiency and effectiveness are terms that are often misunderstood. Some people think that they are synonymous, and freely substitute one for the other. Actually, they represent two different concepts which work best in concert with each other.

If you run an automated car wash business, on any given day, you want to send as many cars through the wash tunnel as practical (efficient). At the same time, each car's exterior needs to be completely, expertly washed (effective).

It would be of no advantage to have a process that offers a complete wash so slowly that you only handle a few cars a day (inefficient). Likewise, it would be deleterious to long-term business to have the fastest car wash in town, but the cars aren't washed that well (ineffective). In this case, efficiency and effectiveness, as so often is the case, are intertwined.

Improving Your Efficiency

So, a quick review: efficiency can be described as doing a job correctly, and effectiveness can be described as performing the right job. Efficiency is the measure of productivity, how swiftly you can accomplish something.

The following is a list of efficiency-related activities:

◆ Establish a routine of departing the house easily in the morning.

◆ Set out your clothes, work materials, or briefcase the night before.

◆ Respond to overnight communications (phone messages, faxes, and e-mails) before mid-morning.

◆ Be professional but succinct on the phone.

◆ Type e-mail responses correctly on the first try by being clear and concise.

◆ Minimize break time, but make breaks effective. Don't lose productivity when a co-worker happens to drops by. Instead, stop at a natural breaking point, such as when work is completed.

◆ Use spare time during the day to complete smaller tasks.

◆ Bring a bag lunch and eat at your desk, but recognize that sometimes you need to get away to be refreshed.

◆ Handle tasks in a circular route; for example, from your starting point, plan your route so as to not backtrack.

◆ Delay tasks that can wait, for example, instead of tackling any project as soon as it crosses your desk, defer less vital ones to a later date, yet allow enough time to be thorough.

◆ Update files as a part of a daily routine; for example, get rid of notes and papers that are no longer germane to your current projects.

◆ Assemble meeting notes and conduct or attend meetings on time.

◆ Stick to daily agendas as closely as possible.

◆ Straighten up after completing a task instead of letting things pile up.

◆ Maintain flagging energy in the late afternoon by having a mid-afternoon snack or by consciously tackling more taxing tasks before lunch.

◆ Finish up as many things as possible before departing for the day.

◆ Exercise right after work, before you go home and you find it more difficult to leave the couch.

Effectiveness Is Mandatory

In the quest to get things done, many career professionals are able to display high levels of efficiency in dispatching this task and that; however, the more compelling issue is whether they are even embarking on the right task. Are they tackling that task or project to which it makes the most sense to be devoting their time and attention?

On a daily basis, recognize that with any type of activity, while efficiency is desirable and admirable, effectiveness is mandatory. Unfortunately, the present-day workplace, as it has evolved, often conveys that motion and activity are more important than closure and results. As a result, you see people dashing about like chickens about to lose their heads.

Those who develop a solid reputation for getting things done, particularly those who aspire to leadership, learn how to master the nuances. They understand that it's one thing to produce, say a new software program, debug it, and ship it out the door to users, and another thing for the software to be effective in the market.

To become a get-it-done type of career professional, make the commitment to perform your work efficiently while supporting the overarching quest to attain objectives effectively. Shield yourself from information and communication overload, and focus on results.

When Pure Efficiency Equals Effectiveness

Oddly, efficiency in itself sometimes is all that's needed for effectiveness. For many years, I heard the stories about Chamra Tasmala (name changed to protect the fabulously wealthy), one of my neighbors in Chapel Hill. She allegedly was a superstar real estate agent. I read that she had won an award for selling or renting $18 million worth of commercial property over so many years. My quick calculation showed that she was raking in more than $400,000 annually.

As time passed, I was considering relocating my office. I called Chamra, who identified several properties that potentially met my criteria. I was eager to visit sites with Chamra because I was interested to see what she had found for me and to witness firsthand a legendary real estate agent in action.

Chamra was presentable, neither striking nor decrepit. She exuded some measure of success—nice car, no flashy jewelry, and the minimum trappings of fashion. I thought she must have a highly engaging interactive style; perhaps her honed and refined persuasive skills coupled with direct eye contact were enough to make anyone think she had found you the location that smartly suited your needs.

To my amazement, she didn't come close to impressing me with her interpersonal or selling skills. Her style consisted of opening the door, showing me around, and saying, "Here's the reception area, here's the bathroom, here's the kitchenette. Well, what do you think?" I kept saying to myself, "There's got to be more to her than this."

Where were the keen insights? The witticisms? The extra touches? The connection with my business dreams? All were glaringly absent. She didn't possess any special skills. She never called me by name. I felt I was with a first-time agent who was unprepared and in a hurry to boot. Her efforts seemed bare-bones.

I soon realized that she had mastered the critical issue in her industry, which was to find many prospects to whom she could show many properties. In essence, she played the numbers game and she played it well. I thought of all those agents, not merely in real estate but also in many other businesses, who earn their living by generating prospects, selling them a product, and earning a commission.

I also thought of all the books, articles, and everything else that's been written on "what you need to know and do" to be successful in such a business. Now, in the span of but a few minutes, Chamra's approach to real estate thoroughly trivialized the importance of these criteria.

As a top commercial real estate agent she was living proof that traditional success advice wasn't necessarily essential for success. I began to understand that the essence of success in most industries is misunderstood by most. All the guidance given by all the *schlockmeisters* is hardly necessary.

Word Power

A **schlockmeister** is a slang term which refers to people who have all sorts of advice to give, some of it questionable, on all sorts of topics.

Efficiency Alone Is Often Insufficient

- Focusing on a few critical elements made all the difference for Chamra. Simply being efficient, in and of itself, usually does not add up to effectiveness.

- In a manufacturing concern, a product manager may be predisposed to ship a volume of products (efficiency) while a marketing manager is concerned with how customers rate the product (effectiveness).

- A human resources manager may be attuned to how well people are fulfilling the roles for which they were hired (effectiveness), while a shift supervisor is more concerned with not exceeding his quarter budget for labor (efficiency).

You might be highly proficient at knocking off one task after another on your to-do list. When you focus more on effectiveness, plowing through your list takes a backseat to strategizing how to best handle the items on the list. Some items, perhaps, can be delegated. Something else might be deferred. Two items might be combined, and so on.

If you're in sales and you're making calls on prospects daily, being efficient would entail calling on as many as you can. Being effective would mean concentrating more time and energy on higher potential prospects and probing for their underlying objectives.

> **Coming Undone**
>
> It's possible to be efficient to the point of losing effectiveness, i.e., win the battle but lose the war. An efficient person is predisposed to staying busy, while the effective person keeps the desired ends in mind.

Some professionals proceed as if they can handle everything as long as they stay focused. This is embodied by the sales manager who wants to increase his department's quarterly volume by 12 percent, inspire his territory managers each day, enroll in an evening course at a local university, spend more time with his wife and kids, rise to a position of leadership in his professional society, and maintain peak fitness.

Such professionals harbor the notion that if they can find a way to work more efficiently, they'll be able to "get it all done." So, they race through some tasks as fast as possible, slow down a bit for others, rarely pause and reflect, and remain in that mode for hours or days or weeks on end.

> **Coming Undone**
>
> Some managers fall into the "I must do it all" trap because they don't trust others. Some fall because they have no inkling of how to delegate effectively (see Chapter 21). Others succumb because they see co-workers all around them putting in exorbitantly long hours. Hence they believe that this is the only way to approach one's work and get things done.

When doing things rapidly doesn't seem to be enough, this manager stays on the job longer each day. To be sure, there are times when it makes sense to put in a long day. When weekly work hours start to stack up and cut into one's personal time, stress, anxiety, and exhaustion are all but predictable. The stakes seemingly increase as one's perspective decreases.

Remember, an over-emphasis on efficiency, often characterized by attempting to handle too much at once, can lead to burnout.

Becoming More Effective

Efficiency is wonderful, especially when handling routine tasks or, in the case of Chamra, when you can make numbers work in your favor. Efficiency is more wonderful when it is combined with effectiveness. Some people mistakenly equate multi-tasking with effectiveness, but multi-tasking is an attempt to be ever-more efficient, and the price can get too high (see Chapter 15).

The ability to stay organized and to manage your own time is critical if you are managing others. For indeed, if you cannot stay organized or manage your own time, how can you possibly manage other people?

The effective manager is interested in how his staff proceeds through their day as well as how they harness their ideas and insights, their knowledge and wisdom, and their energy and enthusiasm. This is the manager who is focused on achieving powerful results and recognizes that sometimes the path to such results involves starts and stops, twists and turns, reformulation and reconfiguration.

The following is a list of effectiveness-related activities:

- Staying on target.
- Focusing on the big picture.
- Matching customer needs with products and services.
- Getting feedback from customers.
- Making mid-course adjustments.
- Minimizing error rates.
- Striving for results.
- Establishing repeat customers.
- Building word of mouth.
- Engendering client referrals.
- Aligning goals with priorities.
- Meeting organizational objectives.
- Staying true to the mission.
- Aspiring to market leadership.

Dyna Moe

Productive managers understand the power of germination, how taking a few minutes break here and there often yields fresh insights that simply weren't available a few minutes before.

Effective managers are open to the ideas of others, be it from bosses, coaches, mentors, co-workers, or subordinates. They know that no one has a monopoly on good ideas. They're willing to study case histories, examine what other people have tried, and learn what worked well and what didn't work so well. They've heard the expression "An ounce of prevention is worth a pound of cure." They're willing to question their own activities, modify plans, and adjust to changing situations.

Effective managers take the time to re-evaluate, not regarding that time as a waste, but as a necessary element on the high road to getting things done. Effective managers can do great things for themselves and for their respective organizations. Effective leaders can do great things for their society. Effective workers can do great things on the job.

The Least You Need to Know

- Knowing where items are located—being organized—puts you in charge and provides freedom to concentrate on creative, fulfilling, or necessary tasks.

- The great secret to time management is that often you first need to slow down and ponder how to best proceed.

- Staying organized and managing your own time is critical if you are managing others.

- Efficiency and effectiveness need to go hand in hand, i.e., wash the cars quickly enough to make a profit and thoroughly enough to please customers.

- No one has a monopoly on good ideas, so stay open to the procedures that work for others.

Part 2

Helpful Insights for Getting Things Done

Each chapter in this part offers insights and perspectives to aid you on the path to getting things done. We will discuss insightful topics such as the importance of your environment and how things that energize you dramatically increase your ability to get things done, and end with an explanation of the work/family connection. Let's begin with a look at the traits of high achievers and what we can learn from them and apply to our own situations.

3

Traits of the High Achiever

In This Chapter

- ◆ Who becomes successful and why
- ◆ Resiliency through trying times
- ◆ Being productive in an ever-changing environment
- ◆ Passion and getting things done

The rich get richer and the healthy tend to stay healthy even at advanced ages. Meanwhile the best at getting things done learn from the best, hence the adept get more adept. Early on, by luck or circumstance, potential high achievers recognize the importance of associating with and learning from other high achievers. Further, they read biographies of people from the last century like Edison, Disney, and Curie, as well Hewlett, Packard, Grove, Gates, Jobs, and the current throng of digital and broadband pioneers.

> **Dyna Moe**
>
> Top achievers have the ability to both stand out and fit in. They understand the importance of being "artful," personable motivators, and good communicators. They seem to intuitively understand or discover how to combine efficiency and effectiveness.

Top-achieving individuals have the requisite energy to succeed, but it's not frantic energy. These trailblazers face the onslaught of information and communication overload much like any other career professional. In both thought and deed, however, they are not inclined to rush around the office, wolf down sandwiches, or jam-pack their schedule to fill every minute. They develop a form of "relaxed" energy that allows them to maintain stamina, tackle complex problems, focus on the matter at hand, and get things done.

The Courage to Act

Deborah Benton, author of *Lions Don't Need to Roar*, is a leadership-developmental expert based in Fort Collins, Colorado. She's observed many hundreds of CEOs, COOs, and company presidents with an eye on what enables them to get so much done.

She finds that while it's essential to be competent in one's position, inspire confidence in others, act accordingly at business functions, and become adept at maneuvering within the firm, "empty suits" don't make it to the top, or anywhere near there. Benton says "top people are not magical, blessed, or dramatically different from you or me. They simply have skills and outlooks that the rest of us don't have, but can get," such as taking calculated risks and enhancing their "people" skills.

Taking Calculated Risks

Top achievers understand that staying put can be risky and so they take decisive action. In their book, *Surfacing the Edge of Chaos: The Laws of Nature and the New Laws of Business*, authors Richard Pascale, Mark Millemann, and Linda Gioja argue that "equilibrium is a precursor to death."

The people who get things done have the guts to speak in front of others, take calculated risks—realizing that the experience will be invaluable—and make that phone call that others would rather avoid. Benton knows of executive managers who have called individuals months after they were fired from their firm to "see how they were doing."

One company executive remarked that when he evaluated a job candidate, he would get leery if the candidate appeared to be too good. "If I see no failures, I assume he's had it too easy." Could this mean that, on the path to accomplishing a lot, now and then you're going to have some failures? Absolutely.

> **Dyna Moe**
>
> The notion of taking calculated risks runs deep among the get-it-done types who are adept at assessing a situation and will go out on a limb to maximize its potential.

People Are the Common Denominator

A popular stereotype holds that those high achievers tend to be stodgy types. However, Benton finds the situation to be the opposite. Get-it-done type executives laugh and smile often, are fond of telling stories as long as they convey a point, and know how and when to physically touch others. They're also well-skilled in the ability to ask for favors and they fully realize how important that makes others feel.

Regardless of how high-tech society becomes, people make deals, make products, and provide services. As we'll cover in Part 6, pacesetters learn the essential elements about interacting with people that many others never do. A veteran manager in one manufacturing company allocates a portion of his day to making personal contact with the people who report to him and the buyers in client companies. He cares, and he wants his employees to care, about their company and customers.

Reading Others

Get-it-done types in larger organizations learn to "read" others in great detail and to recognize the importance of paying attention to others' needs. By "observing aggressively" anyone can learn to read people, and by reading people, work better with them. Meeting those needs enables successful people to negotiate deals skillfully, manage employees responsibly with the least amount of stress and resistance, gain information, or enlist people to support their cause. The crucial characteristic required in this process is that of *aggressive observation*.

> **Word Power**
>
> **Aggressive observation,** a phrase coined two decades ago by the late Mark McCormack, author of *Staying Street Smart in the Internet Age,* requires working with people face-to-face whenever possible because what you observe about a person is far more revealing than what you hear or read.

When two people meet, aggressive observation requires that a person take action, carefully listening to the content of the conversation and watching for signals in body language.

The Brilliance of Resilience

One of the widely observed traits that high achievers possess is *resilience*. Getting big things done at work, or even winning a long-term personal struggle, requires resilience that is demonstrated through patience, alertness, and steadfastness. These behaviors set the stage for adaptation and action.

Word Power

Resilience entails adopting behaviors to meet challenges, but it is more than simply enduring a challenging situation or overcoming an ordeal. It means having the ability to come back even stronger than before.

Why is resilience fundamental to dealing with upheaval in our professional or personal lives? Because, quite simply, those who have resilience flourish!

Resilient people are able to establish a balance—they believe they'll succeed. They sharpen their focus on the tasks at hand, they stay loose, and they roll with the punches. They maintain orderliness and self-awareness largely to avoid becoming overwhelmed and confused.

While resilient individuals are as vulnerable to the anxieties of change as anyone else, they're able to regain balance quickly, stay physically and emotionally healthy, and remain productive when confronted by confusing or gloomy situations.

Recognizing that Setbacks Are Not Forever

When nothing is working, resilient individuals still manage to figure out how to get back on track. They apply such ingenuity to daily tasks, long-term projects, group or team relations, or problems with the boss. If they lose a client, they're willing to undertake the rigorous assessment as to why. If something's going wrong on a project, they jump right in to see why. They consider the possibilities, take each one and follow it through for whatever insights may emerge.

Resilient people are adept at managing sudden, significant, and complex change with minimum dysfunctional behavior. Their capability can be a marvel to behold.

Rather than shrink from controversy, they're more likely to dive into the fray. They take a stand-up role, admitting where and when they were wrong, if that be the case. They assess the choices they made that led to the result and what other choices they could make to achieve a more desirable outcome.

When they find themselves boxed in on all sides, they don't get down or feel sorry for themselves—at least not for long. They're willing to record their feelings, brainstorm, or even clean out the file cabinet, knowing that such activities can be therapeutic. Perhaps most vital, they determine what they can accomplish right now, today. They know that the act of getting things done, in and of itself, generally proves to be an uplifting experience, however small the deed.

> **Dyna Moe**
>
> By identifying, observing, and then incorporating the behaviors of resilient people, it's possible to change your own behavior to better deal with the world around and within you.

So, who in your workplace is great at getting things done, seems to roll with the punches, and doesn't come unglued in the face of setbacks? That's the person you want to emulate.

Realizing that Arrangements Are Temporary

While resilient types have or develop flexibility and know when to roll with the punches, in many instances they are better than average at overcoming attachment to a place, a piece of equipment, a method, or even a business philosophy. They seem to understand that, particularly in the workplace, virtually all arrangements are temporary. For example, your office or work space, the equipment you use, the people to whom you report, the people who report to you, the customers or clients your company serves, the products or services you offer, even the methods of operation, eventually, are all subject to change.

As a lot, resilient individuals don't seem to be as flustered by bends in the road. If they're thwarted in some aspect of a project, they make forward progress in other areas. They use what they have to get what they want.

Don't Let Good Ideas Slip Away

High achievers are in the habit of recording or writing everything down. They understand that, like the late Earl Nightingale once said, "Ideas are like slippery fish."

Nightingale was a soldier stationed on the USS *Maine* when it was attacked by the Japanese in Pearl Harbor. Later he went on to become a high-achieving sales professional, motivational speaker, and audio pioneer. He co-founded the Nightingale-Conant Company, which for several decades was a leader in self-help audio cassettes and CDs.

Nightingale knew that if you were, say, in a conference and it suddenly struck you that arranging your desk in a new way could make a dramatic improvement in your productivity, you'd have to write down that thought if you wanted to be sure that later you'd take action. If you didn't write down the thought and left it to simmer in your busy mind, it might simply slip away. If you didn't act on the thought, you'd probably end up just working the same old way.

Word Power

Singularities are one-time events in the universe, or in terms of your own thinking, one-time events in your brain. You have to make the most of them.

The ruthless reality about novel ideas, especially those that seemingly come from nowhere, is that most that slip away will not come back. You rarely experience the same moment of brilliant inspiration twice. Such moments are what Professor Stephen Hawking refers to as *singularities*.

Use Your Passion as the Driving Force

Some high achievers routinely tap their passions and harness them as the driving force to get things done, particularly when working with others. Many organizations, including yours, have the same basic equipment, technology, resources, and even expertise among their employees.

What, then, makes one company or one branch more productive than another? A growing number of human resource professionals point to the passion that prevails within the organization.

Passion in the Workplace

In his book *The Passion Plan at Work*, Richard Chang cites six tangible benefits that an organization can derive as a result of the passion that its managers imbue upon the staff.

1. **Attracting the right type of employee.** "The passion-driven organization appeals to the superstars of the job market," says Chang.

2. **Direction and focus.** Passion can define the direction the business takes whether at the regional, local, or branch level. The passion of your particular business, office, or store is the filter with which all decisions are made.

3. **Energy.** When a manager is passionate about the company, about his work, and about his employees, everyone benefits. Staff can become supercharged. On a daily level there is an extra level of energy that can empower the company and often make a huge difference between merely getting the job done and performing with distinction.

4. **Loyalty.** Relationships with employees that are built on passion have a higher probability of succeeding. It's shown repeatedly that money is no substitute for the connection a manager can make with his staff, more so with a young staff.

5. **Unity.** When managers, team leaders, and employees share a common passion, they stand on common ground. "They are connected on a deeper level to achieving the organization's objectives," says Chang. Each incident and each day may not go smoothly—this is not to say there won't be some friction here and there—but overall passion is a unifying element for which there is little substitute.

6. **Heightened performance.** Passion helps drive improvements in both the quality and quantity of work that staff will perform. "If passion is alive and well at work," says Chang, "your company has a clear advantage over its competitors."

On an individual basis, many managers can muster significant levels of passion when it comes to facing competition, meeting a sales quota, or some short-term campaign. The passion discussed here, though, involves making a leap from being a reason-based manager to one who is also a passion-driven manager, not that there's anything wrong with reason.

Too often, managers lose touch with the passions that they once drew upon to energize themselves and those around them. Chang says when you re-clarify what you want to achieve and find that your purpose is in alignment with your core passions, it will become a sustaining element of your work.

Influencing with Passion

Be on the lookout for what Chang calls "purpose by default." If your purpose fails to reflect your true, underlying passion, this can lead to a lack of focus and less-than-desirable performance on the part of you and your staff.

Once your passion begins to take effect, you may find it easier to influence staff who wish to be involved with the energy that derives from your passion. Go ahead, ride the wave—we all know take-charge types who, with their positive infectious attitudes, have been able to amass support from others with seemingly little effort.

> **CAUTION**
>
> **Coming Undone** _____
>
> You have to be careful; any changes you may want to introduce could confuse others. Staff may not be able to accept or benefit from new approaches if you spring things on them too quickly.

Stick close to your passion. You may have abandoned it once before—it's all too easy to fall back into becoming a totally reason-based manager. Use your passion to help others latch on to your ideas and to what you want to achieve. Stay close to your passion and diligently seek to preserve it.

The Least You Need to Know

- High achievers have a source of "relaxed" energy allowing them to work long hours and concentrate on big projects.

- Resilience is demonstrated through patience, alertness, and steadfastness that set the stage for getting things done.

- When all else fails, use what you have to get what you want.

- To improve your productivity, capture your best thoughts; don't let them slip away.

- Tap your personal passions and harness them as the driving force to get things done, particularly when working with others.

Chapter 4

Manage Energy, Not Time

In This Chapter

◆ Energy is everything

◆ Sleep, my pretty

◆ Eat and drink to your health

◆ Circulate to percolate

How you manage yourself and your energy level says much about how productive you will be with your time. An *energetic* you is a more *effective* you. Unfortunately, all around us messages lure us toward energy-zapping temptations. Energy zappers come in many forms: getting too little sleep, eating the wrong foods, drinking the wrong beverages, and lying around too much. Let's look at each of these four areas with an eye on what you can do to ensure that your propensity for high productivity hovers at a desirable level.

The Power of Sleep

It's a popular ritual to plop down in front of the TV for at least a half hour or hour before going to bed. You worked a long hard day, had lots

CAUTION

Coming Undone

Most of the shows you watch, whether sitcoms, dramas, reality shows, sports, movies, documentaries, talk shows, or news, tend to arouse, not calm, your nervous system. Rather than going to bed in a subdued state, ready for deep reverie, your nervous system may be working overtime to calm you down as a result of the added stimuli you heaped upon it before retiring.

of responsibilities around the house, and now feel that you deserve to sit and relax. Do you realize that studies show rather than calming people down before they go to bed, TV actually stirs them up?

Before television, more people would actually read before going to bed. Many people today read a little before conking out for the night but usually the reading follows a stint of late-night TV. Regardless of how you feel as your head hits the pillow, if you unwittingly stimulate yourself through TV, your nervous system will respond accordingly. You can't fool it.

Getting Ready for Bed

A survey sponsored by the Serta manufacturing company (you know, the mattress people) reveals that adults actually engage in a wide variety of activities before getting ready for bed. In order, such activities include:

Watching TV	75%
Securing the home	59%
Reading	53%
Setting the alarm clock	50%
Praying or meditating	43%
Checking on children	33%
Snacking	32%
Listening to the radio	26%
Exercising	20%
Surfing the Internet	19%
Drinking a nightcap	13%

Note: these numbers add up to far more than 100 percent since many people engage in two or more activities before retiring.

Most of these activities are not conducive to sleep. Securing the house makes good sense and seems to be an appropriate pre-bedtime ritual, as does setting the alarm clock, praying/ meditation, and checking on the children.

Listening to the radio and surfing the Internet are probably harmless from the standpoint of inducing sleep, depending upon what stations or what websites you patronize. Certainly some people like to listen to a favorite show or visit a favorite website.

CAUTION

Coming Undone

Drinking a nightcap is not recommended for anyone. Sure, a glass of wine or any alcoholic beverage for that matter, will help induce sleep, but the effects are temporary. Alcohol dries out your system and tends to induce waking sooner than you'd prefer.

Contemplating the list from top to bottom, you'd have to conclude that as many as half of the activities that adults engage in during their pre-bedtime ritual do not support sufficient deep, restful, undisturbed sleep. A *Prevention Magazine* survey showed that 40 percent of U.S. adults "suffer from stress every day of their lives and find they can sleep no more than six hours a night."

In a *Time Magazine* feature titled "Drowsy America," the director of Stanford University's sleep center concluded most adults "no longer know what it feels like to be fully alert." The National Sleep Foundation found that almost 68 percent of adults are getting too little sleep, and 58 percent suffer from some type of insomnia at least once a week. These people are not simply a little groggy or sluggish, but completely and undeniably walking around as if in a stupor. This situation represents a cultural dilemma, but not one to which you fall prey.

As a get-it-done type of professional, you've probably already discovered that when you shortchange your sleep too often, your mind and body simply don't respond anywhere near optimal capability. What you do at night significantly affects your ability to get things done the next day.

Most experts agree that three to four hours of sleep once a week won't cause any long-term problems. You might feel awful the next day, but you can recover somewhat by going to bed earlier the next evening, or napping, if that is an option for you. You may have to force yourself to get into bed at 8:30 or 9:00 on evenings when you'd rather be up and about, but do it—your body will thank you.

Factoid

Your immune system and mental skills decline when you habitually get less sleep than you need.

If you're missing out on more than ten hours a week, decide to catch up on your sleep now before you further diminish your capabilities. Recovery may take a month or more but, wow, will it be worth it!

Don't Fight the System

In *The Organic Clock*, author Kenneth Rose observes that each part and function of your body has its own timing. A heartbeat, breathing, speaking, and even hiccupping have their own rhythms. If you sleep too little (or for that matter, too much), you will disrupt internal cycles that required millions of years to evolve.

Rose also found that each of your body's functions is reset every 24 hours, which parallels the natural daily light cycle. Every essence of your being is subject to this circadian rhythm, which is the daily cycle of activity in living organisms. Altering that rhythm for a prolonged period will prove to be contrary to your own physiology. It's like being at war with yourself!

Factoid _____

Your alertness will vary according to hours of consecutive work, hours of work in the preceding week, your regular hours, the monotony you face on the job, the timing and duration of naps you take, lighting, sound, aroma, temperature, and cumulative sleep deprivation, among other factors.

In his book, *The 24-Hour Society*, Martin Moore-Ede observes that certain times of the day are important to sleep through, such as between 2:00 and 5:00 A.M., when human physiology is at its lowest level of alertness. Highest alertness, by the way, is between 9:00 A.M. and noon, and also 4:00 to 8:00 P.M.

If you happen to be short on sleep some particular day, light exercise such as stretching or a brief walk is a good idea. Your energy level may perk up for an hour or two. If you have the opportunity to nap, that would help as well.

All About Napping

Napping can increase your alertness for the rest of the day. Some people nap easily; others can't seem to nap at all. You already know which camp you fall into. Here are some things to consider about napping:

◆ The best nap time is between 2 and 3 P.M. Any later and your nap may be too deep, which can interfere with your nightly sleep.

♦ Your quality of sleep will be much higher and the immediate benefits more apparent if you nap in a bed or cot as opposed to a chair.

♦ Although everyone feels a little groggy for a few minutes after a nap, this gradually subsides.

♦ Short naps are more productive than long naps. A short nap will leave you refreshed; a long nap may interfere with your sleep that evening. Naps of 20 minutes or less usually help avoid REM sleep, a stage where you're likely to wake up groggy and stay that way.

♦ To derive the most from your nap time, safeguard the nap area before you nod off by making sure that phones, fax machines, or other gadgets will not disturb you. Post a "Do Not Disturb" sign if that will help.

Even with all that said, naps are not a good substitute for regularly getting the right amount of sleep.

What You Eat Is How You Think

Eating nutritiously and at the right times can greatly benefit your attitude and capability at work. For many of us, however, heeding the need for balanced meals is yesterday's news and yesterday's discipline. Since Ray Kroc opened the first McDonald's in 1955, society has become a "fast-food culture" ad nauseam. Family and work demands on our time have kept fast-food restaurants in business and despite all the scary headlines in recent years, too many people still have poor diets and poor eating habits.

To get back on track, start with a good breakfast. Studies show that people who skip breakfast are missing out on an important source of energy for their day—and therefore have less energy than those who eat breakfast. People who skip their morning meal also tend to have a higher proportion of fat to other substances in the body. So take the extra 10 minutes, and fuel your body in the morning. Your body will thank you. Also take a multi-vitamin every day to reduce feelings of lethargy and to ensure that you're getting most of the basic nutrients your body needs.

CAUTION   **Coming Undone**

People who skip breakfast are not as mentally sharp, have less physical energy, and tend to put on weight more easily than those who take the time for a good breakfast.

While we're at it, don't skip any meals. If you skip a meal, the ensuing hunger and lowered blood sugar can make you tired. It can also make you want to eat a huge meal later, and you will end up downing a large quantity of unhealthy food to satisfy your hunger instead of eating two smaller, more reasonable meals. This will have the effect of making you feel tired and sluggish afterward and, if you make a habit of it, gain weight.

Hydrate or Die

Nutritionist David Meinz says that every chemical reaction occurring in your body, including all that goes on during the workday, involves water. The brain itself is 75 percent water. Unfortunately, our thirst mechanisms lag behind our true need for water. Even a 2 percent reduction in the amount of body water renders a pronounced lack of productivity. A 5 percent reduction in our body's water supply results in acute decreased mental functioning. Your productivity at work is directly linked to your degree of hydration.

Factoid

Air-conditioned rooms usually have some humidity added, but heated rooms generally are dry. You need to drink more when you stay in heated rooms for prolonged periods. Women are at risk for dehydration since they have a lower water content due to a smaller lean muscle mass than men.

Eight cups of water a day is still the standard, but most people wait until their thirst reminds them. Drink before you're thirsty. When you work out hard, it takes your body 24 hours to regain the water supply it needs. If you constantly work out, you are constantly in need of more water than you think.

Regardless of what you're working on, keep water nearby and take several sips when you can. Here's the truth in black and white: from the standpoint of getting many things done, it is better to pee often than to experience even mild dehydration. Don't wait until you know you're thirsty. Thirst is actually your body's alert that you're dehydrated. So drink up.

Work Out to Work Better

Television and computers and other information and entertainment delivery systems have made our society a sedentary one, and our bodies pay the price. Only in the past few decades has an alarming percentage of adults from industrialized nations become overweight, if not obese. Exercise deficiency is the major culprit. Exercise not only gives us more energy, it makes us healthier, and boosts self-confidence.

You can scream and you can moan, but for all your lamenting there is no doubt, you need some type of exercise every day. Walking 10,000 steps—about an hour for most people—is ideal. If you can't get in more than a few minutes worth of exercise, at least do something.

If you work in a high-rise building, take the stairs when you're heading downward. Also, take the stairs if you're only going up one floor or two. If you're going more than two, feel free to take the elevator.

Look for little ways all day long to engage in a few moments of exercise. For example, park your car a block or two away from a store you're going to. If you're in a mall parking lot, park at the far end of the lot and walk the two to three blocks. If you use public transportation, get off the bus or subway one stop or a few blocks before you normally would, and walk the rest of the way.

And no matter how demanding your schedule, don't forget to make time for leisure. Especially in our supercharged, rushed society, leisure is a vital component of our lives. Creating free time for hobbies and activities is essential to keeping our lives in balance, and helps prevent us from burning out in our primary preoccupations. Fortunately, there are more activities to choose from than you will ever be able to perform, let alone perform well, in a single lifetime.

The activities you choose can help you to be energetic, alert, and ultimately more productive on the job.

The Least You Need to Know

- How you manage yourself and your energy level says much about how productive you will be with your time.

- When you shortchange your sleep too often, your mind and body simply don't respond anywhere near optimal capability.

- Drink before you're thirsty.

- Look for little ways all day long to engage in some form of exercise.

Chapter 5

Accomplishment Is Personal

In This Chapter

- ◆ Leadership begins at home
- ◆ Morning has broken
- ◆ Right time and right mood traps
- ◆ Energy from small maneuvers

This book is about getting things done, and one of the ways to make yourself as productive at work as possible is to make your home life a sanctuary. Increasingly, it can be argued that one's home life is more stressful than one's work life. High achievers and those who realize the importance of managing their energy as well as their time, acknowledge the importance of balancing work- and domestic-related issues. This chapter will explain how what you do at home impacts productivity at work.

Lead at Home, Succeed at Work

At work, for all the demands and pressures, at least there's some semblance of order. You report to someone, others report to you. There are meetings, agendas, goals, and objectives. You're assigned specific responsibilities. You are expected to meet those responsibilities within a given time frame. Your compensation and indeed employment depend upon your ability to deliver on a regular basis. This regimentation, though challenging, also offers a fair degree of comfort.

Is any of the above true at home? Home environments tend to have much less structure. Whether you're part of a family, live with a significant other, or live alone, your home environment may contribute to your sense of fatigue, indirection, and low energy at work. Too much clutter, distractions, responsibilities, and things competing for your time and attention and too little order applied to addressing such issues could well result in a tired, discombobulated, unfocused you.

Take control of your home environment, recognizing that your ability to get things done at work is partially dependent upon it. It all starts with how you get out of the house each morning.

Leave in the Morning with Grace and Ease

If getting out of the house for you each morning represents a time-pressured, hectic routine, then it's more difficult to turn things around when you step into the office. As you learned in Chapter 4, as in the case of watching television before retiring, your nervous system is weathering everything that you feed it.

If you live in a major metropolitan area and you're a good distance from your workplace, you may be battling the crowds every morning. Or your morning commute may otherwise be out of your control. Certainly, you can attempt to get up before the masses, or after them. You may not have leeway as to when you must arrive at work. Hence, make your journey as pleasant as possible. If you drive, then make sure that you have the music or programs that soothe and inspire you.

CAUTION

Coming Undone

If you've left yourself too little time; haven't put important items that need to go with you by the door the night before; gulp down highly sugared, caffeinated, or fat-laden food products; and then fight your way through the masses to arrive at your place of work, be prepared for what might turn into at least a 30- to 60-minute time frame before you finally "calm down" and can begin to focus on accomplishing worthwhile tasks.

Take Steps the Night Before

How you depart your home in the morning is entirely up to you. If you awake by alarm clock, then by definition you didn't get enough sleep. Find that hour at which you can retire and easily wake up on your own the next morning without the aid of an alarm. If you need eight hours, then obviously to get up at 6 you'll have to retire by 10.

If it helps, lay out your clothes for yourself the night before, like your mother did for you when you were young. Have nutritious food ready. You know too well that eating junk at home or eating anything on the run is not going to give you the fuel you need to accomplish one thing after another at work. You'll run out of gas too soon and then look for quick and easy stimulants—did someone say caffeine?—to keep you going. This is no way to work, no way to treat your body, and no way to pass through your life's journey.

Coming Undone

If you're going to bed at 11, 11:30, and still getting up by alarm, thinking you can slug through the day, you're right, you can in the short term. In the long term, it all catches up to you.

Arrive Ready, Progress Steady

When you arrive in the morning, particularly if you're there before the rest of the staff, you have the best opportunity for structuring your day. Envision how you would like your day to go. Review your appointment calendar and plot out the few critical elements that will make your day a success. Keep flat surfaces clear to the degree that you can.

If you work in a home office, when everyone else has departed, give yourself a few minutes to undertake the same type of contemplation. If you stay home with children or other household occupants, carving out a few minutes for yourself during the early morning is even more crucial. How would you like your day to be? What are the critical elements or critical tasks you wish to complete?

Learn Your Productivity Cycle

At all times, the person who knows best about what will keep you most productive is you. As often as possible, you want to work with your internal rhythm so that you

Dyna Moe

Any time you're at your desk and you feel the urge to stand up, do it!

get the best of yourself, while minimizing any stress or anxiety you might otherwise experience. For example, if you've been seated at your desk for twenty minutes or so, it's best to get up and stretch, even if only for a few seconds. Your veins need this, so does your heart.

Physiologically speaking, your body will give you the cues you need at precisely the right moment. It's actually counterproductive to ignore your body's message to you that says it's time to stand up, to stretch, to take a drink, or what have you.

Daily Performance Ability

Although we each have what is called a "normal" temperature, rarely does your body temperature maintain a steady 98.6 degrees Fahrenheit. Body temperature fluctuates over the course of a day in a relatively stable pattern controlled by the brain. Most aspects of your body's performance ability are highest when your temperature is highest. This is true for physical coordination, memory, and alertness—all of which decrease as temperature decreases.

John Poppy, a health columnist whose articles have appeared in *Esquire*, *Men's Health*, and *Look Magazine*, makes the following recommendations for undertaking work-related activities, given your body's natural capacities at different points in the day:

10 A.M. Mental skills begin to rise. From now to noon is the best time to attack a challenging project or to make that pitch for a raise.

Noon. Brain power starts to dip. Contrary to popular belief, this "post-lunch dip" probably can't be entirely blamed on your midday meal. Scientists are not sure what prompts it. Here the dip comes, even though the temperature is still curving upward.

3 P.M. Alertness returns. Whatever the reason for the noon dip, it loosens its grip and you get your mental acuity and efficiency back.

4 to 5 P.M. Best time for exercise. Muscle tone is at its peak at this time of the day. So good, in fact, that for many people, late afternoon is fitness time.

8 P.M. Last call for alcohol … if you want to sleep soundly during the night.

Based on the above, 10 A.M. to noon and 3 to 4 P.M. are the best times to exercise your brain, and 4 to 5 P.M. is the best time to exercise your body.

Tackling the Day's Toughest Task

Has this ever happened to you? You approach the end of your workday and realize that you didn't get to the most difficult tasks. If you're like most people, you're likely to accomplish more of what's on your daily task list if you start with the hardest tasks. Moving on to the easy tasks then seems like a downhill bike ride.

Researchers agree that you are best able to perform your hard tasks well if you do so in the morning. Dr. Norbert Myslinski, a neuroscience professor at the University of Maryland, found that *cortisol* peaks around the time you wake up. Cortisol increases your blood sugar level, better enabling you to handle tasks energetically and with enough momentum to carry you through their completion.

Word Power

Cortisol is a naturally occurring stress hormone that affects your ability to respond to challenges or perceived dangers you face.

Most importantly, tackling tough tasks in the morning generally enhances your confidence level. By increasing productivity at the beginning of your day, you are motivated to perform better and accomplish more throughout the rest of your afternoon and evening.

As your workday winds down, seek to tie up loose ends. Can you put away several file folders? Can you return the one key phone call? Can you get tomorrow's project notes ready? Can you discard junk mail and other unnecessary documents?

As we'll explore more fully in Chapters 16 and 17, the more little things you complete before departing, the more focused and energized you'll be when you return the next day to a clear and clean environment that is conducive to greater productivity, not to mention more visually appealing.

Energy from Switching Tasks

Over the years I've observed that even the most mundane tasks, if approached in a certain way, can help to maintain one's energy level. I'm talking about the energy you can gain from switching tasks.

After school, my daughter sometimes helps me in my office. I might have a number of assignments for her, such as putting labels on envelopes, proofreading a letter, applying postage to a package that needs to be mailed, and so on. Still in her early teens, she finds any one of these done to the exclusion of all else to be boring after

Dyna Moe

Task switching can't be employed all the time for all types of assignments, but it does work well when you can mix the mundane in with the tasks that are a little more challenging.

just a couple of minutes. By giving her bite-sized portions of each and rotating the tasks, she's able to go for an hour or more. This process works just as well for adults.

Suppose you're faced with an assignment you'd rather not be handling. Something as pedestrian as folding newsletters. Instead of tackling the assignment for a straight 60-minute period, if you were to proceed for 10 minutes, then turn to something else of a shorter nature, go back to folding for another 10 minutes, and likewise turn to something else, you can maintain productivity, reasonably high spirits, and energy for what comes next. Because you proceed methodically, in a controlled manner, you avoid the perils of multitasking.

What about Handling Errands?

Everyone has errands to handle—the professional and personal variety. The way you handle errands and when you handle them can make a huge difference in your overall energy level and impacts your performance at work.

IDIOTWE is an acronym for *I'll Do It On The Weekend*. Weekends, if you haven't already discovered, are when everyone else is attempting to do their errands! I suggest using Monday, Tuesday, or Wednesday to handle errands and avoid the IDIOTWE syndrome. The following is particularly useful for entrepreneurs:

- If starting from home, prepare for multiple stops in a circular route. List your stops in order on a Post-It note and affix to your car dashboard or radio.

- To ward off parking woes, stockpile plenty of quarters and dimes.

- Keep a file folder, envelope, or pouch in your briefcase for the various receipts, tickets, and sales slips that you will need or will be collecting.

Coming Undone

Cease and desist if you run into undue delays, traffic backups, or long lines. Chances are, when you handle errands at a different time, delays will be less.

- Keep the passenger side of your car clear for the new buys and pick-ups.

- Shop by mail. There's no need to pick up stamps at the post office when you can order them by mail and have them delivered to you. Similarly, deposit checks and money orders by mail. Ask your bank for self-addressed envelopes, or produce your own set.

Give yourself credit for the smallest of tasks, such as dropping off an item for a client, depositing a check, returning rental equipment, and so forth. As often as possible, however, use retained help to take care of these items instead of doing them yourself.

Forsake "Right Time" or "Right Mood" Traps

When I was 26 I moved from Connecticut to Washington, D.C., the big city. I was excited about my new job. That whole first day at work went by like a dream. When I got out in the evening, I headed up the road to pull onto M Street so I could cross the Key Bridge and go home to Virginia. There was no break in the traffic. I couldn't even pull onto the road.

So I sat there looking at my car clock, and after two minutes there was still no break. Amazingly, after four minutes there was no break. After six full minutes there was no break in the traffic, no opportunity for me to pull onto the major road that led across the bridge.

Think about the times you've been in front of a traffic light for two minutes when you wanted to get somewhere. It turns out that I sat there for literally ten minutes. Think about how long that is. Try to sit where you are in silence for ten minutes to reinforce just how long that is. Even the thought of it seems difficult!

So, what did I do? I decided to head back down the road, drive all the way around, and try another road where there's a traffic light. That way at least I got onto M Street, even though I was much further back than where I started.

The next day I headed into work again, everything was going well, and I was enthusiastic. I was excited to be there. At night I left work, pulled up to the road to turn onto M Street, and guess what? An endless sea of traffic. I thought to myself, "This is not going to become a nightly ordeal. I'm going to get home, and the Key Bridge is my route across."

So, I waited for a minute, two minutes, three minutes, and finally I just pulled into traffic. I made my break. I got home that night and felt like I had achieved a great victory. How many of us, in attempting to get things done, wait for the right time or the right mood instead of making that break, taking that calculated risk that would propel us faster and further? Sometimes the step we need to take does not need to be a large one, but it's critical to propel us forward. For example: initiate contact, make that call, order the supplies, map out a plan, talk to the boss, or commit to the team.

Forsaking the "right mood" trap can be more insidious than forsaking the "right time" trap. Many professionals wait until they are "in the mood" to take action. In doing this, they run the risk of being in the right mood at the wrong time or not at all!

Are you among the portion of the population who happens to "never be in the mood"? Setting a standard for yourself may help overcome the dilemma of not being in the right mood to get started on something. Let's take writing, for example, since many people face the task with something far less than enthusiasm.

Dyna Moe

Forcing yourself to produce a number of words per day accomplishes little if you turn out low-quality writing. However, in the case of writers who set a word quota, many correct themselves as they go along. Therefore, what they write is seemingly effective, potent, and on the mark from one day to the next.

Consider a professional writer. Suppose the writer steadfastly maintains a writing quota of a certain number of words per day. This daily writing quota helps generate a desired level of output, whether or not the writer "feels like it." On occasion, a writer's daily performance level may not be up to par but can be balanced by days when the quality of writing surpasses expectations.

Similarly, you may be highly productive when you are "in the mood" to tackle something, making it more vital to focus your efforts when you are in a less-than-enthusiastic mood. By doing something—regardless of your mood—you're farther ahead than if you do nothing. You may not manage to complete a task on your first attempt, but it's to your benefit to at least start.

Hereafter, when it comes to getting things done, have the mentally clarity and emotional strength to *ignore* your mood. Stop telling yourself that you must "feel like proceeding." Instead, move forward upon your personal desire to achieve results.

Being in the Zone

In my book, *Breathing Space: Living and Working at a Comfortable Pace in a Sped up Society*, I introduce the concept of time warps. Time warps happen when you're not conscious of your output or responsiveness in relationship to fixed time intervals, such as an hour. You can increase the likelihood of experiencing a favorable time warp effect by removing yourself from the time-measured environment, such as by hiding the clock. This is why jotting notes while sitting on a park bench, in an airplane, or on your back porch often yields greater output than anticipated or accomplished during the same interval while at a desk in a traditional office.

Other people have other names that they use for what I call time warps. Some people call it "being in the zone." Some call it "being on a roll." Regardless of what you call it, would it be useful for you to know how to get into a time warp on a more-consistent basis? You bet it would!

Here's a simple exercise you can undertake to help create that environment in which you can work at your best:

1. Think back to when you were highly productive:
   Where were you?
   What time of day was it?
   Was anyone else around?
   What was the temperature?
   What was the lighting?
   What resources were available?

2. Think about yourself at that time:
   What were you wearing?
   What did you consume the night before?
   How long did you sleep the night before?
   How did you feel?
   What was your level of fitness?
   What did you eat that morning?

3. Think about the time of day and week:
   What time of day was it?
   What day of the week was it?
   What had transpired earlier?
   What was forthcoming?

4. Think about the tools available:
   Were you using a computer?
   Were you using other equipment?
   Did you have a pen or pencil?
   Did you have a blank pad?
   Were you online?
   Were other resources available?
   Were periodicals, books, or directories present?

5. Consider other factors that were present:
   Did you have a view?
   Were you in a comfortable chair?
   Were you at a desk or at a table?
   Were you in a moving vehicle, i.e., a plane or a train?
   Was there quiet or soothing background noise?
   What were the colors of the walls surrounding you?
   Were you in a room with rugs?
   Could you hear others?
   Was water nearby?
   Were you near the bathrooms?
   Were you near the coffee machine?

As you recall the situation when you were in a time warp, circle each item above that was present or was a factor at this time. New insights may emerge.

If you can, recall a second time in which you achieved a time warp and run through each of the questions above once again. What items have now been marked or circled twice?

If you have the momentum, use this list for a third or fourth time in which you were highly productive. You may see a strong pattern emerge. You'll uncover the specifics as to what factors were present at those times when you were highly productive.

Your goal is now to emulate the scenario to increase your probability of achieving similarly pleasing results. I've used this technique to isolate those factors that are present when I've given dynamite, rousing keynote presentations—the kind that the audience members remember long after the event. To the best of my ability, I seek to ensure that future speaking engagements have all of the key factors present. And you know what? A large percentage of the time, it works!

Master Your Immediate Environment

Take charge of your immediate environment to the degree that you can, as often as needed. You may find that a lack of productivity stems from the feeling of not being in control. When you creatively carve out sanctuaries for yourself, they give you both the quiet you need to get quality work done, and serve as a reminder that you're in charge of your career.

High Energy When Working with Your Computer

Whether you work with a desktop, laptop, or palm top computer, or some combination thereof, it's too easy to fall into unproductive, energy-draining customs and postures. This is especially so when you sit for prolonged periods, fixated on a screen.

Here are some simple exercises you can undertake right where you are that will help to keep you on a more-energetic keel:

- To experience an energy boost, breathe in slowly through your nose, and hold your inhale for two seconds and then exhale through your mouth. Repeat this often.

- To loosen up your shoulders and upper torso, using a wide circular motion, roll your shoulders forward four or five times. Then do the same thing in reverse.

- To stretch your neck, turn your head slowly from side to side and look over each shoulder. Count to three and then repeat the exercise several more times.

- To stretch your back, while seated (and with no one looking!), slowly bend your upper body between your knees. Hold this position for a few seconds, then sit up and relax. Repeat this exercise a few more times.

> **Dyna Moe**
>
> There's something about taking control of your immediate environment that enables you to get the best from yourself, to work with your internal rhythms, and to more easily and effortlessly produce superior results.

- To stretch the muscles in your forearms and give your wrists some relief, hold your arms straight out in front of you and raise and lower your hands bending them at your wrists. Repeat this several times.

- To give your upper back and shoulder blades some relief, fold your arms in front of you, raise them up to your shoulders, and then bring your elbows straight back. Hold this for several seconds. Repeat several times.

- To relax your fingers and hands and make them feel more nimble, make a tight fist with your hands and hold it for several seconds. Then, spread your fingers as far as you can and hold for another five seconds. Repeat this exercise several times.

These exercises are appropriate in or out of the office, whenever your muscles feel tense, but not so frequently as to disrupt your work.

Better Eye Health at Your PC

Your computer screen is comprised of pixels, dots of light that are bright at the center and dimmer at their borders. It is hard to read the screen of your PC for a prolonged period because your eyes have nothing to "lock on to."

Common ailments people feel when looking at a PC monitor for extended periods include headaches, itching or burning eyes, blurry vision, fatigue, aching shoulders, and an aching neck.

Factoid _____

Gazing at a screen for long periods of time, day after day, quickly adds up to eye strain, which directly contributes to a drop in energy. Eye strain is now the single most prevalent office complaint in America. One government study estimates 91 percent of people who use a PC for more than three hours daily experience eye strain at one time or another.

Here are some simple exercises that can help you minimize or even ward off eye strain associated with too much time in front of a monitor:

- Reduce any glare from the walls surrounding you, especially if it reflects back onto your screen.

- Seek to match the brightness of your room to that of your monitor.

- Refocus your eyes on distant objects every few minutes, then turn back to your monitor. Also, blink often!

Also, at least once every twenty minutes stretch or get some water. That way you can be at your best pretty much close to all day.

The Least You Need to Know

- How you leave your house in the morning and in what frame of mind can impact how your day goes at work.

- Work with your internal rhythm so that you get the best of yourself, while minimizing any stress or anxiety you might otherwise experience.

- Handle the day's toughest task at the start of the day whenever possible.

- When it comes to getting things done, have the mentally clarity and emotional strength to ignore your mood.

- Take charge of your immediate environment to the degree that you can, as often as needed.

Part 3

Workplace Organizational Issues

Thus far, we've eased you into the get-it-done frame of mind. This part will cover observations and suggestions that require a little more work on your part! To get things done, more often than not, you have to get your act together, and that means dealing with workplace organizational issues. Your desk, your office, the paperwork all around you, your computer, the web, and e-mail: all these arenas require some type of order so that you will be able to work comfortably, find things when you need them, and be in command of your resources.

Chapter 6

Your Desk, Your Office, Your Career

In This Chapter

- ◆ Your work environment
- ◆ Rule your desk
- ◆ A new set of commandments
- ◆ Love your surroundings

Let's face it, your productive work life is finite. You will only be able to work for so many years at such-and-such a pace, and then one day that will end. When it comes to getting things done, taking control of your immediate environment works wonders.

This chapter is all about the direct connection between how you manage your desk and office and how that ultimately impacts your career.

Filing and Organizing Effectively

Practically speaking, much of getting things done comes down to how well you're able to retrieve what you need, and much of that adds up to a single concept: filing.

Filing is a non-glamorous tool for getting and staying organized. Filing involves allocating information and materials into their best home, for now. What do you need to be a good filer? Clear objectives and the space to put a chair in front of a filing cabinet. If you fear that filing means you're becoming a caretaker, remind yourself you are taking care of items or information that you deem to be important. If it isn't important, don't save it. If it is important, file it with gusto.

Conditioning your environment is a crucial step in organizing and filing effectively. This means that you arrange, stock, and maintain such spaces in a manner that supports your efforts. For example, organizing a desk drawer initially takes time and may be slow going. Thereafter, finding what you want in the desk drawer is simpler and faster.

If you avoid organizing the drawer all together, always have things strewn about, and go on a "hunt" each time you need to find something, in little ways you're hampering your productivity potential rather than devising a system that will support you every time.

Managing the Beforehand

With the vacant space you have created, you now have a clearing for the things that you'll be receiving. These include new policy memos, articles you want to save, meeting notes, and course information that you want to review at a later date. The items may be different for each person. The important point in an over-information society is to take control in advance—*manage the beforehand*—as opposed to dealing with the aftermath of too much information.

Word Power

Managing the beforehand means to prepare for something in advance of a need, such as to prepare your files in anticipation of new items that are coming. Rather than having files and cabinets filled to their brims with information, strip them of all excess materials so that you have some vacant space.

Once you develop the habit of clearing space in all the compartments of your life—your desk, your car, your closets, etc.—you accomplish many things: you demonstrate to yourself that you do have enough space to manage your career and conduct your affairs, and you keep in a ready state to handle what is next rather than trying to figure out where to store things or how to create ad hoc piles.

The table below presents eight typical mismanagement scenarios in the left column and corresponding preventative measures in the right column.

Dealing with the Aftermath	Managing the Beforehand
Not knowing where to put things and hence creating ad hoc piles on your desk and around your office.	Creating space in advance of the arrival of new information or items in your life.
Returning to your office from a meeting lugging mounds of new information.	Returning from a meeting with a thin, highly potent file of key ideas.
Panicking when a key employee calls in sick one morning and no one else is prepared to handle the job.	Having already cross-trained your staff members so they can ably fill in on short notice or having good relations with temps!
Leaving for work in the morning in a mad rush, forgetting things and feeling stressed to start the day.	Leaving with grace and ease because you have already assembled everything by the door or in your car the night before.
Heading into the city without the quarters and dimes needed for parking meters and pay phones.	Having at least 50 dimes and 40 quarters (a roll of each) safely and subtly stashed in your car.
Being totally surprised when your primary customers change their focus and hence what's important to them.	Not being surprised that your customers change focus, because you subscribe to their industry and in-house publications.
Having a pile of magazines and other publications stack up because you can't keep up with them, let alone identify relevant articles or information.	Having no piles because you've dropped most subscriptions, and you quickly strip those you receive to get the few relevant pages before recycling them.
Pretending that the six things currently competing for your attention are there because that's just the way it is in your office or line of work, or with your boss.	Remembering that typically you're in charge of your situation. Putting systems in place that limit the number of things competing for your attention.

Conditioning Your Office

Conditioning your work environment, coordinating the arrangement of physical spaces in your career in an anticipatory, supportive manner, works well on many levels. You can apply the principles to your entire office. Whether yours is a corporate or home office, you can discover how to gain greater balance. Obviously, you will have more leeway if you are self-employed, or the "boss," but the principles work pretty much the same.

If you need them, room dividers and sound barriers are available in a wide variety of shapes and sizes and can improve upon any existing sound barriers. The gentle, rhythmic "white noise" of a small fan's motor serves as a sound buffer to many of the sounds that may distract you. Maybe you want a couch for quick cat naps during the day. The quality and ambience of your work space works best when it demonstrates the quality and ambience of your life or how you would like your life to be.

The table below presents five examples of working in an unconditioned environment and corresponding antidotes.

Unconditioned Environment	**Conditioned Environment**
Being inundated by junk mail on a daily basis at work and not liking it.	Hardly ever receiving junk mail because you methodically remove or prevent your name from being entered on mailing lists.
Frequently getting up in the middle of a phone conversation to find a pen or paper.	Always having a pen and paper near your phone, because you've secured them so that they can't be removed.
Being embarrassed all afternoon because at lunch you spilled ketchup on your white dress shirt.	Not experiencing embarrassment for your earlier accident because you always keep an extra shirt stowed in your office.
Fumbling through your wallet or with a palm-top computer at the airport to find a phone number.	Having your key phone numbers on one master sheet on the inside back flap of your pocket calendar.
Being interrupted by all manner of phone calls put through to your office all day long.	Having concentration time scheduled every day and telling the receptionist when callers can best reach you or when you'll call back.

Your other environments, including your car, briefcase, and remote work station, each have a pronounced impact on how you get things done. To ensure that your home environment supports your sense of balance, don't allow ad hoc outposts to build up. Take the trip receipts out of the folder right after the trip. Adopt supportive docking and unloading techniques. Always bring important paper items, such as mail, office work, tax receipts, warranties, and other purchased items to their final destinations—that is, bring them to your administrative outpost for processing and integration into your organization system.

The more you are able to keep flat surfaces clear—your desk, tables, shelves—the greater your ability to manage the flow of items in your career, deal with them capably, and move forward. You experience a sense of balance.

Factoid _____

The London subway system was experiencing a growing problem of unwanted vandals and thieves in their tunnels. So they devised a plan to play classical music and opera, such as Vivaldi, Mozart, and Pavarotti in the effort to make unwelcome visitors uncomfortable with the subway environment. Studies have shown that this type of music is unfamiliar and unacceptable to the thugs who hang out in the subway. Making them miserable with music they don't enjoy will drive them away.

The 10 Commandments of Deskmanship

Keeping in control of your desk is divine. Speaking of which, if Moses himself climbed to the top of Mount Sinai today, considering all the desks that are hopelessly disorganized, here's what he might bring back:

1. Thou shalt clear thy desk every night. Yes, every night.

2. Thou shalt continually refine what goes on thy desktop.

3. Thou shalt not use thy desktop as a filing cabinet.

4. Thou shalt predetermine what belongs inside thy desk.

5. Thou shalt keep 20 percent of the drawer space vacant.

6. Thou shalt furnish thy surrounding office to support thy desk.

7. Thou shalt take comfort when at thy desk.

8. Thou shalt keep clean thy desk and thy surrounding area.

9. Thou shalt leave thy desk periodically.

10. Thou shalt honor thy desk as thyself.

It's Divine to Refine

Let me expound upon a couple of the essentials:

- *Furnish thy surrounding office to support thy desk* with familiar and comfort inducing objects, for example, plants, pictures, slogans, and anything that supports your efforts.

- *Clear thy desk every night. Yes, every night.* Joe Sugarman, in his book *Success Forces*, explains the values of clearing your desk every night. He says it essentially forces you, the next morning, to start on those things that are truly important and not to continue with what happens to be cluttering your desktop. I practice this and find that it pays off.

Factoid

Researchers at the University of Texas conducted a study that found people with cluttered offices get very little done, are less efficient, less organized, and less imaginative than people with clean offices.

- *Keep clean thy desk and thy surrounding area.* This is crucial if only to maintain the perception of being in control. Also, *take comfort when at thy desk.* In other words, your desk should be a comfortable place for you, not a war zone.

- *Continuously refine what goes on thy desktop.* What you used to keep on your desk because it was convenient and useful may no longer be so. Also, continuously assess different items that support your desktop arrangement, such as computer trays, hanging lamps, and swivel mechanisms to conveniently move equipment as needed.

Always remember, *keep 20 percent of thy drawer space vacant*—in an information-overload society, your desk will not serve you if all available compartments are filled to the brim. Cut back now and acknowledge what is coming; i.e., manage the beforehand to stay in control.

The Perils of a Messy Desk

In the over-information era, your desk needs to be a comfortable place for you. What does it say if your desk is continually a mess? You met the din, and the din won? Beyond the logistical problems of not being able to find things, a messy desk sends the wrong message to those who might otherwise include you on big, important projects!

Personal organization is fundamental in the quest to get things done and disorganization is costly. A cluttered desk reflects poorly on one's efficiency and capacity for clear thinking. If you want to stifle your career, having a messy desk will help. When your desk is a mess, it appears that you're not in control, whether or not you actually are!

A messy desk makes it look as if you cannot handle your responsibilities. When a supervisor is delegating assignments, you may be passed over out of the fear that the assignment will go into a pile and never find its way out. In working with others, appearance matters and your desk is as important as appearing professional in formal business meetings. Besides doing good work, to make a positive impression on co-workers and bosses, take control of your desk and office environment.

> **Dyna Moe**
>
> If your situation currently appears hopeless, at the least establish a drawer where you can temporarily house what you want out of sight, and keep the drawer closed.

Getting Things Done with Grace

I often have readers and audience participants ask me questions about taking control of their work environment. The issue behind such queries? How to get things done throughout the day with greater grace and ease.

Q: I may be responsible for how organized I am each day, but I don't feel that way. There are things that I have to do that seem to throw everything off. How do I increase my feeling of control and sense of responsibility for how my space is arranged?

A: Begin to recognize behavior that you practice that is comfortable but outmoded and time consuming; ceremoniously (but not strategically) arranging the items on your desk, over-surfing the web, and dozens of other habits qualify here.

Q: Many days I am in control for at least most of the morning, sometimes even into the afternoon, but then all of the sudden, like a train derailment, everything seems disorganized and out of control.

A: Take mental pauses throughout the day, particularly as new developments occur. The best-laid plans often go astray, and those who are able to maintain order know when to let go of one activity and redirect their focus toward another.

Being in control often is more related to how you feel about a situation than the presence of evidence. Ten minutes before the end of the day, if your boss springs a one-hour assignment on you that must be done immediately, you can regard this as a major intrusion in your day and an affront, or you can see it as a professional challenge or an opportunity to demonstrate your overall value to your company.

Make a note of the times you have taken on such challenges and bring them up particularly at raise times. Also, before, during, and after handling the late assignment thrown on your lap, keep considering the many benefits of completing it. These include learning something new, practicing maintaining grace under fire, and serving as a reminder for you to discuss this type of situation with your boss so that it doesn't happen too frequently.

Q: How do I determine what items I need on or around my desk?

A: Surround yourself with what supports you! When deciding whether to have a particular item in your office, ask yourself, "Does this item deserve prime real estate?" This includes those gifts from family and friends. In most cases, hold on to the love and let the gift go!

Q: Are there any early warning signs that indicate when I'm heading for disorganization?

A: Anytime you start stacking horizontal piles on your desk indicates that you are operating in a malfunctioning mode. If you find yourself perpetually five to ten minutes late for meetings and always handling activities up to the last minute before turning your attention to what is next, you're leaving yourself wide open for some anxious moments. If you don't give yourself enough space—physical space—to handle a task, you are also likely to feel a bit disorganized.

If it helps, for each item that crosses your desk, ask these fundamental questions:

- Why did I receive it? Should I have received this?
- What's the issue behind the document?
- Why keep this? (Is it vital? If it will be replaced soon, I don't need it.)
- How else can this be handled? Can I delegate it?
- What will happen if I don't handle this?

At every juncture, avoid playing the victim, believing that circumstances of others cause you to be disorganized while not acknowledging your participation and willingness to be a victim. Take ownership; that is, lay claim and accept responsibility for what occurs in your career. You'll go further and faster, and you'll get more done.

The table that follows serves as a quick guide to keeping your desk and office in order.

Items	Feel Free to Toss or Recycle if ...	Feel Free to Retain if ...
Business cards, assorted notes	You have many cards and never call anyone, or you can't recall someone or his goods or services.	You can compress and file them, and know you will use the information.
Paper, files, documents	They're old, outdated, uninformative; they've been transferred to disk; or they no longer cover your derriere.	It's your duty to retain them, you refer to them often, they have future value, or they simply comfort you.
Reports, magazines	They're outdated or stacking up; you think you need them to keep up; or you fear there'll be a quiz.	They're vital to your career or well-being, you choose to retain them, or there will be a quiz.
Books, guides directories	You've copied, scanned, or made notes on the key pages; they're obsolete or have updated versions.	They're part of a life collection, you refer to them monthly, they have sentimental value, or you simply want them.
CDs, cassettes, videos, and A/V	You never play them, and, if you do, they don't evoke any feelings or memories. They play poorly.	You play them, you like them, and you couldn't bear to part with them. They're keepsakes.
Outdated office equipment	You can donate or sell it; it's collecting dust, takes up valuable space, or it's simply in the way.	It serves a specific purpose, it adds to the décor, or it can be overhauled or revitalized.
Mementos, memorabilia	They no longer hold meaning, you have many similar items, you don't have room, or you've changed.	They still evoke strong memories, you will hand them down someday, or they look good on display.
Gifts, cards, presents	They're never in use or are not wanted, and the bestowers won't know or care that you tossed them.	You use them often, are glad you have them, or are saving them for some special reason.

High Accomplishment Through Shelf Management

Shelf management and self-management are not dissimilar! Your shelves are generally home to items you'll probably use in the next two weeks, items too big for your filing cabinet (or collections of such items), current projects that you'd rather not file, and supplies (that ought to go in supply cabinets).

It makes sense to shelve the following: items that you might use within a week or two include reference books, directories, books, phone books, manuals, instruction guides, and large magazines. Items that are too large to put in a file cabinet might include books, large reports, and any item that is part of a series. If you're working on a task or project that requires a variety of materials and they can be neatly housed on your shelves, go ahead—as long as the project has an end, and these items don't linger there forever.

What doesn't go on your shelves? Anything that belongs in a supply cabinet! Now you know.

The Least You Need to Know

- ◆ How you previously got things done or what worked yesterday will have less and less value with each passing day.

- ◆ When it comes to getting things done, taking control of your immediate environment works wonders.

- ◆ Develop the habit of clearing space in all the compartments of your life and you can accomplish many things.

- ◆ In the over-information era, your desk has to be a comfortable place for you.

- ◆ Surround yourself with what supports you! When deciding whether to have a particular item in your office, ask yourself, "Does this item deserve prime real estate?"

Chapter 7

Paper Rules

In This Chapter

- ◆ Paper offenses
- ◆ Forms beyond reason
- ◆ Merging and purging
- ◆ Quiet contemplation works wonders

Even with the dramatic rise and popularity of the Internet and e-mail, when we talk about information deluge, paper remains as a major culprit. In the United States, we have the lowest postal rates in the world, which contributes to a huge direct mail industry. We also have the highest amount of paper-generating equipment per capita, and more fax machines, laser printers, personal computers, and personal copiers. We nearly paper each other into oblivion.

Increasingly, the sheer volume of paper that we all face is, in and of itself, an impediment to productivity as well as to staying organized.

Pounded by Paper

When my daughter had just entered high school, I attended parents' night. Going from class to class, as she does during the day, I met each of her teachers. In the first class, the science teacher handed us a syllabus, a reading list, a list of rules and regulations, another page with his website and homework for the next several months, and other sheets related to the class. Before I left, I had seven sheets in all.

Factoid

The United States consumes more paper per person than any other country on Earth. By some estimates, the typical U.S. office worker consumes 60 sheets a day or 12,000 a year.

In the next class, I received another eight or nine sheets. Thereafter, the teachers gave me seven to nine sheets per class. I left that evening with 50 sheets of paper, when receiving maybe two or three had been my expectation.

When I arrived home, I said to my daughter, "Look at this! I attended parents' night for freshmen and ended up with 50 pieces of paper! Here, you take these. I've already been to high school. I graduated. I can prove it."

How about your workplace? Despite the cyberworld or, as some say, because of it, a preponderance of paper plagues each of us.

Another Form to Fill Out

A stifling array of government laws and regulations hampers business, allowing the United States to support 70 percent of the world's lawyers, says Barry Howard Minkin in *EconoQuake*. It is crucial for you, a mere pawn in the game of rules and regulations, policies and procedures, to keep your own systems as uncomplicated as possible. It won't be easy; there is a pervasive tendency among organizations and individuals to over-complicate things. You can see its effects every time you have to fill out some new form at work.

Are such forms getting any easier to fill out each year, despite many organizations' long-term commitment to streamlining information, or are they becoming more difficult and involved? Have you bought any office equipment recently? Are there more forms, or fewer? Some companies have double the number of approval and reporting forms that they had 10 years ago.

If you're an entrepreneur, or if you supervise others, think about the last time you tried to fire someone. Is it getting harder or easier from the standpoint of completing paperwork?

Examine Your Own Forms

Examine the forms you've created in your organization, department, or venture, and re-examine them. What can be eliminated? Here are some immediate potential benefits you might experience from combining two or more forms into one or eliminating a single form:

◆ Reduced paper consumption: less ordering, fewer costs, less receiving, less handling, and less storing

◆ Reduced printing and associated costs: less retrieving, less printer use, less electricity, and lower cartridge and toner costs (or lower outside costs if purchased from a printer or forms vendor)

◆ Reduced need for storage: less collecting, less transporting, less storage space used, less employee time used

◆ Reduced distribution costs and labor: less retrieving, less disseminating

You're not the only one who'll benefit from the reduction or elimination of forms. Here's what you'll be doing for the people who used to have to fill them out.

◆ Less writing, less handling, less ink used to complete them

◆ Less walking, less faxing, and less mailing or e-mailing because there's no form to have to submit

Finally, there are benefits for the people who used to have to process the forms:

◆ Reduced collecting: less walking, less opening mail, less handling faxes

◆ Reduced compiling: less sorting, less calculating, less totaling

◆ Reduced reporting: less writing, less presenting, less mental energy expended

Any way the wind the blows, when you successfully reduce or eliminate forms multiple benefits accrue.

> **CAUTION**
>
> **Coming Undone**
>
> All too often in the business world, if you can create a new reporting form, you do. Thereafter, it becomes difficult to eliminate. If anything, such forms get longer, more complicated, and more time-intensive.

Rule Paper Before It Rules You

Any way you cut it, handling paper is still *numero uno* when it comes to becoming and remaining organized. Your organizing mission, and there is no choice but to accept it, is to persevere in the quest to stay in control of the paper that comes your way.

> **Dyna Moe**
>
> Dr. Terry Paulson, author of *They Shoot Managers Don't They?*, suggests that if you touch a piece of paper, at least advance its progress. "If you read it, at least identify what file it belongs in and write it on the top right hand of the document so you can file it without re-reading it," advises Paulson.

Be cautious in deciding what you do and do not want to file away. Don't pitch everything coming in, but recognize that problems begin when you allow even one unnecessary piece of paper to enter your office. Every unneeded page helps derail your ability to stay organized.

Each day, fight to keep your desk clear. In the evening, after you've cleared your desk, acknowledge yourself for what you accomplished that day. As you learned in Chapter 6, if you keep the spaces of your life clear, especially flat spaces like the tops of your desk and filing cabinet and the corners and windowsills around the room, control of your time and control of your life tends to follow.

Never Volunteer to Be Inundated

Sometimes the piles of paper and documents all around us that thwart our ability to remain organized arrive by our own invitation! I was phoned one afternoon by a marketing representative from a well-established investment company. With such calls, after a couple lines of their spiel I find a polite way to quickly end the conversation. This particular caller seemed to be different, so I listened a bit longer. He discussed his company's various investment options. He offered to send a brochure that listed the 35 different investment vehicles available, plus his company's annual report, and a prospectus.

"Wait a moment," I said. "I have no interest in reading about 35 different investment options. Please, do us both a favor by confining your information to a single page. You know, a paragraph or so on the three best options you think would be right for me." I told him I wasn't going to read his firm's annual report, so there was no reason to send it. If I liked what he sent me on the single page, I could always request the annual report at another time.

I explained further that while I have an MBA and have earned the certified management consultant (CMC) designation, "I'm not fond of reading prospectuses, so please don't send that either."

As our conversation drew to a close I repeated to him that I only wanted to see a single page with the three investments he thought were best for me. If he wanted to send one other slim brochure that contained data about his company's latest financial standing, that would be okay. Seemingly he agreed to send only those two items.

Several days passed, and I forgot about the call. In Monday's mail, I noticed a thick package from his investment firm. Uh-oh. I opened it and saw everything I had asked him not to send. I took the assemblage and with one flick of my wrists, sought to tear it in half, but it was too thick. I quickly tossed it, and you may rest assured that I did not become a client.

Never volunteer to be inundated. If that agent had sent me what I asked for, who knows, I might have made his day.

Take In and Retain Less, Starting Now

People make excuses at work all the time about why they are overloaded with paper. Someone else is forcing them to receive more periodicals and subscriptions than they can handle or is forcing them to put their names on more mailing lists. No one is doing this to you—you are doing it to yourself.

Curiously, the more information we attempt to consume, the more we seek to acquire. We are like information switchboards, marveling at how much we can keep our fingers on. To ensure there's never a dull moment, we open up yet another piece of junk mail or we look at yet another non-essential bulletin.

Factoid _____

Wired Magazine (06-03) ran a feature that stated that "clutter is among the lowest forms of spatial organization. A pile simply allowed to stack up contains items, that, if not retrieved, will lose their previous usefulness. Massive clutter lacks geometry. Stuff that is haphazardly strewn across one space has little—if any—value where it currently lies. What's more, it diminishes the value of the space it occupies, ultimately offering the perpetrator less value, less freedom, less control, and greater poverty."

Accumulations, by their nature, steal your time. First you receive them, then place them somewhere, look at them, move them, arrange them, perhaps file some items and discard others, move things yet again, and then put up your hands and fall into despair.

How would your career proceed if you merged and purged on a regular basis, as these items came across your desk? You'd likely have more time and ultimately get more done.

The Surge to Merge and Purge

In the course of a workday, week, month, and year, you encounter memos, reports, newspapers, newsletters, faxes, bulletins, magazines, calendars, promotional items, and all manner of sundries. Right now you're hanging on to too much paper and that is slowing you down on your path to getting things done.

Grasp the information that impacts your career, stay on top of that, and have the strength to leave the rest behind. Not to suggest that you ignore things willy-nilly, but make conscious choices about where to give your time and attention. Most of what competes for your attention needs to be ignored.

To stay organized and get things done, I advocate that you can take in even less paper and less information than you're currently doing. Actively choose where you will give your time and attention.

If you're concerned that you'll miss some vital piece of information, fear not. The redundancy in our information channels, be they publications, the Internet, key newsletters, or your organization's intranet, increases the probability that you won't miss some major development that merits your attention. If you use e-mail effectively, you can quickly establish a peer group of cyber associates that trade and share information with one another on a regular, if not on an ad-hoc, basis.

What to Do with All the Paper

At work when you receive a magazine or other periodical, even one that you actually want, do you need the whole magazine? Continually strip down magazines to the basic elements relevant to you. Usually you can pull out the few articles that matter, and recycle the rest. Develop the habit of streamlining the information you receive, regardless of how big and thick the item. You can probably peruse a 250-page book in ten to fifteen minutes, picking out the eight or ten key pages.

When confronted by a large packet of information I swiftly break it down to the few pages that appear most useful. I use the edge of a ruler to deftly and neatly extract only the bits of information from each page that I need, then quickly assemble such tidbits on the copier and create a one- or two-sheet composite of what might have been many, many more pages. This affords quicker review in the future, keeps my files leaner and more targeted, and is anxiety-reducing.

If it helps, buy a paper puncher for a three-ring notebook and group like materials in one- to two-inch binders. Particularly in areas where you are collecting information in periodic fashion, assembling a notebook can be more practical than accumulating files in a filing cabinet or contributing to multiple piles.

After you've collected information in a notebook for a while, you can rearrange it and introduce sub-dividers for easier use.

Streamline the Information Mine

Straightening up your desk, handling paper, re-arranging files, answering mail, and updating your lists help in feeling and being in control. Then, like clockwork, more "attention grabbers" will arrive. E-mail requests appear and require effort. Mail arrives presenting at least an item or two worth your attention. A critical fax comes through. The phone rings. Suddenly, that newfound sense of order seems to evaporate.

Increasingly, each of us encounters waves of "attention grabbers" throughout the day that render our sense of order and control futile. Yet, there are some simple ways to stay in control in spite of the obstacles.

As piles on your desk mount up, the task of dealing with them soon becomes overwhelming, at least mentally. "How am I going to deal with that information?" When you keep them to a minimum, they seem manageable. Perception is an important tool. When you believe you're on top, you tend to act accordingly. It's not merely positive thinking—a chain reaction occurs, and it works.

Remember: to help stay organized, reduce voluminous materials to the slimmest, most potent file folders or packets that still retain the essence of what you need to have for the task or project at hand.

> ### Dyna Moe
>
> Strip arriving mail down immediately—discover what parts are vital, and what can be tossed or recycled. When you receive a large packet of information, immediately go through it and extract the key pages, paragraphs, or contact information.

Fast-Forward Replies

To quickly and adroitly handle much of the correspondence and paperwork that crosses your desk, particularly if you do not work for a large organization that has formal structures, think "speed reply."

Too much time goes into re-reading what you receive, composing a letter in response, proofing it, and printing or sending it through fax machines. When a response doesn't require formal business protocol, there are many ways to handle it quickly.

Not So Formal

When you receive a letter that merits a reply, if you already know the other party or it's not essential to maintain professional protocol, write your reply at the bottom of the letter or on the reverse side, make a photocopy and mail or fax it back immediately. I often write "speed reply" and the date, quickly jot down a note, put my initials and then send it back within a matter of minutes.

> **Dyna Moe**
>
> Some organizations have stamps and stickers, "Please excuse our informal reply, we wanted to send the information to you quickly."

You can clip the return address label when it is provided on the envelope. Then use that clipping as the label to send something back to them. Not many people find this objectionable. Of course, don't do this for first-time contacts or official business. However, you'll have a sense of when you can; for example, personal correspondence with people with whom you have had long-term relationships, who know you well, or who see you often.

Easy Label Making

You can buy a rubber stamper that says, "speed reply"—I have a big red one. I use the stamp on the letters I receive, handwrite my response on that actual letter, and fax it back to them, or copy the letter and mail it. Then the letter is off my desk, and I have a written record of our correspondence.

Create a fax label or stamper that includes your name, address, phone, and fax. When many people send me messages, the first page reads, "Fax message coming through"—unimportant information that no one needs. You can create a label, one inch by three inches, that has everything that anyone needs to know in terms of the first transmission page, "Fax reply to so and so, from so and so, here's my phone and fax." Then your message should only take half a page or less.

Get Off Extraneous Mailing Lists

It's a wonderful morning when you open up your mailbox and see only six pieces of mail, instead of 18 pieces of mail and 12 of them junk. Develop a standard letter, sticker, or stamper that you mail back to the other party saying, "Please take me off your list."

The myth of "handling each piece of paper once" and others like it must give way to the reality that most pieces of paper should never cross your desk at all.

A vital part of reducing correspondence and paperwork is to get your name off the junk mail rolls. Write to the DMA or register online at www.dmaconsumers.org/consumerassistance.html and ask to have your name removed from their lists. This will reduce your junk mail by 40 percent for about the next six months, after which time write them another letter requesting the same thing.

Mail Preference Service
Attn: Dept: 16433070
Direct Marketing Association
PO Box 282
Carmel, NY 10512

Quiet Contemplation

It is helpful to actually schedule time to peruse the material you've retained, in a quiet place away from phone, fax, and e-mail. Your concentration powers will be at their best. You'll be able to zip through the folder at a much quicker pace than if you attempt to do so on the fly. As you review the items, pare them down further.

Instead of a two-page article, perhaps you need only one key paragraph. Instead of a flyer or brochure listing some offer, maybe you only need the toll-free 800 number or URL. Simply log in the important information on a palm top, note pad, or pocket dictator and then chuck all the pages. Hence, you are lighter, freer, and able to handle whatever else comes into your work area. In a single file or two, you have the essence of what you need or want to pursue.

Dyna Moe
Clearing out what you don't need to retain is good house-keeping, as well a vital discipline among those who win the paper war. Merging and purging is essential because even with all the new technological tools, paper will continue to proliferate the foreseeable future.

The Best Times to Merge and Purge

In the course of your year and career, when are the best times to merge and purge what you've retained? Here are some suggestions:

♦ *As you're approaching New Year's.* When the end of the year approaches I find it easy to rip into files and get rid of half the stuff I know I'm never going to use again. I clear more room in my files, enabling me to be more organized, and am ready to face other things that compete for my attention.

♦ *Spring cleaning.* This has traditionally been a time for clearing out the old and making room for the new. The arrival of fall works as well, toward the end of the summer around Labor Day. Having the crisp, cool air return is a stimulant for getting your desk, office, home, and car back into top condition.

♦ *Whenever you move offices or work locations.* There's no sense in hauling stuff to your new location if you're never going to use it. Make giveaways to co-workers if appropriate and helpful, but don't transport items that you can do without to a new location.

♦ *Obviously when you change jobs or careers, you'll clean out your desk and office or work station.* Again, don't make the mistake of carting unnecessary paper, documents, and files with you that are best recycled and out of your life.

When is a good time to get back in control? The answer is almost anytime—whenever the spirit moves you is an opportune time to merge and purge. You don't need to wait for any of the above. Begin to sense the power inherent in regaining control of your files, your possessions, and your career.

The Least You Need to Know

♦ Examine the forms you've created in your department or venture with an eye on what can be reduced or eliminated.

♦ Streamline the information you receive regardless of how big and thick the item.

♦ Never volunteer to be inundated with materials, and get off extraneous mailing lists.

♦ Schedule time to peruse the material you've retained, in a quiet place away from phone, fax, e-mail, and other distractions.

♦ Eliminate extraneous paper and documents at opportune times throughout the year, i.e., New Year's, the arrival of spring, your birthday, or when relocating.

8

Operation Clean Sweep

In This Chapter

- ◆ Important versus urgent
- ◆ Where and when considerations
- ◆ Pile it up as high as it goes
- ◆ Act, file, toss, or delegate

Thus far in Part 3, we've covered the mechanics of organizing your desk and office, and of handling paper. Now we turn to a surefire way to quickly break down the mounting, recurring piles and accumulations that cover your desk, can hamper your productivity, and certainly diminish your sense of control. I call the procedure "Operation Clean Sweep."

To make the procedure work best, we first need to classify what the paper, documents, messages, piles, and accumulations represent, namely tasks and projects of wide-ranging importance and varying urgency.

Now That's Important

In recent years, the work of Steven Covey and his approach to handling *important* and *urgent* tasks has been given much attention. The basic concept is that everything that you want and need to get done falls into one of four quadrants:

The Four Task Quadrants.

Important

Quadrant 1	Quadrant 2
Quadrant 4	Quadrant 3

Urgent

Not Urgent

Not Important

Ideally, you want to devote the brunt of your time and energy to Quadrant 2 types of tasks: *important, but not urgent.* Type 2 tasks include:

♦ Long-term planning

♦ The big picture focus on the direction of your career

♦ Key company projects

♦ Maintaining a harmonious team

> **Dyna Moe**
>
> Taking a big-picture look at *important* projects enables you to identify potential obstacles in advance, again helping you to avoid crisis management.

When you're able to concentrate your efforts into *important* but not *urgent* tasks, many of the other things that you need to get done at work fall into line. Having a well-oiled, smoothly functioning team translates to less time having to put out fires and, hopefully, fewer crises.

Important and Urgent

At first, it seems odd that merely *important* issues generally outrank *important and urgent* issues represented by Quadrant 1. These tasks, *important and urgent,* need to be addressed right away. This could involve:

♦ Tending to the budget

♦ Conducting meetings

♦ Conducting and attending appointments

Understandably, items that are *important and urgent* are more likely to demand your attention. *Important and urgent* tasks don't tend to go away, they'll always be with you. However, your ability to focus on purely *important* tasks (Quadrant 2), eases the burdens you face in regards to *important and urgent* tasks (Quadrant 1).

Not Important, Possibly Urgent

Quadrants 3 and 4 are below the meridian. Quadrant 3 represents *urgent but not important* tasks which can include:

- Returning phone calls
- Addressing e-mail
- Filling in time sheets

Here, you may be able to efficiently dispatch such tasks because you have handled them before. You know the routine and completing them speedily is desirable. No real need to worry about effectiveness for many *urgent but not important* tasks.

Quadrant 4, *not important and not urgent*, often represents trivial activities. Many of the websites we visit, and much of the mail and e-mail we dwell upon, do not merit the time or attention we devote to them.

Some of the reading we undertake at the office falls into this category as well. Sometimes we delude ourselves into saying that this or that is vital to our overall understanding of the customer, the market, the industry, or society at large. Minimize how much time you spend on the *nonimportant and nonurgent*, while recognizing that occasionally we all dip into this realm and it does help to fulfill some basic human needs, such as providing escapism and mental vacations.

Many of the crises you face and deadlines you fail to meet are a result of something being *important*, not *urgent*. The wise manager understands the necessity of carving out the short-term portion of long-term tasks and addressing those short-term activities on a regular basis. I'll explain this in greater detail in Chapter 11, on creating the super to-do list.

> **CAUTION**
>
> **Coming Undone**
> The paradox of addressing *important but not urgent* tasks is that often they have no specific deadline or the completion date is sometime in the distant future. So it can be easy to give them no attention. Then, when that future does arrive, one ends up resorting to crisis management to accomplish the task.

Avoiding the Urgency Trap: Assessing Tasks as They Emerge

The proliferation of office technology has a profound effect on our sense of urgency. Suppose one morning you receive an overnight package. You're probably willing to devote your attention to that package more readily than others you receive via first-class or even priority mail. Then you receive a fax message from a key customer. You're about to deal with the fax message when you receive an e-mail message from another customer.

So, which form of communication merits your attention first? Whatever your answer, recognize that the form of technology employed in no way equates to the importance of the messages' content.

The typical response is to address the latest communication, independent of its importance. Hence, the e-mail would trump the fax and the fax would trump the overnight package. Watch out! Managing by e-mail is an insidious trap. Remember to continually assess what is *important*, versus what is *important and urgent*, versus what is merely *urgent*.

The Highest and Best Use

Allen Lakein, in his 1973 classic book *How to Take Control of Your Time and Your Life*, suggests monitoring yourself by determining, "What is the highest and best use of my time?" If you fail to consciously assess how you are allocating your time, then you will disproportionately skew toward the *urgent*, independent of its importance.

In the short run, skewing toward the *urgent* can be okay. If this is a long-term habit, then you will become more and more adept at handling the minuscule, while failing to accomplish the grand achievements that you seek to accomplish—the same achievements that your boss and others will notice. And, make no mistake, the higher-level achievements are what count with your boss and are typically goals set for your performance reviews.

> **Dyna Moe**
>
> If heretofore you have been the kind of person to throw your time or energy at everything, all day long, week after week, taking a more structured approach can yield tremendous benefits in as little as 2 to 3 weeks, depending on the project!

Developing the discipline and ultimately the habit of focusing on *important but not urgent* tasks followed by *important and urgent tasks* pays off faster than you think.

Stop and Consider

If you're the type of person who arrives at the office and jumps right in, perhaps you need take a few minutes to:

◆ Pause and reflect on how you'd like your day to proceed.

◆ Contemplate which tasks you'd like to handle and in what order.

◆ Consider whom you'll be meeting and what results you hope to achieve.

◆ Determine how you choose to feel throughout the day.

Rather than check e-mail right away, curb your raging inclination and simply sit there. Take out a pen, or with your keyboard, capture your thoughts.

The five minutes or so that you invest in simply pausing and reflecting, repeated each morning for several weeks, can have a profound impact on your ability to get things done. I've employed it and found the benefits to be enormous.

As time passes and you permit yourself such intervals at other times throughout the day, you may pleasantly surprise yourself as you ascend to a new and uninterrupted level of accomplishment. You may even unwittingly improve both your efficiency and effectiveness.

Handling Tasks Based on *Where and When* Criterion

David Allen, in his book *Getting Things Done*, says that attempting to address tasks and projects based on *important* and *urgent* criterion is not always the best way to proceed. He overlays the *important* and *urgent* approach with a mild adaptation: tackling tasks and projects based on *when and where* it is most appropriate to handle them.

For example, all the things you need to do at the copier, on the phone, or via e-mail, in Allen's approach, are best handled in clusters. I agree; as long as you don't become obsessive, hence deciding to address all e-mail during the same interval or to make all phone calls during the same interval, even when you've exhausted the *important* and *important and urgent* ones, and on impetus are now dipping down to the merely *urgent* or *not important and not urgent* categories. Otherwise *where and when* considerations in getting things done can prove to be most worthwhile.

Important and Urgent: Preparing for Operation Clean Sweep

Now that you understand the distinction of *important* and *urgent* tasks, we're ready to discuss the all-time desk-clearing, energizing, get-it-done technique: Operation Clean Sweep.

Accumulations cost you double—you don't take action on them and you keep confronting them. To handle the array of items competing for your attention, and to balance big goals with the daily grind, collect everything on your desk and elsewhere that may need attention.

Coming Undone

Don't attempt Operation Clean Sweep when you are weary or otherwise not fully alert because this procedure will seem overwhelming.

Have you collected everything? Wonderful. Stack it high in a temporary pile—the higher the better. This will enable you to have a much clearer idea of what you've allowed to accumulate. Within a span of thirty minutes or less, you're going to rip through this collection of breathing space–threatening items. Without hesitation or sentiment, you'll allocate each item to one of four designations: "Act-on-it" Items, "File-it" Items, "Toss-it" Items, or "Delegate-it" Items.

Top-of-the-Pile Decisions

How do you handle each piece of paper, document, or artifact currently at the top of the pile? The short answer is lady's choice, or gentleman's choice. As you confront each top-of-the-pile item, quickly decide what to do with it. There are four categories for dealing with the top-of-the-pile items, including *act-on-it items, file-it items, toss-it items*, and *delegate-it items*.

If you are unsure of any particular item, you may place it at the bottom of the large stack, but only once for each item. On the second encounter, you have to classify it.

Act-On-It Items

Ideally, only a fraction of what makes your clean sweep pile will actually end up in the act-on-it category. This is because these are the handful of things that are *important*, or possibly *important and urgent*, and those that you otherwise deem appropriate for addressing in rather short order. You can collect these items in a file folder if that's convenient, or if the tasks represent something on your PC, then start listing them or filing them in sequence by when you wish to tackle them.

File-It Items

Many items in your clean sweep pile are best filed rather than acted upon. Some items require no action. The items simply represent information you wish to retain and hence go into a file. Remember, filing, a nonglamorous tool of organization, supports you because that which you file presumably has future value.

Many people have 43 rotating tickler files that they label with the 12 months and 31 days (to accommodate the longest months). Tickler files automatically remind you of when you need to deal with a particular task that does not have to be handled today. So, when a task comes your way, you can place it in the tickler file for the appropriate future date. Then each day of the month, you check your tickler file to identify the tasks that need to be handled or at least initiated.

> **Dyna Moe**
>
> This system of using tickler files works particularly well with smaller and recurring tasks that you'd just as soon bother including on a to-do list or as part of an electronic calendar or scheduler.

If you receive something on the third day of the month but don't have to deal with it until the 24th, put it in the file marked the 22nd. Or, to give yourself some extra time, put it in the file marked the 20th.

The monthly files and 31-day tickler files aid you in staying organized and reducing office clutter. Also, when you view something several days, weeks, or months after first filing it, you may have greater objectivity and a new chance to act, file, toss, or delegate it.

If you maintain a tickler file, then you may place the item in that file near the date when it makes sense to take action. It may make sense to add the item to the long-term portion of your super to-do list. In any case, the item is off your desk and out of your mind for the time being, and can be found and handled at a more suitable time.

For those items that can be handled another day, simply slip them into a daily or monthly tickler file. If the materials are too big to go into the tickler file, put a project note in the file, and neatly house the materials in another location, but away from your desk and not in sight.

Toss-It Items

Prior to filing any particular item, assess whether or not it should be filed at all! Much of what we file, unfortunately, represents information crutches—stuff we're never going to use again but somehow it makes us feel comfortable if we retain it. Many documents we save represent old or obsolete information that has already been updated or can quickly be found someplace on the web if we need it. So, items that make your toss-it category should add up quickly. Ideally, your toss-it items will represent the largest of accumulations.

If you have trouble tossing any particular item, sometimes it helps to identify others within your office who might benefit from the item. If you find someone else who would be grateful for receiving what to you represents nothing new, nothing vital to you, you may find it a lot easier to part with the item.

Delegate-It Items

As you continue with Operation Clean Sweep, seek out those items that can be delegated. The more items you can appropriately delegate (see Chapter 21), the clearer and cleaner you keep your desk and work environment, and the more energized and focused you may remain on other, more important tasks.

Look to delegate every single activity that you can possibly delegate. If you and you alone have to tackle something, then that item does not get delegated, and all else does.

If it helps, with a pencil and Post-it pad mark the items with the names of those to whom you will be delegating.

Clear and Clean and Ready for Action

As soon as your Operation Clean Sweep pile is down to nothing—and yes, I mean nothing—immediately allocate the tasks that you have identified as suitable for delegation. Toss or donate that which you do not need to retain, and file those things that are most suitable for filing at that particular time. What's left are the handful of items that you need or want to act upon: the *important* and the *important and urgent* tasks you face today, this week, this month, and on a periodic basis.

Thirty minutes and, poof, the mess is gone. Starting with the act-on-it items, estimate how long it will take to complete each item. Add all your estimates and multiply that number by 1.5 (to account for your optimism or naivety!).

As the number of task hours before you climbs, as it may, you can see dramatically that there is no point continuing as you have. So, get meaner and leaner, and more focused. What else can you chuck? What can be combined, ignored, delayed, delegated, done in multiples, farmed out, automated, or systemized?

> **Dyna Moe**
>
> As each new day or period of high anxiety over all the tasks you face ensues, repeat Operation Clean Sweep and remember to include the items in that day's tickler file.

Anti-Pile Behavior

The best of all worlds, in terms of controlling your sacred turf, is to engage in a routine that heads off piles before they even begin. For example, as soon as the mail arrives, open it—over a wastebasket. Constantly be on the lookout to reduce key data and vital information to its least voluminous form.

Whenever you see a pile starting to form—not just those on your desk—on top of the filing cabinet, around the corners of your room, and covering flat surfaces and ledges, break it up.

Whenever you find folders and tasks mounting up on all sides of you, remember how they got there, and that you are in charge of them, not vice versa. I've found that nothing else will get you moving as fast and as focused as Operation Clean Sweep. You'll also find yourself dropping *nonimportant*, *nonurgent* tasks.

After you've identified the most important project or task, begin working on it to its completion. If you can't complete it because it requires input from others or for some other reason, proceed with it as far as you can go. Then go on to the next item.

Trouble Getting Started?

If your desk is such a mess that you don't know where to get started, first re-read Chapter 6! Otherwise a nice, quick step could be to round up all the pens and pencils that populate your desk from the far corners to those right in front of you. Put them in a pencil holder or pencil can or whatever you want to call your container.

Next, grab all the Post-it pads, small notes, and scraps of paper that contain some type of vital information, be it an address, a phone number, a website, or what have you. Decide here and now to do the following: (a) enter the information on your hard drive in a folder that is typically designed to be a catch-all for such tidbits of information, or (b) lay down these Post-it pads and scraps of information on the copier to create one or two collective pages to be neatly filed, or folded and parked in the corner of your desk for quick reference. (Clue: if you have all such tidbits in one place, you have a far better chance of finding and using them as needed.) Ideally, you don't let such tidbits pile up to begin with. However, human nature being what it is, you are probably going to keep doing this.

> **Dyna Moe**
>
> I've seen people clear up and re-organize a desktop in a few min-utes when they put their minds to it. You'll never know how much you can accomplish in a brief stint.

Now collect all the papers, documents, and file folders on your desk. Also gather up any books, reports, or other large documents and place them on appropriate shelves. If you need specific pages from such documents, copy them on a copier, put those pages in the appropriate file folder, and put the books, documents, and reports on shelves or in appropriate file folders.

If you have trouble getting started, you can schedule your session in your appoint-ment book or calendar as you would any other important obligation. Wait! Schedul-ing Operation Clean Sweep? Won't that represent another burden in a long line of tasks you face? Actually scheduling such time increases the probability of your success! Formally scheduling Operation Clean Sweep sessions to stay organized automatically raises the status of the procedure.

File with Style

As you begin to allocate the top-of-the-pile items during Operation Clean Sweep, once again you'll find yourself doing significant filing. As we've discussed, in this information overload era, filing is essential. What you file, given that you've made good choices about what to retain, supports your career. The goal of filing is to withdraw what you need when you need it (whether it's on a hard drive or in a filing cabinet). The basic tools you need for effective filing are a wastebasket, file folders and labels, a magic marker, and a chair.

I file for several hours once a week. To file intelligently, acquire colored file folders, colored file tabs, and dots. You can set up a system similar to what you would see in a dentist's office with visible, color-coded files. You could have everything related to clients in red files, and everything related to marketing in green, and so on.

The more files you have, the more difficult it is to find any particular file. You are better off with a handful of large files than many small files. This way, you have a much greater chance of choosing the right file.

Found in 60 Seconds

Generally, if you can't find an item in about 60 seconds, you're not organized. This may seem like a stern standard, yet how long should it take you to open up a file cabinet, flip through a couple of files, and find exactly what you're seeking? Organized managers don't require more than about 60 seconds.

Getting to this hallowed state is not going to happen overnight, particularly if you haven't given your files supreme attention in recent weeks or months. But cut yourself some slack, you can make it.

You'll probably have to expend the equivalent of three weekends, or about six days, metered out a half day at a time. If the prospects of killing half a day doing nothing but organizing is going to throw you out of whack, then come in on a Saturday morning when no one is around, and you can work undisturbed.

Periodically, sort through your files, look for outdated items, and chuck them. Make it fun. Pare down those files until you have only the essence. Regardless of your particular inclination toward organizing (some people seem to enjoy it), practically speaking, you have little choice. When others are counting on you, you need to have your materials in order and easily retrievable.

> **CAUTION**
>
> **Coming Undone**
>
> Disorganization can cost you the trust and confidence of those to whom you report and those who report to you. If you have a reputation for mislaying what others have given to you, they begin to change their behavior around you, and not in ways that would please you.

Creative Filing

Be creative when you file. Feel free to experiment—create files that say, "Check in a month," "Check next year," or "I don't know what to do with this." Feel good about your style of filing.

You might establish a "rainy day" file. You would include handwritten notes from other people, pictures, memos, and anything else that helps brighten your day. It could even include performance appraisals, evaluations from speeches or presentations you have made, or simply your bosses' handwritten words or praise accompanying something that you have submitted. Anything and everything that will lift your spirits is fair game for this file.

In closing, if you can't find what you have, your files are of no value. When you're in control of your information and files, you're able to retrieve items easily and use them to get things done. The information your files contain, appropriately used, equals power!

The Least You Need to Know

- ◆ If you fail to consciously assess how you are allocating your time, then you will disproportionately skew toward the *urgent*, independent of its importance.

- ◆ Seek to devote the brunt of your time and energy to tasks that are *important*, but not *urgent*.

- ◆ Prior to filing any particular item, assess whether or not it should be filed at all.

- ◆ In Operation Clean Sweep, top-of-the-pile items fall into one of four categories: *act-on-it*, *file-it*, *toss-it*, or *delegate-it* items.

- ◆ If you have trouble starting Operation Clean Sweep, schedule your session.

- ◆ Use tickler files to park items for a later date when it might prove more advantageous to deal with them.

Chapter 9

E-Mail as an Organizing Tool

In This Chapter

- ◆ Does e-mail dictate your day
- ◆ Why e-mail is addictive
- ◆ Ground rules and common sense
- ◆ Take an e-mail vacation

In preparation for my presentation to an annual convention of commercial printers, I visited the office of one of the larger printers in my area. I had an appointment with the vice president of operations. He made an observation I've never forgotten and which I seek to practice myself every day, which has a tremendous implication regarding getting things done: *don't let e-mail dictate your day*. The savvy executive talked about the people on his staff who receive e-mail in the morning and let it rule the rest of their day.

E-Mail Is a Tool

Certainly vital messages you receive in the course of the day or a week merit a significant allocation of resources. When your time and efforts are driven by e-mail, however, as opposed to what you've listed to get done (the subject of Chapter 11), the type of things you're going to complete will likely be different, lesser in magnitude, and less satisfying than those you achieve when you stick to the items and the course you've plotted.

E-mail is a tool, something like mail, something like the phone. E-mail and instant messaging take the place of face-to-face communication, special deliveries, occasional meetings, and having to verbally converse with others. All of those functions, as convenient and critical as they may be, do not represent a substitute for you taking control of your activities, time and day.

So much has been written but so great is the problem about the crushing burden of e-mail with which managers contend every single workday and then some. I wanted to glean the advice of someone who constantly deals with e-mail issues and who provides solutions to executives in a broad swath of industries and occupations. I turned to one of North America's foremost experts on getting things done via e-mail, Wayne McKinnon, author of *The Complete Guide to E-mail* (Ryshell Books, 1998) and director of www.ITcoach.com.

Wayne's pearls of e-mail management wisdom extend throughout the chapter. As you proceed, notice the ways in which skillfully managing your incoming e-mail parallels managing your desk and office—*act, file, toss,* or *delegate*—via Operation Clean Sweep (discussed in the previous chapter).

The Wisdom of Managing Your Messages

It is Wayne's contention that most people have a hard enough time managing the stacks of paper on their desk, let alone the piles of information in their computers.

CAUTION

Coming Undone

In a corporate environment, your e-mail administrator will not like you if your messages remain undeleted on the e-mail server. If everyone left their junk on the server, it could soon fill up and we would be unable to receive new messages.

"The amount of junk you will collect is directly proportional to the space available, says Wayne. "Computers encourage us to keep more information than we otherwise might."

Keeping the number of stored messages to a minimum saves time.

If you have to sort through hundreds of messages each time you seek information, your search will be inefficient. Many stored messages become redundant once you receive a more recent message. It's easier to clean things up as you go along than to face the daunting task of tackling a mountain of unsorted messages.

Move Your Mail Messages to Your Own Hard Disk

If you work in an environment where your e-mail might be stored on an e-mail server, to eliminate the possibility that your e-mail server will fill up, the system administrator may impose a limit on the size of each user's mailbox. Find out the limits in your system, if any, and consider what you will do if you approach those limits. Depending on your type of system, move your messages to e-mail folders on your own hard disk.

If you decide to store your messages locally rather than on the e-mail server, then of course, you and you alone are responsible to back up those files. As a precaution, store critical information on disks, CDs, or as a permanent archive.

Read Your E-Mail in the Morning

By getting an early start, you can arrive at work relaxed and ready to take on the day. Spend your first quiet moments before the day piles up doing the necessary things—plan your day before the hectic pace takes over.

For some people an efficient start includes checking their e-mail. Perhaps your daily plan depends on the e-mail you receive. Depending on the nature of your work, you may check e-mail once at the start of the day, or only after all of your other tasks are complete.

Your answer will depend greatly on how strategic e-mail is to your job function. If you are in a support role and your e-mail tells you that you have a fire to put out, then by all means make checking your e-mail a morning priority. But don't waste your most productive time of the day checking discretionary messages. Focus on the important ones at the time when they need your attention.

Assign and Delegate Tasks Before You Respond

If you begin your day by reading new mail, delegate what you can before you respond. You may find that others can handle the tasks better, or provide you with useful information to help you respond. Where appropriate, ask the person to whom you delegate the message to respond directly to the original sender, with a cc to yourself. This saves time and keeps you from being an e-mail bottleneck.

Dyna Moe

Most people, most of the time, simply want an answer to their e-mail questions ... and they don't care where it comes from!

The remaining tasks have to be done by you, but is today the best day, or should they be scheduled for another time? Plan your day. If you have an integrated contact manager, such as Microsoft Outlook, you can prioritize and schedule your tasks all in one place. If not, enter your tasks in your calendar, daybook, or personal information manager.

Save Most Replies 'Til Later

Reply to all other messages in the afternoon. Once you have collected the necessary details, and received answers from those you have delegated the tasks to, you are ready to respond. Your goal is to reply to everyone who e-mailed you that day by closing time, or at least before the next morning, when they'll likely sort through their e-mail.

If you're really swamped, respond with a standard reply stating that you have received the message and it will be X days before you can reply in detail. Also consider if you can forward the e-mail to someone else who can handle it. (Be sure to keep the sender in the loop.)

CAUTION

Coming Undone

Everyone needs to understand that the value of sending a message marked "high priority" is lost when all messages are set to that level.

Not all messages are equal, so mark your messages with the proper priority. Messages from customers and your boss generally are *important* and may be *urgent*. Read those messages before the rest of your in-box. Since many e-mail systems allow you to mark an urgency level on the messages you send, encourage your colleagues and any staff to use this feature appropriately.

If your e-mail system does not provide a priority feature, write a subject line that will help the recipient classify the message.

Rules of Engagement

Long after clearing out the spam and junk, resist the temptation to read all of your remaining messages. Information messages from listservs and other sources may be worth retaining, but these can be read when you choose. They can be stored for later reading or for reference.

Where there are several messages with a common thread, read the latest first. You may not need to read the earlier messages at all.

Create folders on your computer for each project you work on. Move all correspondence into the appropriate folders. If a particular response is part of a project, move the message to the appropriate project folder. This way you will have both sides of the conversation on file for future reference.

When the project is over, you can delete the entire folder, combine it with something else, extract relevant parts, or archive it.

Practically speaking, there's no danger in "losing" an e-mail because logically it has to be in one of two or three places: either date-related files, project-named files, or some other category. With the find and search capabilities of major e-mail software programs, even if you did temporarily lose track of where you moved an e-mail message, you can find it by the date it arrived, the subject line, the sender, or part of the message text. So, keep your in-box organized and clean. This is habit-forming and a good thing!

Dyna Moe

Get creative when it comes to establishing electronic file folders that serve as holding bins. You can create files based on the project name, a team member name, the client or customer name, and so on. You can also create files for the day of the week, the weeks in a month, the months in a year, and so on. It takes less than half an hour to set up this file system and the dividends pay off, over and over again.

Set a Time Limit

If e-mail is not a business-critical application for you, in other words if you're not hired specifically to handle e-mail, don't let it distract you from your work. Determine what times of the day are your most productive and make these e-mail blackout periods.

If you typically run out of steam at 3:00 in the afternoon, schedule half an hour or so then to review your messages. Stick to the time limit you have chosen. Without time limits, you could spend an entire day sorting and reading the in-box on your desk.

By quickly sorting discretionary mail into one pile, you can simply throw it away if you run out of time. If you have been out of the office for a while, scan your messages and read the newest ones first. If you see more than one message from an individual, chances are the most recent contains more information, or tells you that they have already received the answer they need.

Some companies discourage the use of e-mail during certain hours in an effort to get employees talking again! Douglas Richardson, in careerjournal.com, says while on the job "don't rely on e-mail too much when you're just getting to know someone. E-mail may be easy for you to create, but it's also easy for the person on the receiving end to destroy. You're at the recipient's mercy." Also, not too many people will open up a morning list of 71 new e-mail messages and think, "Oh wow! 71 opportunities for meaningful human interaction."

Set Aside Items You Receive

Do you regularly read the messages that people copy to you for your reference? If your in-box is jam packed with cc'd items that you can't seem to get to, you may miss some of the *important* messages sent directly to you.

Set up an e-mail rule that automatically moves all carbon copy items to one folder so you can refer to them later if you wish. Establish a reasonable time limit by which you will delete these messages.

If you subscribe to mailing lists, make sure that your e-mail client provides you with a way to automatically sort messages and store them in specific folders. You can set up your rule to recognize the subject of the message and automatically file information-only items away. You might never look at these items, but they are filed for future reference if you ever need them.

If you have an automatic rule that sorts messages based on the subject, be aware that if the subject line is not exactly the same for each message, your rule will not work.

Dyna Moe
E-mail comes in waves all day long, pretty much whether you want it to or not. Most of it is junk, but much of it requires attention. To engender a feeling of accomplishment and completion, and at the same time actually get many things done, maintain zero e-mail in your in-box. It sounds difficult, but in practice is easy. There's no justification for having a huge number of e-mails build up in your in-box and a great case for maintaining zero or close to zero mail in the in-box. The same can be said for the sent box. Once you've sent an e-mail to someone, simply allocate it to one of the types of folders previously discussed.

Keeping It Moving

Set up a rule to automatically move material—newsletters, for example—to appropriate folders. Begin by moving new messages to a subfolder titled "Just Arrived." At the end of, say, each week, move unread items from "Just Arrived" to a subfolder called "Recent," and move the items in "Recent" to a third folder called "Remove."

If you decide that any information more than a month old can be discarded, then every month delete the entire contents of the "Remove" folder … without reading a single message! Once this folder is empty, move the contents of the "Recent" folder to the "Remove" folder, and move the "Just Arrived" to the "Recent" folder.

Any time during the week you can read the contents of any of these folders, keeping in mind that at the end of the cycle you must throw away the contents of the "Remove" folder without looking at it.

You Can't Read Them All!

If you receive relatively few e-mail messages daily, this is likely not a problem for you. If you're swamped, it is useless to try to keep up. Be selective about which information items you read. Remove yourself from mailing lists that you never get around to reading. If you are fortunate enough to have an assistant, prepare a list of criteria that he or she can use to evaluate whether or not you need to personally respond to each message.

Don't jeopardize your time, your income, or your sanity by becoming a full-time message handler and personal advisor to the world. Some people will take everything you give them and still ask for more. By answering their questions, you invite them to ask again. If you find that your willingness to help is being taken advantage of, refer the offender to a book or other resource.

Alternatively make your response very brief. In trying to be polite, we often send out the message that we would be happy to continue helping. This example shows a polite but conclusive response to a request for help:

Question: Hi! Could you tell me how to do ABC?

Answer: Please refer to page 10 of your user manual.

If you have to respond to the same question repeatedly, save the response and re-use it the next time you need to answer that question again. Better yet, post the response in a public area such as your website. You can build a list of frequently asked questions (FAQs) where others can find their answers.

Dyna Moe
Be sure to write informative sub- ject lines yourself. If your mes- sage requests action, mention that right at the top, so your reader doesn't have to wade through the message to prioritize it. If everyone you communicate with uses this procedure, you won't need to read most mes- sages past the header—you'll see it's not critical information.

Decide and Move On

Go ahead and make decisions based on the subject line! Most times, you should quickly be able to make filing or action decisions based on the subject. This is more crucial when you are traveling, since palm top e-mail allows you to view the headers even before downloading the messages.

Use previews to sort and delete and resist the temptation to read! If you're swamped with e-mail, quickly scan your messages. If the subject line does not provide enough detail, the preview function pro- vided by many e-mail programs allows you to see the first few lines of text without opening the message.

Filter Out the Junk

E-mail software increasingly offers more-sophisticated filtering systems. By setting up specific rules, you can automatically sort, respond to and delete messages. If you receive junk mail from a particular address, set up a filter that will automatically file or delete any message they send to you. You already know this, but are you using your filter to the best advantage? Largely for review, here are basic examples of what filters can do for you:

- Maintain a list of your top-priority contacts, and move everything else out of your in-box.

- Weed out unwelcome known addresses.

- Filter based on message text (look for common phrases).

- Find what works for you depending on the types of messages you receive.

Marketing companies that are notorious for spamming cruise on-line areas of the Internet to collect e-mail addresses. Sophisticated "robots" search for text that looks like e-mail addresses. Prevent your address from being picked by making it invisible to these robots. One way is to change the format of your e-mails. For example, on Wayne's website, *Info@ITcoach.com* can instead be written as *info(at)ITcoach.com*.

This format looks enough like a typical e-mail address for most people to under- stand, but the robots will likely miss it. The downside is that if someone does want to contact you, they cannot simply click on your e-mail address. Instead, they will have to compose a message manually and enter your proper address.

Give Yourself a Break

Psychologists have started diagnosing a new psychological disorder called *communicative enslavement*. Communicative enslavement is characterized by obsessively checking and rechecking e-mail for new messages, or by refusing to leave the vicinity of the computer, so as to always be available to someone else via chat or e-mail.

Word Power

Communicative enslavement is the desire to stay in constant communication to the point of interfering with the activities of daily living.

As you read in Chapter 1, information and communication overload is a sociocultural phenomenon impacting virtually every adult in society. This phenomenon has reached pathological proportions for many individuals. I hope you're not among them.

Unquestionably, e-mail can be addictive. It is gratifying to receive thanks for a job well done or for information you forward to someone else. For people working from home, e-mail may be one of their only contacts with the outside world. For their corporate counterparts, it can be an escape from the office while still at one's desk.

These little gratifications throughout the day can be addictive. Like a kid waiting for a letter from his pen pal, you anxiously await a new e-mail message … from anyone!

In a corporate network or with cable, DSL, or T1, you are always connected. If you are automatically notified when a new message arrives, you may not waste time checking for mail, although you may waste a great deal of time reading frivolous messages. And your concentration and ability to get things done may suffer from the constant notices.

Sure, many people need to check in regularly for messages so that they can reply in a timely fashion, but for e-mail addicts, popping out to the Internet just one more time to check the mail is no different than popping just one more quarter in a slot machine or video game.

If you are starving for attention or gratification, sometimes it is best just to give in. Pick up the telephone and complete an entire conversation in minutes instead of dragging it out over days. Once satisfied, move on and get some work done.

Take an "E-Mail Vacation"

Many tasks require concentration. When you're in a state of "flow," you can accomplish your work more easily. E-mail is supposed to be unobtrusive, so why do you let it interrupt you when you are busy? If your e-mail system automatically notifies you of each incoming message, turn that feature off when you don't want to be distracted, which ideally is much of the time.

> **Dyna Moe**
>
> Schedule a time to check your e-mail. Plan your day in constructive blocks of time dictated by the types of tasks you have for that day or week. Allow yourself to check your e-mail only after you have completed a task. Even the biggest projects can be broken down into smaller chunks that will give you a sense of accomplishment.

Many people find that checking e-mail is a good way to wind down before leaving the office. Others find it a terrific way to raise their stress level. If you find that work has taken over your life, a few evenings per week make a point of not checking your e-mail before you depart from work. Cut yourself loose and enjoy some down-time away from e-mail and any other form of communication with the office.

The Least You Need to Know

- If you have to sort through hundreds of messages every time you look for information, your search will not be efficient, so manage and weed out as you go along.

- If you begin your day by reading new mail, delegate what you can before you respond.

- Create folders for each project and move all correspondence including responses into the appropriate project folder so that you'll have both sides of the conversation on file.

- If the e-mail subject line does not provide enough detail, use the preview function to see the first few lines of text without opening the message.

- If work has taken over your life, a few evenings per week don't check e-mail before you depart.

Chapter 10

The Hard Drive for High Productivity

In This Chapter

- The rise of megalomania
- Don't fight the system
- Handheld and powerful

In the first four chapters of Part 3, thus far we have addressed organizational issues related to your desk, files, shelves, and office; paper and correspondence; *important* versus *urgent* criteria, and e-mail. Now we turn to the issue of organizing information per se, as in what do we do with all this stuff?! What do we make of it? How can we classify information and benefit from it?

The Rise of Electronic Addiction

One of the strangest phenomena I've encountered in my 22 years as an author and speaker is the rise of electronic addiction among career professionals. Electronic addiction is the overarching desire to stay connected and seemingly on top of things—to be control, to be in the driver's seat.

In our over-information society, where people are bombarded on a daily basis with more information than they can comfortably ingest, oddly enough, they often go out of their way to take in more than they know they can handle!

"Search" and "find" techniques have become a breeze. The Internet has both elevated and exacerbated our ability to gather information in a hurry. All you have to do is go to one of these high-flying search engines, type in a few key words, and voilà, hundreds if not thousands or tens of thousands of hits. As one observer put it: "the Internet is so big, so powerful and pointless that for some people it is a complete substitute for life."

On the road, you can take your notebook computer, your Blackberry, cell phone, pager, and presto chango, you can still keep your mitts on things. The quest to stay on top of it all, however, is not solely related to online and voice communications. People subscribe to another magazine or another newsletter. People sign up for more catalogues, more brochures, and more information coming their way.

With the flood of e-mail in everyone's in-boxes these days, along with the abundance of informative and entertaining Internet sites, on top of all the printed information that comes one's way, it's almost as if people are equating being deluged with being alive. "I'm overwhelmed by information, therefore I am." In 1844 Henry David Thoreau succinctly summarized his approach to a satisfying life: simplify, simplify, simplify. Today, it appears as if we can't even follow a third of his advice.

A Little Bit Can Go a Long Way Toward Wisdom

By continually assessing the information that comes your way, staying organized, and applying what you've learned or know in ways that yield usable, transferable knowledge, you can become more valuable in the work place, get more done, and rise faster and further in your career.

Here is a basic classification system for the progression to knowledge and even wisdom:

- The lowest level of input is **bits,** single packets of information that essentially say yes or no, left or right, on or off. In combination, bits add up to data. Mostly, this stuff doesn't affect you.

- **Data** are raw numbers in chart form, equations, lists, and so on. Ideally, they are objective, readily observable, and readily understandable. When worked upon, data has value.

◆ One step up from data is **information,** which, as used in this classification system, is the manipulation of data, analysis, interpretation, and reporting. For example, virtually every article that you come across in magazines and newspapers contains information. Some even share knowledge or convey wisdom (see below). Authors of articles, books, and other documents draw upon some data or observable phenomena, make some conclusions, and offer commentary.

◆ When information is added to experience and viewed with reflection, depending upon whose brain is in the driver's seat, it can yield **knowledge.** Think of knowledge as the product of lots of information that somebody gathered, thought about, and started to draw conclusions from. The most knowledgeable people in your profession, not by coincidence, tend to read considerably, organize their notes, develop original thoughts, and then postulate (and draw conclusions) from what they have taken in.

> **Dyna Moe**
>
> Comparing knowledge with others makes one valuable both within an organization and with clients and customers. The most knowledgeable salespeople, all other things being equal, have the best chance of achieving greater results.

◆ When new knowledge is gathered and added to one's existing knowledge, **wisdom** becomes possible. This is as true for organizations as it is for individuals.

Wisdom often comes slowly, sometimes only after years of accumulated knowledge. In your career, it's exceedingly easy to get caught up in the glut of data and information. It may be temporarily satisfying to maintain an unrelenting pace of reading everything that crosses your desk, downloading files, subscribing to publications, and so on. Indeed, much new knowledge can be generated from such efforts.

> **Dyna Moe**
>
> As you begin to draw upon your own accumulated knowledge and the wisdom that you develop, you will be able to free yourself from ever-accelerating flows of information, save time, get more done, and be more valuable to those around you.

Wisdom, in an age where far too much information confronts each of us, often comes in the form of the ability to recognize broad-based patterns and long-term trends rather than being caught up in short-term phenomena and, worse, fads.

Jumping In Versus Establishing Control

Here's a bit of organizing wisdom to which we can all readily relate. How often have you slugged your way through a new software program without bothering to read even the summary card of instructions? You learn enough to be proficient, but you never master the program. You're willing to undertake trial-and-error approaches to getting things done.

Coming Undone

In our culture people often work 50 to 55 hours a week for 40 hours' pay. Many "throw their time" at problems as opposed to establishing control over the immediate environment and thereby devising useful systems for accomplishment.

Sometimes you get lucky and things work on the first couple go-rounds. Buoyed by a few successes, trial and error becomes your method of operation. Too often, you're frustrated and stymied. You spend endless amounts of time going down wrong paths, experiencing more errors for your trials, and still you have no intention or even a notion of actually reading the directions.

You fail to stop and take the time to devise a system, which initially makes for slow going, but ultimately pays off in terms of increased time savings with each deployment. Many of the systems that we could devise, to make us more productive and to help us avoid throwing our time at a problem, simply require taking an organized or more methodical approach to learning.

Learn or Devise a System

Submitting a monthly report that requires consistent headings and format is best facilitated by learning your word-processing software's style-management function. That takes time and effort, but represents a viable approach to succinctly accomplishing what you need to do.

Refusing to learn the style function and manually formatting each month's report is analogous to throwing your time at a problem. You'll get the report done, but the 10 to 15 minutes you lose each time in preparing it has a cumulative impact. Now, add this behavior and time loss to all the other ways in which you throw your time at problems rather than devising or taking advantage of pre-established systems.

It becomes clear that the time cost of getting things done, for you, is significantly higher than it needs to be. This cost, in turn, exacerbates other time pressures you may be experiencing in getting other things done. You're on a downward cycle that knows no end. You stay at work longer, enjoy yourself less, and wonder why others are passing you by. You don't seem to be completing the critical tasks and have little hope of tackling larger, longer-term challenges.

Minor Changes, Major Results

Along your career path, it's a guarantee that how you previously got things done or what worked yesterday will have less and less value with each passing day. You certainly want some stability, but don't fear change or close yourself off to it.

Peter and Rosemary Grant, Princeton University biologists, have spent the last 30 years in the footsteps of Charles Darwin in the study of mate selection. Cactus finches, for example, breed based on what nature provides for them. In 1977 they only had a few seeds left from the year before, as a drought devastated the landscape. Breeding was down. As a result, the next generation, actually evolved larger, blunter beaks. Six years later, there was a surplus of seeds along with heavy rains. The finches bred profusely.

In 1985 there was another drought, leaving only small seeds in the ground. These seeds favored smaller, quicker birds with thin beaks. The Grants came to an astounding conclusion: *even the most minor changes in the environment*, such as an increase or decrease in rain or rising temperatures, *can have a huge impact* on the course of evolution. In many respects, the same holds true for your career: even minor changes in how you manage your environment (i.e., organizing your desk, your office, your time, your approach to learning) can yield great payoffs.

A Simple System and You're Welcome to It

Have you ever considered the number of options you have when you load a new software application or make a new connection to the Internet? Toggle this on, toggle this off, choose this, elect that, ignore this, make this your default, customize this, ignore that. So many options, so little time!

Sure, there are people who understand these things, and they're usually under 20 years old. If you were born before the personal computer came along, however, then it's not as likely that it will become second nature to you. With this as a backdrop, the real issue becomes, how much time do you want to waste in your life and in your career fiddling with such stuff?

Factoid _____

Thomas A. Edison, on accomplishment: "Hell, there are no rules here—we're trying to accomplish something."

I am among those who won't read the instruction manual or card. In fact, I refuse to open an instruction book, and I refuse to look at the laminated instruction card that comes with so many products today—are you with me on this one? For me, the issue is clear. I want to spend _zero_ seconds fiddling with hardware or software instructions and spend the brunt of my time getting things done that I seek to get done.

Help Is at Hand

I bring in a junior instructor, a web guru, a PC specialist, someone who knows the Internet like the back of his hand, someone who is either majoring in computer science or already has his home wired from basement to ceiling.

Word Power _____

When you **codify** something, you organize it into a system, such as a body of laws or instructions.

Item by item, function by function, we review both what I reasonably ought to be able to do with the equipment and what kinds of things I want to get done as a result of being able to use the equipment. Then, we _codify_ everything. We list the steps, item by item, make labels; no problem. Gadget by gadget, item by item, function by function, we list the instructions that I need to know.

Dyna Moe

The larger your organization, the greater the chance there is someone with whom you can strike up a business relationship. They help you with all things technical and you help them with some skill you can teach which they wish to master. Or you pay them!

We go over it until I have it down cold. It's called "Jeff-proofing," instead of calling it idiot-proofing. After my guru departs, I have the sacred set of instructions. Now and then, yes, I still run astray. No problem, I'll park that one for now, and at the next possible opportunity my guru makes whatever modifications necessary to the instructions. Sometimes, it's simply a word change, "enter" versus "click" versus "return."

By and by, we hone and refine any set of instructions that requires modifications. No endless bouts with the instruction manual for me, no siree.

Creating a Computer and Software Instruction File

I haven't opened a computer or software instruction booklet in more than ten years. Yet, I know exactly how to operate my hardware and software to accomplish what I choose to accomplish.

I've learned the importance of creating one master file, alphabetical by topic, of all the instructions that I need. Whether I learn these instructions on my own, attend a training session, or am told specifically by a computer guru "how to do it," everything I may need to refer to is housed in one ever-growing file.

Currently my instruction file is 26 pages, but it wouldn't matter if it were doubled in length. I can find what I need in a hurry. Whether it's how to use the print screen function, the actual specifications for each of the computers that I own, how to access the server to make changes to my website, or how to synchronize the database on my main computer with my networked computers, I have all instructions boiled down to the essence in this single, amply backed-up file.

Any time I learn a new routine, a new way of doing something, I immediately codify the procedure and save it in my instruction file.

Over the years, I've had different computer gurus instruct me. As one departs and another arrives, the new one is always ably aided by my instruction file. Using the convenient word-search function, we can quickly get to any topic and any set of instructions.

Scheduling Software, Calendar Systems, and Organizers

Here is another area where operating proficiency sometimes requires some organizing groundwork. Since the technology for what we're about to discuss changes so quickly, we'll focus on general capabilities and basic principles upon which you can rely.

Scheduling software, calendar systems, electronic organizers, and the like fall into the category of personal information managers (PIMs). The nomenclature is not standard, some people simply call them organizers, some refer to them by brand name such as "Blackberry." Keep in mind that even with the vast array of information and communication capabilities that such devices provide, the four principal Operation Clean Sweep alternatives—*act, file, toss,* or *delegate*—still apply.

The features at your disposal vary. PIMs today come with clocks, timers, and alerts. You can send and receive e-mail, websurf, or take pictures. Electronic scheduling tools, or ESTs for short, are software that enhance your hardware, be it your desktop PC or a notebook-size computer. As basic features, scheduling tools provide an appointment book and calendar, a to-do list, a database, and a notepad.

All-In-One

You can, of course, store names and addresses, keep appointments on your calendar, record notes, and maintain lists. You can generate business correspondence with an integrated word processor and transfer it via e-mail. You can manage your schedule with a built-in appointment calendar, use drag 'n' drop capabilities to move a name and phone number onto or off of an appointment calendar, and personalize the way you search and retrieve records. You can search through thousands of records to quickly find the contact person or information you need.

You can insert icons both on appointment calendars and lists you're maintaining. Icons could include a sun, a rose, a star, or a smiley face. You can print your calendar or any key lists. You can toggle on alerts to remind yourself when to make a call, and have the call dialed for you. You can color-code files and bits of information for easy retrieval. Thus, you benefit from color-coding in much the same way you do when dealing with manual files (see Chapter 8).

ESTs enable you to consolidate other calendars that you maintain. They'll prompt you as to meetings, appointments, and any other notable event. They enable you to identify scheduling conflicts. You can change priorities, move items around on to-do lists, and delete them instantly. You can engage in keyword searches. Online and connected via global positioning satellite, you can initiate vendor searches of the variety "where's the nearest printer from where I'm standing?"

> **Dyna Moe**
>
> When shopping for a palm top, keep it simple—identify the four or five major features that you require. This will help you screen out the majority of products that are available. You can then give a closer look to the few remaining ones that make the initial cut.

As hardware and software capabilities advance, the list of options will become endless. The systems will more closely emulate your PC, i.e., you can load in what you want and you can move data around as you wish. Hence, more and more people find these units to be daily essentials to getting things done.

What Can Go Wrong Will

With any tool of productivity, keep in mind that over-use as well as mis-use can diminish, not enhance, your productivity. The potential downside of using palm tops, or computers for that matter, for getting things done is significant. No gadget can re-schedule a one-time meeting for you. Anytime you enter incorrect data, it will give you incorrect data until you fix it—the old garbage-in, garbage-out problem, except this time you may be relying heavily on the garbage.

Dyna Moe

Until such devices can decode your brain waves, any time your priorities change or your schedule changes, you need to add the information to your system. In this respect, nothing is new under the sun, your schedule is up to you, and your effectiveness is up to you. So what does portable computing power add to your life? More organization, reminders, less clutter, and perhaps peace of mind.

If you're away from your palm top, you're going to resort to notes and Post-it pads when new items come up, and add them later, as you would with any system. For any device to be supremely effective, they'd have to accompany you wherever you go.

The handheld transfer option allows you to transfer data from your PC to a palm top and back. Thus, you can overwrite old data with new information. If a phone number or someone's address changes, and you transfer the information between different-size computers, both will carry the correct and latest data.

The systems are getting more powerful by the day, but as with all of the recommendations in this book, keep your files lean and mean. Record what you want and need to, but have the strength to leave out that which need not be entered at all. You'll be way ahead, and get more done.

The Least You Need to Know

- ◆ Instead of throwing your time at a problem, have the patience to learn or develop systems that will make you more productive and stay better organized.

- ◆ The hardware and software capabilities of handheld devices are more closely emulating your PC, and so these units are regarded by many as essential to getting things done.

- With any tool of productivity, over-use as well as mis-use can diminish, not enhance, your productivity.

- When adding data to any of your systems, record what you want and need to, but leave out that which need not be entered at all.

Part 4

Becoming More Efficient in the Workplace

Efficiency at work! Now there's something worth attaining. The chapters in this part of the book help you become more efficient in getting things done. We'll cover the importance of codifying everything you want to get done, the delicate difference between being proficient at longer-term tasks versus accomplishing things right now, tools to help you stay on track in accomplishing what lies in your path, and how to stay in control on the bigger and more-involved tasks and projects you face.

From Your Head to the Page

In This Chapter

- Keeping it all straight
- To-do lists forever
- One giant list for everything
- Short circuits with the shock

Once upon a time the typical worker in our society sweated a little more, but was anxious a little less. Actual physical work would tax one's muscles but would not contribute to the mounting form of stress that so easily builds up when handling office work. When you could physically see what you had done—say, moved all the boxes from this side of the room to that side of the room—there was less of a chance of misunderstanding how much you had accomplished.

Today's workplace presents you with a never-ending stream of information and communication, much of which needs to be addressed. Often little barrier exists between professional tasks and personal tasks, and it's hard sometimes to know when your working day is actually "done." This chapter presents a guide to making the kind of lists that will help you to stay organized and productive.

The Best Chance to Keep It Straight

In days of yore, the factory whistle at 5 P.M. signaled the end of the work day. What signals the end today? Virtually nothing. With so many items begging for your attention and your unvoiced commitment to attend to them, the state of being over-whelmed never seems to subside. Considering everything on your plate, how are you going to keep it all straight?

As I speak at conferences and conventions, it never ceases to amaze me: to this day, people are always asking me about to-do lists. Do they need to have one, and perhaps more appropriately, how do they best maintain them? I can't think of anyone in the workaday world who doesn't use some form or variation of a to-do list as a primary tool for getting things done.

I don't believe there is a tactic as appealing or that proves to be as useful as a classic to-do list. It seems the more you do, the more you need them.

The more responsibility you have at work, the more you need to write down and codify everything you need to get done. Especially when you have two or more people reporting to you. There will simply be too much floating in your head.

Except for the brief tasks that confront you, for which it makes sense to take care of them on the spot without ever entering them on a to-do list, everything else needs to be recorded in one way or another.

> **Dyna Moe**
>
> It's a semi-bonus anytime you can knock out something without it having to make your to-do list, but the brunt of the tasks and projects that you face, being longer and more involved, don't necessarily fall into that category.

Count on this: the to-do list is not going to go away soon (nor should it). The human brain, the wonder-ful contraption that it is, has trouble retaining lists, specific sequences, and minute detail. If you doubt this, try reciting the phone numbers, right now, of several different friends, or the sequence of digits of the two credit cards you use most often.

In this era of unprecedented, non-stop bombard-ment of information and communication, to-do lists have become a quintessential tool in furthering our careers. They help shape what we do, when we do it, and even how we do it. A career professional without a to-do list is worse off than a ship without a rudder. At least the crew might be able to conjure up some makeshift means of navigation.

Proceeding without a to-do list is a recipe for going over the rapids. You could recall some things that you need to tend to, but you'd forget others for days or forever.

Those items screaming for your attention, the *urgent*, would keep jumping up to the front of the line, squeezing out the *important* and the *important and urgent*. Worse, the *unimportant and not urgent* would see the light of day, and a bit too often at that!

What's more, the items that you do not get done, incompletions, have a way of reverberating in your head (see Chapter 16), coming back to you over and over, hence magnifying and multiplying themselves. Since the number of responsibilities, tasks, and projects that you face far exceed what you can keep track of in your head, you have to get it all down on paper, disk, or microchip. Otherwise, you'll face mounting forms of anxiety that can lead to all kinds of trouble.

So, one of your primary tasks is to log in everything—everything that you want to get accomplished. If you don't, you're liable to receive intermittent alerts from your brain all day and all night long.

> **Dyna Moe**
>
> To be in control of your career and your life, to squarely face the age-old dilemma about how to stay on top of what you need or want to get done, and to maintain your sanity, you've got to embrace the concept of creating and using to-do lists with the enthusiasm of a crow in a cornfield.

A Brief History

Who knows when the first to-do list first saw the light of day. It might have happened in the caves of France along with those early drawings depicting "the hunt" with some fresh croissants afterward.

More likely, soon after human-kind gravitated towards carving messages into the bark of trees and logs and stone slates, somebody somewhere probably recorded a list of stuff they wanted to get done:

- Hunt the mastodon
- Gather firewood
- Make new war clubs
- Repair bow and arrow
- Grab woman by hair and drag back to cave …

The Paper Chase

Invented by the Chinese in 105 A.D., paper proved to be a handy media for marking notes. Undoubtedly, early forms of to-do lists flourished after this invention. By the height of early Greek civilization, and certainly by the time the Romans ruled the Western world, the head slave of any household probably found it convenient to go to the market with a list.

Flash forward a millennium and a half and you have Martin Luther nailing his 95 *theses* to a church door in Wittenburg. Okay, they were more like grievances but, inverted, could be seen as a grand to-do list containing all kinds of changes that this protestor felt were necessary in the Church.

> **Word Power**
>
> **Theses,** as used here, refers to strongly suggested reforms—items that needed to be changed.

The Western Swing

Add a century or two, skip over the Atlantic to the new world, and you have Ben Franklin publishing gazettes, writing almanacs, and turning the to-do list into a near art form. Let's see:

- Start the first public library
- Perfect bifocal lenses
- Launch first volunteer fire department
- Discover electricity
- Become governor of Pennsylvania
- Help draft and sign the Declaration of Independence
- Sign the U.S. Constitution
- Raise funds in France for the Revolutionary War

You get the idea ....

Quills gave way to pens, and ratty paper gave way to smooth sheets, 500 to a ream. Here and abroad,

> **Dyna Moe**
>
> Documenting all that you want to get done from this afternoon's tasks, to forthcoming trips, to long-term goals, to retirement puts you on the path to greater control and greater accomplishment.

the world of to-do list makers were on an upward trajectory. Aided by manual type-writers, then IBM Selectrics, then Lexigraphs, then computers, along with copiers, fax machines, and printers, the to-do list as notation of desired personal and professional accomplishments became the most ubiquitous productivity tool in the world.

To-Do Lists Rule

Today, among career professionals, do you know anyone who proceeds throughout the workday and -week without some written or recorded compilation of what they want, need, or have been told to get done? To-do lists appear in notebooks, on notepads, on single sheets of paper, and on Post-it pads. They appear on-screen in desktop PCs, notebook computers, palm tops, and cell phones.

They're transmitted via disk, e-mail, and fax, and copied in duplicate and triplicate. They're posted here, there, and everywhere. People carry them in their front pocket, back pocket, purses, briefcases, billfolds, satchels, and everything in between.

People are forever updating, merging, losing, rewriting, and becoming frustrated by to-do lists. Many people have more than one to-do list! They have one for a particular project, one for recurring items, one for longer-term distant types of objectives, and so on.

Utility Over the Top

When you maintain a to-do list, and any of its kin such as an appointment schedule, or plain old rosters of stuff that you need or want to get done, you accomplish several things:

◆ You have a document you can refer to, amend, and update, as well as print, copy, and bring with you.

◆ You free your mind from having to carry and dwell on such items. You know that you've put it on paper. That in itself is highly comforting.

◆ You have a better chance of taking an organized approach to handling these tasks and responsibilities. You can rank them, schedule them, rearrange them, and even eliminate them when you've either accomplished the task or the situation has changed such that the task no longer needs to be done.

Dyna Moe

A free and clear state is a license to create, perform, and achieve—like a person finally giving a speech who is no longer concerned about the preparation, rehearsal, and coaching, and is now simply in a pure delivery state.

♦ You get the satisfaction of crossing things off your list when you have accomplished them. A cheap thrill at the list, such cross-offs can be quite gratifying.

Independent of how much you rely upon to-do lists, in general, if you've gone too long with too much dancing in your head, and I'm not talking days or weeks but rather months or years, it may be hard to recall when your mind was free and clear. A cluttered mind is a terrible thing, as is a cluttered desk, office, and e-mail in-box.

Getting Clear

To embark on the magnificent road of establishing a viable to-do list, you want to move everything from your head to the page. Whether you use a simple pad and paper, a palm top or Blackberry, a notebook or desktop computer, or something else, once you have listed every thing that you want and need and are directed to accomplish, your anxiety level begins to simmer down.

What are the processes by which you will collect everything floating around in your world, desk, office, home, car, briefcase, and wallet, as well as your head? I prefer to use a pocket dictator to quickly generate lists and then have such lists transcribed and saved on disk. Many career professionals swear by their palm tops, Blackberrys, or other form of personal information manager. You may use whatever tool you find to be comfortable and convenient.

Aligning Your World

You may need to tap a variety of source materials: lists, rosters, notes, business cards, outlines, phone messages, etc. Recognize this, however: you and you alone are responsible for generating this grand compilation. Unquestionably, you are responsible for initiating and maintaining the pipeline of source materials that ultimately will be organized and captured on your to-do list. This requires setting up the various environments in which you dwell to support this effort.

You may need pads, pens, tape recorders, disks, and electronic tools in the stations of your life when you are most likely to need them. This means allocating your tools so that they are near your bed, in your glove compartment, in your briefcase, in your suitcase, and what have you.

CAUTION

Coming Undone

If you haven't aligned your life with the implements that would enable you to jot down what you want to record or what you want or need to add to your get-it-done compilation, then you're not serious in your approach to getting things done. You'll get some things done, those that are easier to recall, and you'll leave off others, those that momentarily crept into your consciousness and just as easily crept out.

Collecting Bins

Many people find it convenient to maintain a catch-all folder in their briefcases or desk drawers so that all the notes, lists, receipts, article clippings, business cards, and announcements can be temporarily housed. Then when you return from a convention, travel, or simply a meeting down the hall, you can quickly allocate and address the items in the folder.

If you're a palm top devotee, your mission is to list every inkling of an idea, such as a phone call you need to return, notes you want to review, a book you want to buy, as soon as you have the first idea at all.

From Making Lists to Taking Action

You've undertaken the exercise of listing what you want to get done, but now what are you going to do about it? Some of the smaller, less-critical stuff is easier to tackle than the larger, more intricate, and important stuff. A solid approach is to rank the tasks from "1" to the end. Regardless of the size of the project, if you break it into steps and have a clear and bite-sized task before you, you can build momentum more easily than you imagined.

Divide and Conquer

For each item that makes your list, go ahead and record a first, second, and even third step as to what you're going to do to realize its accomplishment. For a small project, the steps may be as simple as visiting a website, calling for information, or walking over to the file cabinet.

Dyna Moe

You can't always proceed on every task project as swiftly as you'd like. Sometimes you have to wait for other people. Sometimes there are delays in obtaining information, and so on. Fear not, there's always something else you can work on for a while.

By perpetually having a next step ready, then a next and next, none of the items that make your list need to linger forever. Certainly, you don't want to bite off more than you can chew by engaging in too many first steps on too many projects at once. However, identifying a few first steps for a few projects should be sufficient to get you rolling.

Once you're comfortable with the sequence of steps you've plotted for the various projects before you, reinforce your progress by further honing and refining your environment to support your various quests. For example, set up a 12-month and 31-day tickler file system (explained in Chapter 8) so that you'll have a place to park and locate associated task documents in a timely manner. You may also group projects and associated steps by where you'll actually take action, such as at the copier, telephone, fax machine, and so on.

You may wish to prepare a series of checklists for recurring tasks such as visiting branch offices, the company library, or select clients.

Physically Arrange Your Spaces

People reflexively put things by the door when they need to take items with them to meetings or with them at the end of the day. It makes sense to put a small table or set of shelves by your door. Likewise, as you look around your office and other workspaces, think about how you can arrange them to accommodate the tasks on your list, the steps you've identified, and the associated actions you want to take to further your progress.

Coming Undone

Getting things done means acknowledging the reality of working and living in an era of information and communication overload. The manner in which you set up your desk, files, shelves, and office right now may be insufficient as change occurs and as the months and years roll on. Getting too comfortable can cost you.

If you find yourself needing various organizing items from your organization's supply center or office supply stores, don't be surprised. Arranging your environment to make you more productive, at first, often leads to the installation of some items and/or the removal of others.

With all that you want to get done and all that competes for your time and attention, if you're not occasionally shifting things around on your desk, in your files, or on your shelves, then your efforts are suspect.

When and Where

If you tackle tasks based on when and where you're probably going to handle them, you tend to get a whole lot of things done. In our daily high-wire balancing act, handling dozens of e-mails, scads of inter-office messages and phone calls, and "gotta have it now" assignments dropped in your lap, when we group tasks based on *when and where* considerations we generally handle the *important* and the *important and urgent* items in the mix.

Review and Conquer

As you proceed down your to-do list, stick to the basics, one of which is to continually peruse your list, cross out those things that you've completed, add next steps as they become apparent, and consolidate all items.

Now you're cooking. You've written down your to-dos, identified next-step activities, and aligned your environment to support your efforts. Continually reviewing your grand list helps you mentally reinforce your commitment to getting those things done. A few minutes here and there throughout the day work wonders. Also, one good long review (say, every Friday or Monday), if that suits you, is recommended.

I take a weekly, hour-long review in a quiet place away from the phone, where I can't check e-mail and where I otherwise won't be disturbed. These precautions give me the best chance to let the ideas on my to-do list linger, which enables me to more fully understand them.

> **Dyna Moe**
>
> Review your to-do list enough so that your projects and activities stay in mind, but not so much that the review itself becomes burdensome. If it helps, actually schedule your long review. Perhaps you want to do it on the same day at the same time each week. You'll find that long after, it becomes automatic.

Managing Your To-Do List, Long-Term Versus Short-Term

What if you could maintain not just a handy to-do list, but a comprehensive single list of everything short- and long-term, minuscule and grand, now and for a lifetime that you want to get done? The primary dilemma we face each day is balancing short-term versus long-term tasks and activities. My solution to the dilemma is to compile and maintain a super-long to-do list, sometimes 12 pages!

In my career, I have hundreds of things on my to-do list arranged by major life priorities. How do I keep from (visibly) going crazy? Most of what's on the list are medium- to long-range activities.

Turn to Page One

The first page of my list represents only the short-term activities—the things I've chosen to do now or this week. I continually draw from the 12-page list, and move items to the top as it becomes desirable, or necessary, to tackle them.

It is a dynamic to-do list in the sense that it contains everything on this earth I want to get done, but the key is that at any given time, I only need to look at one page, and it's always on top.

All the anxiety about the things you want to get done diminishes once you put every-thing down on paper. My list is long, and it will stay long. I am forever updating the list and running a new printout of it, but that's fine. I wouldn't think of doing it any other way.

I don't worry about all the things on the list, because I know I can only get so much done in one day or one week. I know that I'll periodically review the entire list, and continually move items from, say, page 8 up to the front. Sometimes, I extract a small portion of a long-term task and move it to page one.

Suppose many of you are organized and use lists, but you don't know if a 12-page list would be such a good idea. Perhaps with this approach you feel like everything is *too* planned out. Relax. The items that make your back pages can ably serve as mental placeholders—they may change in many ways, many times, and even be dropped, but for now at least, you have them all listed in one place.

Not Everything Everyday

The super to-do list enables you to keep an eye on balancing long-term *important* tasks and projects with short-term *important and urgent* and merely *urgent* tasks and projects. If I'm working on something during the day and it appears that there will be a break-through in my ability to tackle something buried on page 9, I'll certainly consider it. Many days, however, I don't look at pages 2 through 12.

Maintaining a long to-do list helps me to become more proficient in managing long-term or repeated tasks. If something represents a long-term project, I can continually draw from it those portions that can be handled in the short-term and move them up to the front page. Likewise, if something is a repeat or cyclical project, something that I need to do every month or every year, I can move the item up to the front page.

> **Dyna Moe**
>
> Consider using the super-long to-do list. At the least, you'll have identified everything you face, and have it all on one gigantic roster. At the most, you'll have a tool that will support you for years to come.

Short-Circuiting the To-Do List

Most people who encounter information worth retaining make a note or add it to a list. The information stays there for days, weeks, or months. On occasion, you may wish to short-circuit the to-do list and get stuff done without entering it on your list.

Sometimes a task you want to accomplish is small enough that you can launch right into it. No need to write it down because that would be more work than it's worth.

Since whatever information you encounter usually involves calling or writing to someone else, rather than adding it to your to-do list …

- ◆ Pick up a pocket dictator and immediately dictate a letter or memo to whomever you need to be in touch with; take action on what it is you've come across.

- ◆ Type it on your computer and send an e-mail or Internet message for immediate transmission.

I was talking to someone who said they enjoyed the *Readers' Digest* section by Peter Rich. In this section, he reviews vocabulary words from books he's read. Years ago, I would have made a note about this and done something about it sometime in the next few months.

Instead, I grabbed my pocket dictator and dictated a letter to Mr. Rich on the spot, indicating which vocabulary words I thought his readers might enjoy. Once my transcriber types the letter, I send it. Hence, the item never goes onto a to-do list.

You'll find when you short-circuit the to-do lists for some tasks and you get on a roll, you begin to knock out other smaller tasks that may be on your super to-do list. That's fine. Your goal is to get things done, and practically speaking, any technique or strategy that happens to work at any given time is worth pursuing.

The Least You Need to Know

- ◆ The more responsibility you have at work, the more you need to write down and codify everything you need to get done.

- ◆ Break projects into steps to have a clear and bite-sized task before you, and you can build momentum more easily than you imagined.

- ◆ When you tackle tasks based on when and where you're probably going to handle them, you tend to get many things done.

- ◆ No law says you can't maintain a comprehensive, single list of everything short- and long-term, now and for a lifetime, that you want to get done.

- ◆ Short-circuiting your to-do list for some tasks puts you on a roll that can extend to larger, longer-term tasks.

Chapter

12

Getting Things Done Right Now

In This Chapter

- ◆ Over-preparation and underestimation
- ◆ The costs of tackling projects
- ◆ Productive resources
- ◆ Rewards system to encourage productivity

Now that you know a thing or two about composing, maintaining, and implementing to-do lists, let's focus on immediate measures for getting on the golden path to accomplishing shorter-term tasks, particularly those things you want to complete today, this hour, or right now!

Avoiding Common Mistakes

The two most common mistakes that people make on the path to accomplishing short-term tasks are *over-preparing* and at the same time, paradoxically, *underestimating* what will be necessary to succeed.

Over-preparation has stopped many would-be get-it-done enthusiasts right in their Bass Weejuns. Consider the sales professional who makes few sales calls per week, and as a result closes even fewer sales because he or she gets stuck in the semi-perpetual state of over-preparation.

The over-prepared professional means to do well. His anxiety level, however, may prompt him to over-complicate one sub-task after another en route to actually calling on the client. This is the person who, on the day he is finally ready to make a sales call, is bound to blow it. Why? He's *soooo* ready, that he has more information than he'll ever be able to succinctly present in the time allotted for the appointment.

Coming Undone

Besides hogging the conversation, the over-prepared salesperson may be too quick to respond to the prospect's objections. He may come off as a know-it-all, or unwittingly offend the client by displaying too much zeal.

If you can, forsake the crutches that seemingly aid but often impede your progress. The crutch that most often impedes most individuals is information. Too often, many people want to have the broad swath of information, data, figures, statistics, you name it, all assembled before launching a task.

More data is not always the answer, especially in a society where we're deluged with data. Enough data exists to lead to all answers, which clearly gets in the way of choosing. Forsaking crutches simply means you will not allow extraneous factors to impede your progress. If you have five magazine articles that support your argument, having an additional four or five articles is not going to make that much of a difference.

You don't want to fall into the trap of rounding up resources that, in retrospect, will prove to be only marginally helpful and unnecessarily draw from the time you expend on the task at hand. These wretched souls, the type who tend to over-prepare, either truly believe or have deluded themselves into believing that all the crutches that they've assembled will somehow accelerate their progress once they actually launch into a task. Too late, they find that they've allocated their time and energy in the wrong places.

The other most common mistake on the path to getting things done is to underestimate what will be required to succeed. The antidotes to this pitfall are to sum all costs, and marshal one's resources. Each antidote will be explained in the sections that follow.

Sum All the Costs

Forsaking crutches is not a contradiction to the summing of all costs. On any project or task, big or small, it pays to total up what it will cost in terms of time, energy, dollars, or other resources. The paradox faced by otherwise popular professionals is that they often underestimate the time that it will take to complete a task—even short-term tasks. This is the person who is perpetually racing the clock. His to-do list grows longer and longer because he is inappropriately optimistic about how much he can accomplish in a day, an hour, or other short time span.

Understandably, in the information-based society engulfing us, it can be difficult to estimate how much time it will take to complete a particular task, especially in those cases where we're undertaking a task for the first time. You may ask yourself:

- Who knows how long it's going to take to learn a new software routine?

- Who can say precisely how much time it will take to complete a particular form?

- How much time will be needed to review a team member's first interim report?

- How long will it take to respond to the 3 critical e-mails that just arrived?

You can make a strong case that a large proportion of the tasks you face on any given day are "first-time" type tasks, and the time to complete them in is not abundantly clear at the outset. That's why it's useful to establish *benchmarks*, set time limits, and use fudge factors.

Word Power

A **benchmark** is an indicator or reference point that you can use to compare a current outcome or experience to one previously documented or noted.

Benchmark Your Tasks

Suppose you have to read a team member's eight-page report. From past experience, you've found that your reading time is roughly three minutes per page. This task may not be so different from reading other reports. For effectiveness and efficiency, you'll be reading slowly and carefully, line by line.

Hence for an eight-page report, with a benchmark of three minutes per page, you can figure that you'll need about 24 minutes. With an occasional interruption, a rough spot that may slow you down, or other unforeseen factors, it may be better to make it 28 minutes.

Suppose you have no benchmark for a report of this length or of this nature. How else could you approach the task without underestimating what it would take to get it done? Set a time limit!

You could give yourself 15, 30, or 45 minutes to handle this report. In the case where you've given yourself 15 minutes and you notice, with about 3 minutes to go, you're still on page 5, you have a good indication that you underestimated the time.

You now re-compute and see that 25 or 30 minutes might be more realistic. You may not have the extra time to devote to the report right now, but at least you have useful information. Alternatively, you could greatly increase your reading speed for the last 3 pages and still finish within 15 minutes, recognizing that you may need to review the last 3 pages again at some other time.

Take Advantage of a Miscalculation

Suppose you picked 30 minutes as a time limit to review a report, the likes of which you haven't tackled before. In this case, you may finish after 24 minutes or 28 minutes with 2 to 6 minutes to spare. Is that so bad? Actually, that's a nice state of affairs.

> **Dyna Moe**
>
> Ideally, you want to have little slack at the end of a task. This enables you to collect your thoughts, finish up your notes, and file, return, or otherwise process what you've been working on.

> **Word Power**
>
> A **fudge factor** is a numerical adjustment you make to an estimation. In this case, we are applying it to time limits in completing tasks.

Suppose you allocated 45 minutes, and you finish after 28 minutes? "Oh my goodness, what am I going to do with the extra 17 minutes?" Have there been any days in the past 10 years where you couldn't use 17 minutes to accomplish other small things?

Maybe 17 minutes from now you have a meeting, you have to make a phone call, or something else has been scheduled. Those 17 minutes represent prime time in which you could handle smaller things that have accumulated, prepare for what's next, or simply take a mental or physical break.

Thus, the last of your strategies in summing the cost of completing the task, and in this case we're focusing on how much time the task will cost, is to apply a *fudge factor* to curb your optimistic estimate.

The Fudge Factor

Many otherwise competent career professionals seem to perpetually underestimate the time it will take to complete certain tasks. There's a practical solution that will help alleviate this problem. If you initially estimate that a task will take, say 24 minutes, automatically increase your estimate by 50 percent. In other words, allocate 36 minutes for a task you initially estimate to require 24 minutes. Allocate 90 minutes for a task you initially estimate will take 60 minutes, and so on.

Coming Undone

Your reflexive tendency may be to use the +50 percent fudge factor a handful of times, and find that it works reasonably well. Then, you'll slip right back to what you've been doing for years—being unwittingly optimistic about the time it will take to accomplish short-term tasks.

Forgetting What Works

If you're like many others, despite its effectiveness, in time you'll forget about the fudge factor. In the blink of an eye, you'll revert to making estimates that are at or under any previous benchmark, that don't represent appropriate time limits, and don't encompass a fudge factor. In short, you'll be underestimating too many of the tasks you handle in a given day, and hence your day will seem like an endless struggle.

As you learned in Chapter 11, feeling good about your accomplishments, maintaining your buoyancy, and sustaining yourself workday after workday are as essential as anything on the road to getting things done.

The notion of summing all costs actually extends to all dollar outlays, and includes the energy you might expend on a project, staff resources, equipment, etc.

All of this leads us to the second major approach to avoiding common mistakes: marshaling your resources.

Dyna Moe

In all cases, having a realistic notion of what it will take to accomplish the task will serve you far better than finding out midstream that you're not going to be able to coast into completion right now because you underestimated what it would take.

Marshal Your Resources

Consider the activities you undertake when you move to a new town. You obtain local phone books and other directories. You find a doctor, a dentist, and other health-care providers. You call utility companies to make sure your services are running the first day you move in. You get to know which stores carry the kinds of goods you desire. You meet people at work, around the neighborhood, and around town.

Soon, you develop a network of resources that enable you to get domestic things done, like eat dinner, have a well-functioning car, have a dental checkup, and so on.

At work, when you assume a new post, you arrive at a desk that is, hopefully, clean and clear. Soon enough, you'll fill it up with supplies, files, directories, and personal items. You align your office, cubicle, or workspace with those things that help keep you productive, and ideally, balanced and happy.

Surround Yourself

The road to accomplishing both short- and long-term tasks works much the same way. You surround yourself with that which will be useful in the clutch. For short-term tasks in particular, it makes sense to have adequate supplies. If you're writing with pen and paper, the old-fashioned way, then you need to have those ready. If you're making conference calls, then the equipment, numbers, pass codes, and such resources need to be in place.

If you're tackling first-time tasks, those of which you have little or no experience, marshaling your resources takes on an added level of importance. What mentors and gurus can you contact to give you a crucial bit of advice, the right file path, or key phone number on your way to accomplishing something right now?

Get It Together

As a useful task before tackling the next short-term project, flesh out the resources you'll need to successfully handle a short-term task. List what you might need in terms of equipment, supplies, staff help, guidance, money, and time. The more involved the short-term task is, i.e., a half-day or day-long task, the more valuable this exercise becomes.

For any given short-term task, variables such as equipment, supplies, staff help, guidance, money, and time may or may not be significant. Making notes about those that will be significant will serve you well.

The exercise itself takes no more than a minute or two and costs nothing. The added measure of using insight and perspective is invaluable.

Start Simply

Much of the hesitation that occurs before the start of a short-term task is due to erroneous assumptions. For example, if you have to compose a letter or brief report, you might be hung up on starting with that perfect opening sentence or that powerful opening paragraph. Yet, launching into the letter or report is not contingent on nailing the opening part from the outset.

It's often to your advantage to simply start writing and later go back and determine what sentence or paragraph makes for the best lead. Likewise for other tasks you face.

If it helps, allow yourself to take a small step to get started. This might represent simply opening up a file folder, making a phone call, arranging a meeting, or finding a website. The strange and wondrous thing about the human brain is that it likes to continue progressing on the same path it is already on.

> **Coming Undone**
>
> You may not be able to get the task started in exactly the manner you prefer. It might be raining outside. Construction crews may be making noise on the next floor. If you had your way, you'd rather get started on something else. Start on the task anyway.

One minute of activity in pursuit of a task helps lead to the next minute and the next. Almost independent of how you get started, for most short-term tasks, the fact that you did get started clears a major hurdle on the path to completion.

Tap the Power of Immersion

Develop a skill that is becoming rare among professionals today—practice the art of doing one thing at a time and become immersed in that task. When you put all your energy and concentration into one task, great things will result.

Fight the tendency to multitask. It seems easy enough, but the practice of doing one thing at a time, today, rubs against the grain of society, which delivers the message that you need to do many things at once to be more productive.

Even for tasks that take five minutes or less, you can achieve great productivity by immersing yourself in the pursuit. The impetus and even pure joy of getting one thing done, and done well, can carry you to the next task and the next and the next.

> **Dyna Moe**
>
> Allow yourself to become immersed. By tapping the power of immersion, you can mow down 5, 6, 8, or even 10 minor tasks that collectively loomed large as hours or days passed without you tending to them.

Giving your total attention to the task at hand yields wondrous benefits that may not otherwise be achievable. Step away from your online connection. Switch your phone to voice mail. Close your door. Focus your efforts and reap the rewards!

Create a Rewards System

Much of human behavioral psychology can be explained by the simple phrase "Behavior that is rewarded is repeated." This is true even when you reward yourself for your own behavior. To accomplish things right here, right now, identify in advance a "reward" that you'll bestow upon yourself for completing a desired task.

The reward may be as simple as making a phone call. It might be taking a stroll around the block. It could be checking e-mail, having a cup of herbal tea, totaling up your earnings for the last quarter, or any other small, favorable event.

If you're facing an unpleasant task, it makes sense to follow that up with something you enjoy doing, instead of the other way around.

Dyna Moe

It's possible that you're one of those few diligent types who are able to receive a reward first and then make good on the silent, unarticulated promise to yourself, go ahead and complete the task that remained to be done. For most people, however, life doesn't seem to work this way.

After having the reward first, i.e., doing the pleasant activity, what's to stop you from having another reward and another?

Instrumental Temptations

High-speed online connections, such as cable, DSL, or T1 lines, guarantee a virtual smorgasbord of infinite and never-ending temptations. With a couple key strokes and mouse clicks, you can be whisked away on your screen to any one of multimillions of websites.

While previous generations of career professionals faced temptations and distractions, nothing from yesteryear rivals the power, lure, and availability of the Internet. It's always there, it's always on, and meanwhile, you've got tasks to accomplish.

If you are subject to temptations—and who isn't—find a way to include them in your rewards system. Rather than entirely succumbing to such distractions, you get to enjoy them periodically throughout the day in small measures not detrimental to your productivity or long-term career prospects. To do otherwise is to flirt with disaster.

Thereafter, you go from hour to hour, day to day, week to week, without getting the small things done and having them build up, each one looming larger than they actually are, while impeding your progress on longer-term projects and tasks.

> **Dyna Moe**
>
> If surfing the Internet is one of your temptations, then make it part of your rewards system. Then that way, you maintain a modicum of control.

The Long and Winding Road

Even if you maintain a super to-do list with a large, long-term portion, you'll still find it a challenge to maintain vigilance on long-term tasks. Moreover, in many respects, accomplishing long-term tasks requires a different approach, execution, and set of behaviors than accomplishing tasks of a shorter-term nature. Chapters 13 and 14 will help you with larger, longer-term challenges.

The Least You Need to Know

- Over-preparation gets in the way of accomplishing many short-term tasks.
- Having a realistic notion of what it will take to accomplish a task helps you find completion in a shorter time period.
- The human brain likes to continue progressing on the same path it is already on, therefore one minute of activity in pursuit of a task helps lead to its completion.
- Giving your total attention to the task at hand yields wondrous benefits that may not otherwise be achievable.
- Find a way to incorporate temptations into your rewards system rather than entirely succumbing to them and inhibiting your productivity.

Accomplishing Longer-Term Tasks

In This Chapter

◆ Win more battles with clarity

◆ Charting your path

◆ Software to keep you in control

◆ Keeping up

From presidents, prime ministers, and heads of state to CEOs, COOs, and CIOs, the reputation built during one's tenure is largely defined by the longer-term tasks and projects that the leader is able to make happen. You can mess up here and there on the smaller stuff, as long as bigger issues and challenges are tackled and resolved.

This chapter contains strategies for approaching problems followed by a discussion of project-management tools, including timelines, flow charts, and other visual aids. These tools provide both an interesting and useful means of tracking productivity and detailing where you are going.

Clarify the Challenges

Sometimes problems await when you first arrive at your post. You might be hired to tackle specific issues; the direction of your course is pre-established. Other times, issues knock loudly at your door and your ability to get things done is based on the course you set, and how you respond.

In August 1981, some 13,000 of the nearly 17,000 U.S. air traffic controllers went on strike. As you might guess, this caused a near-panic throughout the nation's transportation network. Managers worked overtime to handle most air traffic control shifts themselves. The airlines took it hard. They were only able to operate at about 70 percent of capacity.

The air traffic controllers all belonged to the Professional Air Traffic Controllers Association (PATCO). The organization felt reasonably confident that the strike would work—their members would win the concessions they were seeking. They knew that such a strike, if prolonged, would cause a critical blow to the U.S. economy. By striking, PATCO's members had defied federal law, which prohibited strikes by government employees. Every air traffic controller was required by law to take an oath not to strike when they were first hired.

Reagan saw the strike as illegal and coercive. These federal workers were hired to serve a mission. The actions they were taking put the government, the airline industry, and the nation's transportation system under duress.

> ### Dyna Moe
>
> The PATCO strike was a stern and rigorous early test of Reagan's administrative capabilities, and he was not going to stand down. One could surmise that the Soviets were watching. Years later, in his memoirs, Reagan said that the decision he made "convinced people, who might have thought otherwise, that I meant what I said."

Right up front Reagan stated, "There is no right to strike against the public safety by anybody, anywhere, any time." With the support of the secretary of transportation, Reagan gave the controllers 48 hours to return to their posts. The vast majority disobeyed and 48 hours later found themselves unemployed.

Unquestionably, firing the thousands of air traffic controllers was a bold and decisive move. Reagan knew that if he gave in to this group, in time, his administration would have to continuously bargain with different groups. Rather than bargain with PATCO leaders, the administration hired more controllers, increased the overtime of those who were still onboard, and made do with available resources until the situation calmed down.

Certainly if there had been a single commercial airline mishap during this interval—and fortunately there wasn't—his plan might have backfired. If Reagan hadn't safeguarded the nation's air transportation system and his administration's budget while conveying the message that no such tactics would be tolerated, he might have had a tragedy on his hands.

At the time, President Reagan had a choice; he could back down and allow PATCO to dictate on what terms his administration could negotiate. Or he could stand his ground and bolster his credibility in following through on his verbal promises. This was no easy decision, but President Reagan saw his options and contemplated the consequences and their implications. This situation is a practical application of problem solving by clarifying the challenge.

Specificity Matters

The challenges you face are as likely to come in the form of surprises and emergencies as they are based on your own defined objectives. In either case, when you clarify the challenges confronting you and take into consideration both short- and long-term ramifications, you're in a far better position to solve problems.

Henri Poincare, the nineteenth-century French mathematician, devised a four-part strategy for creative problem solving that still has great utility today:

1. Preparation

2. Incubation

3. Illumination

4. Translation (application)

> **CAUTION**
>
> **Coming Undone**
>
> If you skip the incubation step in creative problem-solving and immediately try to devise solutions, you might be successful, but sometimes you miss out on more innovative or unique solutions.

Poincare said that *preparation* is the first step, wherein you immerse yourself in a problem and collect all relevant information. Depending on how big the problem and the resources that you are already privy to, preparation could last a few minutes, several hours, several days, or many weeks.

The next step is *incubation*. After gathering the most relevant data and framing the problem to the best of your ability, you clear your mind through meditation, taking a walk, even taking a bath—whatever works for you. Let the problem simmer.

The third step is *illumination*. After having totally immersed yourself in the problem, collected all the relevant information that you can, framed the problem, and allowed the situation to simmer for a while, invariably a solution comes to mind. Even the most creative people of Poincare's day couldn't say why, but at this point, feasible ideas sprang forth.

Illumination leads directly to step four: *translation*. Apply your potential solution, make observations, make calculations if applicable, and determine if you have a practical solution. If not, try a second solution, then a third, and so forth, until one of them proves to be a true and winning answer.

Tools To Stay in Control

For much of what you wish to accomplish, or challenges or problems you need to resolve, particularly those that represent longer-term tasks, a variety of leadership and management tools exist that can help guide you every step of the way. The bigger the project, and the more steps, dollars, people, and interplay between players, the greater the need for specification.

> **Dyna Moe**
>
> Plans can always change, contingencies arise, roadblocks emerge, and course alteration may be necessary. Still, as you plot your path at the outset and as you proceed along it, specificity matters.

The tools discussed in this chapter are tested and proven. We'll review them in their most basic forms so that you'll have a clear understanding as to how to employ them. Each tool is available in analog (a wall chart) or digital (software package). Happily, you probably have some experience with each of them in one form or another. So the following need not be foreign to you.

Gantt or Milestone Charts

The *Gantt chart* or "milestone" chart is a basic tool for staying in control on your path to getting things done and one with which you probably have some familiarity. Gantt charts help you to both plan and monitor tasks and projects.

> **Word Power**
>
> A **Gantt chart** basically is a bar chart that aids in planning and scheduling, with activities or tasks shown graphically as bars or line segments with specific time frames.

You update the chart as you make progress on each task. You can determine whether tasks are on schedule, ahead of schedule, or behind schedule by comparing your actual progress to where you're supposed to be based on the chart. An example will make this easy to understand.

Map It Out

Suppose you've established, or been handed, a goal of increasing your company's visibility in the marketplace over the next five months. To support that objective you've identified five activities:

1. Finishing the XYZ project for release to the trade press.

2. Getting an article published in a key industry journal that highlights your firm.

3. Completing a pilot program for employing interns.

4. Establishing an 800-number hotline program so that clients can call any time.

5. Hosting a local forum where subject matter experts discuss critical issues in your industry.

All of these activities are to occur within the next five months. How can you best allocate your energy and resources to accomplish all of the above, thereby increasing your company's visibility?

Map out what you need to do and when, on a Gantt chart such as the one that follows, to gain a clear, graphic representation of the sequence and time lines for each of the five activities.

Activity	Month 1	Month 2	Month 3	Month 4	Month 5
1. XYZ project	Bxxxx	xxxxxxxx	xxxxC		
2. Article published	Bx	xxxx	xxxx	xC	
3. Intern program		Bxx x	xx xxx	xxC	
4. Hotline program		Bxxxxx	xxxC		
5. Local forum		Bxx	xx	xxxxxxx	xxxxxxC

The most basic of information is easily conveyed in the chart above, including the activity, sequence (1 to 5), begin (B), progression (x's extending month to month), and completion time (C). In developing a pilot program for interns, for example, there are several intervals because the action required is not continuous.

Utilize Symbols for Added Meaning

At your discretion, you may employ whatever symbols to add detail to and clarify your chart. For example …

◆ Numbers could refer to chart footnotes.

◆ A dotted line can denote germination.

◆ Initials could represent other people involved in the activity.

Here is a variation of a Gantt chart that yields a bit more information:

Activity	Month 1	Month 2	Month 3	Month 4	Month 5
1. XYZ project **JS, CG, IR**	Bxxxx	xxxxxxxx	xxxxC		
2. Article published **JS**	Bx	xxxx----	--xxxx--	--xC$_1$	
3. Intern program **JS, FG**		Bxx x	xx xxx	xxC$_2$	
4. Hotline program **JS**		Bxxxxx	xxxC		
5. Local forum **JS, BM, IR**		Bxx	xx	xxxxxxx	xxxxxxC

1: delays based on editor's responses
2: scheduled around school vacations
Note: broken line denotes germination

If you so choose, you could employ colors to indicate progress. For example …

◆ Green could indicate the start of an activity.

◆ Red could indicate a critical phase.

◆ Blue could indicate completion of an activity.

For greater sophistication, you could devise a Gantt or milestone chart for each of the five activities, indicating all of the substeps involved in completing them. Armed with project planning and scheduling software (discussed shortly), you could plot the time lines for all activities and all substeps on one master chart.

Program Evaluation and Review Technique—PERT Charts

PERT charts, which are also referred to as network charts or logic diagrams, are diagrams used to manage projects where scheduling is critical. The PERT highlights tasks and interdependencies between tasks. To employ a PERT you identify the activities you've earmarked as crucial, the order and time line of each activity, and the critical path. This indicates, with a given outcome, whether you then take path "a" or path "b."

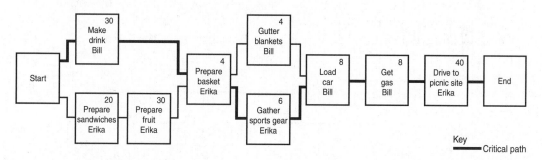

PERTs can be intricate, and depending on the outcome of specific activities, you may need to revise the chart to reflect constraints, setbacks, or opportunities.

PERTs are somewhat like Gantts but the sequence of steps you complete for an activity are interdependent. As the chart shows, steps that need to be completed can intersect and converge at critical junctures. In the case of developing a pilot program for interns, you may have to:

- Develop a manual.

- Have several peers make critical reviews.

- Schedule a proofreader.

- Obtain approval from department heads.

- Initiate a test phase.

- Refine the program.

- Re-circulate it for a critical analysis.

Dyna Moe

When you're tackling a project with multiple activities involving other people and various resources, PERTs enable you to remain on course, identify critical junctures and potential bottlenecks, and in general, stay on schedule.

To consolidate the inputs of others, some of these tasks have to be completed concurrently before you can proceed.

Using Flow Charts

You've been exposed to flowcharts since you were very young. Your third grade teacher might have drawn a big circle on the board, followed by an arrow that led to a second circle, or a square or triangle, and then maybe another arrow extending from that figure to a third figure.

Although flowcharts traditionally are used to convey a process, i.e., how something happens, they also can be used to help you stay on-target in terms of completing a project within specific time lines.

Looking at both the previous PERT example (on successfully completing the pilot intern program) and the flowchart that follows (which includes time lines), you can quickly surmise that the PERT chart and a flowchart have similarities.

Flow charts also help you stay on course.

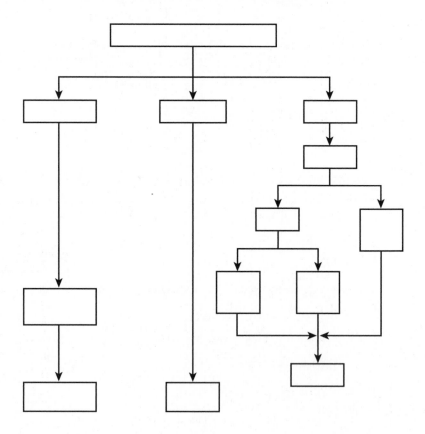

As with the other types of charts, you can employ colors on a flowchart as you choose. Also, geometric shapes are often employed to convey additional information when constructing flowcharts. For example:

- Circle—connecting points

- Square—information

- Triangle—*yes* or *no* decision

Other symbols are often used to convey information as well:

- Straight line—direct connection

- Squiggly line—interrupted or undefined connection

- Broken line—one way or partial connection

As with any chart you create, you may devise your own symbols as well. Initials of another party could represent the need for their input. Stars, X's, check marks, and other symbols can convey other information, as long as you're consistent throughout your chart, and you keep a key handy, so you don't forget what the symbols mean!

The Calendar Block Back Method

To get things done according to the time lines you've established, the calendar block back is a viable way to ensure completion. This method involves creating a process to complete your task, using a calendar either from an appointment book or a large monthly calendar.

Suppose you are seeking to achieve a 4K increase in salary. From the starting date to the ending date, you would identify the five key subtasks. You would also list the interim steps you must complete to attain your specific increase in salary.

Suppose you need to deliver a test program to new employees by the 31st of the month. You decide that you'll need to schedule a conference

Dyna Moe
It is best to use a larger monthly calendar to plot out a five-month-long project, displaying each month in a manner so you can keep track of the coming months. You can start from the completion date and work your way backward, listing the subtasks or specific activities for each day or week according to your plan.

by the 22nd and the training manual must be critically examined by the 9th, proof-read by the 15th, and finalized by the 19th. The month-long plan you have laid out will look like the figure that follows.

The Calendar Block Back chart is the most basic of all.

MONTH *March*   YEAR _____

SUNDAY	MONDAY	TUESDAY	WEDNESDAY	THURSDAY	FRIDAY	SATURDAY
	1	2	3	4	5	6
7	8	9 *Critical review of Training Manual*	10	11	12	13
14	15 *Proofread Manual*	16	17	18	19 *Assemble Training Manual*	20
21	22 *Schedule Conference*	23	24	25	26	27
28	29	30	31 *Deliver test program for new lines*			

Coming Undone

Plotting too many sub-goals and related tasks will make your calendar too difficult to follow. This method works best and can be an extremely useful tool when you keep it simple and thorough.

You will then fill in this calendar with the activities you're implementing and interim due dates accordingly. Symbols and colors can be used here to organize the process further.

You're doing well when you can track your tasks in reverse and in a manner that reflects your available resources, as well as taking into account events during the month, such as weekends, holidays, time off, and vacations.

Meanwhile, to get some of the big things in life completed, it makes sense to lay out a plan with the end in mind. An example would be reaching retirement at a certain age with X amount of savings.

Suppose you want to have $500,000 in savings by age 65. If you're currently 36, taking into account a certain rate of interest, inflation, and taxes, it is possible to estimate how much money should be saved per year, and more specifically, how much you must save per month.

If you work in an office where employees, vehicles, or goods need to be scheduled for optimum efficiency, this method isn't news to you. However, this type of calendar plotting works especially well on a personal basis because you are the boss of the calendar. You get to shift things around according to your own preferences.

Factoid

Office supply stores in your area offer a variety of wall charts to aid you in getting things done. You can use these supplies to implement a Gantt, PERT, flowchart, or the calendar block back method for plotting and monitoring your progress. Some charts are erasable and can be modified if needed.

Project Managing and Scheduling Made Easy

The job of project managing and scheduling is increasingly easier thanks to ever-more powerful computer software. So, no matter what I describe to you now, it will be quickly superseded. In general, however, scheduling software, calendar systems, and other types of project organizers share some common principles.

All such software provides some type of calendar system where you can keep appointments, readily identify schedule conflicts, and be alerted as to when you need to engage in some critical activity.

Project-scheduling software allows you to choose the form of chart, be it Gantt, PERT, flow, calendar block back, and so on, that's most convenient for you. Using pull-down menus, familiar icons, and drag-and-drop techniques, you can quickly cue in the subgoals and tasks or activities associated with them, in the sequence you desire, indicate start and stop times, and add various other symbols as well as color to give you a vivid portrayal of the time lines you've established and your overall progress.

You are also able to print your charts and calendars to keep with you at all times, and create buzzers, bells, and alarms that remind you to send a fax or e-mail, make a call, or anything that encourages you to get things done.

As you have probably noticed by now, the most critical factor in getting things done is managing yourself. All the scheduling tools in the world can't ensure that you yourself will remain on schedule.

While the scheduling tools can help, you alone have to make critical decisions as to where to proceed, and where to drop back. For example, if you don't keep your charts or graphs current, the whole process may become worthless. Or, if you attempt to take on too much at once, the tools may help you realize that you've done so, but largely it's up to you.

The Least You Need to Know

♦ If your time lines are too stringent, any project can quickly become jeopardized. If too lenient, you may lose focus.

♦ Once you actually take steps toward accomplishing something, you have a clearer idea of how long things will take.

♦ Stuff happens. Allow for contingencies and some slack in your schedule.

♦ Use charts to more easily establish time lines, monitor your progress, and reach your desired end.

♦ Any sophisticated project manager or scheduling software will let you down the moment you don't keep them up.

Monitoring Longer-Term Tasks and Projects

In This Chapter

◆ When confidence or optimism hinders efforts

◆ Course correction is the name of the game

◆ Smart managers anticipate

◆ Metrics as progress indicators

The greater the deed you want to get done, the more essential it is to monitor your progress. Suppose you have responsibility for some long-term project that involves many different types of resources over a prolonged period. Not monitoring your progress on large projects is synonymous with failure.

If you happen to luckily catch resultant problems in time, you may end up scrambling for weeks on end, putting in overtime, and causing others to work longer and harder. You'll get things done, but no one may like you.

This chapter is all about how to monitor your progress on longer-term projects so that you are prepared and ready to turn problems into solutions by anticipating potential problems ranging from laissez-fair project management to miscommunications among co-workers.

Been There, Done That

Perhaps no phrase in the English language more closely belies the dangers that can befall a veteran manager than "Been there, done that." Projects can exceed the budget or the schedule by more than 50 percent because the manager did not feel compelled to monitor sufficiently.

In some organizations, a rookie manager with finite previous experience is specifically sought to work on projects. This person doesn't need to be shorn of any unwelcome project management styles. One such unwelcome style is the nonchalance some veteran managers bring to projects resulting from their comfort level in working on projects.

> **CAUTION**
> ## Coming Undone
> If you're brought on to manage a large task or project, consider that there is no "automatic pilot." There is no cruise control with which you can simply lock onto and have the project take its course.

From manufacturing to government, and to education, projects (often called programs) widely miss the mark because somebody who otherwise should have been in control felt confident in his or her ability to revert to cruise control. And as discussed in the preceding chapter, project management software alone cannot ensure that you'll stay on course.

Over-Optimism Contributes to Project Pressures

Not allowing enough time for a particular task is a pervasive problem which is easily remedied by monitoring progress.

For example, I once had the assignment of driving from the consulting firm where I was employed in Rockville, Connecticut, up to Bangor, Maine. My boss told me that it would take about three to three and a half hours. I left at 8:00 A.M. for a 12 noon appointment in Bangor. I figured that with at least a half hour of slack time, it would be no problem. I brought food with me and determined that I'd probably only take one bathroom break along the way.

I'd been on the road already for three hours, and the road signs in New Hampshire indicated that Bangor was still another 64 miles to go. There was no way this trip was going to take only three and a half hours at the most. I put my foot to the pedal, averaged 75 the rest of the way, fortunately didn't get stopped, and made it with about six minutes to spare. However, I was stressed and anxious the whole way.

My boss wasn't trying to do me wrong, he simply did not have accurate information. I should have looked on a mileage chart before leaving, or perhaps visited an online driving directions page, and planned my trip accordingly. You can bet that on the way back, I allocated 4 hours and 20 minutes and as it turned out, came in just about at that time. The point is that no matter how sophisticated your scheduling may be, if you input faulty data, you can't expect to proceed as planned.

Never forget: all project manager or scheduling tools can only be as good as what you enter into the system. Hence, the ability to reasonably estimate how much time a particular task will take is no small matter. A little extra time always helps. As you get to know yourself better and better, you realize allowing somewhat generous time allocations for certain tasks is not going to turn you into a laggard.

Any time you create time savings through this method, apply it to other things that you want to get done. You'll be just as productive as before, but mentally, you'll have set up your day in a manner that enables you to feel less frustrated, more content, more energized, and ready for what comes next.

Often we over-optimistically underestimate the time necessary to complete a particular task. When we fail to monitor our progress—which might have identified the earlier miscalculation—we end up feeling intense pressure to get things done. Sometimes, at the outset, we are given misinformation as to how much time a task will take. Building a little leeway into your schedule improves the psychic satisfaction that can't often otherwise be generated.

Monitor or Die

Planning a project may involve talking to people, experiencing quiet reflection, and working at a table or a desk. *Engaging* a project mandates that you are up and about, checking on this, checking on that, calling here, and making notes there. Project managers should be adept in all of these situations.

> **Dyna Moe**
>
> When you are driving down the road in your car, you need to be good at many functions. Likewise, a good manager heading up a long-term project needs to adequately perform many functions.

A One Percent Shift Early Means a Lot

In project management, veering off course is an everyday phenomenon, while making course corrections follows closely on its heels!

For example, most passengers aren't aware and perhaps they're better off not knowing that the typical airline flight is off-course most of the time. The pilot takes off, and plots a course heading. Then, because of prevailing winds and a host of other factors, the pilot finds himself off-course by a slight degree. He adjusts—he gets back on course. A few minutes later, he might be off a couple of degrees in the other direction.

> **CAUTION**
> ### Coming Undone
> Being only a few percent off in the early phases of a project can yield dramatic negative results later. The only thing that makes sense is the continuous monitoring of your progress.

For the duration of the flight, the plane veers this way and that off the path of the desired course. Through enhanced navigational systems and the work of the pilot, the plane continually readjusts and gets back on-course.

Eventually, as the plane approaches the runway and course settings become critical, all attention is focused on assuring a safe landing.

If the pilot were to announce over the intercom every little deviation in course, the passengers would be aghast. They would lose confidence in the pilot, the crew, and the airline in particular. Yet, continual monitoring and adjustments during flights is the norm, not the exception.

The Right People for the Right Job

The more people you manage, the bigger the budget. The more resources involved, the more interconnectedness there is. More connections between resources uniformly lead to higher levels of complexity. But the right components can yield amazing results.

> ### Dyna Moe
> At every step along the way, ask yourself if you are merely making checkmarks on charts, or performing high-quality work that will please everyone associated with the project.

Assembling a winning team takes skills, hard work, and a strong dose of luck (see Chapter 24). As the project moves forward, ideally team members cooperate with one another at even higher levels than at the outset of the project, much like a winning baseball team progressing toward the pennant. Efficiencies occur that enable you to save time and resources on some tasks. Team members leave at the end of the day feeling good about what they have accomplished and looking forward to what comes next.

Make It Through the Day with Essential Feedback

In project management, you wake up some mornings thinking, "How am I ever going to get through this day?" Miraculously you do, and then you repeat the process again the next day. Depending on the project, simply completing everything on time and on budget and achieving the desired outcome—with nothing extra or particularly spectacular, just a bread-and-butter performance—will get you a feather in your cap. Using feedback can make acquisition of the feather even less strenuous.

Sometimes, even though you are up-to-the-minute in terms of your reporting requirements, you don't get timely, crucial feedback that would enable you to better do your job. If this is so, what alternative strategies do you have in place?

- ◆ Who else can you turn to?

- ◆ What other resources can you tap?

- ◆ How can you expedite the feedback process?

You need feedback!

Top executives and managers may not be the most equipped or readily-available individuals to give you the in-depth regular feedback that would be so greatly appreciated and helpful in ensuring your success. So, you have to proceed as if you alone are responsible for monitoring your own progress. If others are involved, then they may serve as project safeguards. If no one else is involved, then tackle the issue head-on.

Reporting results may merely be a requirement of your position, but monitoring progress accurately is crucial. As many project managers have found out, it is all too easy to get side-tracked in the course of your daily activities. Something comes up that is enticing, but objectively adds little to the overall project. This is where you have to have the mental and emotional strength to let go of the "nice, but not necessary."

CAUTION Coming Undone

Do you find yourself so involved in the nitty-gritty that you can't see the proverbial forest for the trees? It is too easy to get caught up in the capability of the technical tools while missing fundamental project issues occurring right before your eyes. An objective, fresh perspective on the material can help unveil the forest and pinpoint the ailing trees.

Anticipate Challenge

Consider what roadblocks and barriers loom in the not-so-distant future. Can you incorporate them in your thinking so as to be better prepared? What can you head off today, even though it is not at the top of your list to ensure smooth operations several weeks or months down the pike? Like the driver barreling down the highway, you still have to pull into the right lane and slow down when your exit is coming up.

Factoid

There are organizations in this world that have existed for decades and have a single mission posted on the walls and every place in between. Yet, untold numbers of employees still cannot state the organization's mission!

Maintain effective communication with your colleagues. Keep others focused. Even if everyone was on the same page when you started the project, don't count on it staying that way for too long. A miscommunication could cause a costly wreck, but if you let others in on what's ahead, they can avoid the pile-up of misunderstood project goals while feeling far more comfortable with your leadership.

Your project plans, which are bound to be a bit more involved than a company mission, run an even greater risk of not being read, not being understood, and not being followed. Too often, people simply do not read project reports, or if they do, they do not comprehend them. Some circle a few items here and there and feel that they now have the adequate background that they need.

Initiatives Worth Considering

How can you monitor project progress for little or no investment and get a great return? Assign one of your key staff members the task of spending an hour or two some afternoon to do a thorough project review for which they will be thanked profusely, regardless of what shortcomings they may identify.

Alternatively, find another project manager within your organization with whom you can make a reciprocal agreement. Periodically, you might monitor progress on his project, and he monitor progress on yours. Or simply find an accountability partner, whether it is a superior, mentor, fellow project manager, or peer who will cooperate with you on scheduled times to co-monitor your progress.

Whenever your monitoring activity uncovers some variance between the plan you are following and what is actually occurring, certainly you want to take action. As with the pilot, the earlier you start making course adjustments, the easier it is to proceed along the chosen route.

Metrics for Success

Proceeding as scheduled, and on budget, which is a mark of efficiency, represents one indicator of project success—although that alone is not sufficient. Is the desired level of quality, a mark of effectiveness, being met? Are the higher-ups pleased with the project? Will the customer, client, or other end-user sing the praises of the organization as a result of the work on this project? These and other types of feedback indicators are most telling.

Numbers as Indicators

Sometimes, a simple tally is highly useful in indicating project success. For example, if you are cast to design a new safety program and are running a test case in one of your organization's divisions, the good old metric "X number of days without an accident" prominently posted can be adequate.

Similarly, if you are working on a new software package counting computer bugs in the program, a reverse metric can be put to good use. In the previous example, a large number indicates success, while a smaller, hence reverse metric system, indicates success in the de-bugging software example.

For items not readily countable, create a subjective numeric rating system. For example, when you watch divers in the Olympics plunge into the water, there is no absolute indicator of how good the dive is. Judges hold up their signs saying 8, 9, or 10 and through a simple mathematical formula, an overall score for the diver results.

> **Dyna Moe**
>
> The best rating scales are those that remain simple: such as 1 to 5 or 1 to 10. Nevermind this 87.2 stuff.

Your team members, as well, can provide their own assessments of project performance for the day on specific tasks or subtasks or on any aspect of the project. If you can get their attention, and they are willing to participate, top managers, executives, and other stakeholders can do the same. These outside views are always only an addition to your own ratings. What aspects of the project do you rate? Any issue that is deemed to be of importance.

Metrics of Another Kind

Sometimes symbols can be used in place of numbers. Think of a weather chart, where sunny equals a smiling face, cloudy equals a neutral face, and heavy rain equals a scowling face. In like manner, you can design and post charts that elicit the feedback of project team members, and do so in a nonintrusive, somewhat humorous way.

You can also use a form of questioning to help monitor your progress. For example, how will we know when we have completed Task 2 to everyone's satisfaction? The answers may be:

   ◆ When the top boss immediately flashes a big smile upon hearing the news.

   ◆ When the typically hands-on boss takes a hands-off approach.

   ◆ When everyone on the project team is so pleased they spontaneously decide to rendezvous after work at the nearest watering hole.

   ◆ When team members leave for the evening with any take-home work.

> **Dyna Moe**
>
> If you work for a boss who keeps his mitts on everything, then one potential indicator of your progress can be his lack of participation. As one manager observed, "Virtually any project can be successful given enough executive meddling, brute force, and big sticks."

These are subjective to be sure, but if indicated in advance of the completion of some task, subtask, or event, they serve as better indicators of progress than any pre-established indicators.

The Project Auditor Cometh

For larger and longer-term projects you may be subject to the uneasy experience of having your project audited.

> **Word Power**
>
> An **auditor** is usually an experienced expert or team of experts who rapidly familiarize themselves with the requirements of your project and what you are trying to accomplish.

Auditors generally come on-site. Depending on your project, they may examine your records in detail, interview your staff, and/or interview clients or customers. They also may trace the flow of funds, observe and time project management staff, examine equipment, and visit facilities.

After they have completed their efforts, they will usually debrief you as project manager, on their way to producing a written report that you can bet will be seen and read by all the people you couldn't get to read your own reports.

If you are fortunate, the auditors' report will contain observational gems and lead to key opportunities for progress. If you are unfortunate, the report will slash you to ribbons and you will be spending untold hours trying to undo its effects. In any case, a project audit is certainly an eye-opener. If you must endure one, cooperate fully; anything else just tends to work against you.

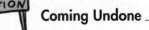

Coming Undone

If you are audited, it doesn't necessarily mean that somebody above thinks that the project is in trouble. It might be standard fare, or there might be something unique about your project that prompted the process. Or you're in major trouble.

Maintaining Momentum on Longer-Term Projects

Here's a handful of other tips to keep you going in pursuit of the things you want to get done when they may extend over weeks or months:

 ◆ Monitor some aspect of the project every day, even if it's the smallest of tasks. You'll be amazed at the usefulness that some kind of daily monitoring provides.

 ◆ Alternate when you'll examine the largest versus the smallest segments of the projects. While it's best to stay focused on the large segments, sometimes you can't make yourself get going. At least review something.

 ◆ Often the need to tackle tasks beyond those of your original plan pops up. Look for help along the way. The kinds of assistance you might need at various junctures might not have been easily identified earlier on.

Dyna Moe

Have the wherewithal to make that call or send that e-mail when your monitoring efforts indicate that the help of someone out there will be crucial to your momentum on longer-term projects.

At all times proceed with a "divide and conquer" mentality. No matter how well you've planned and how well you've plotted, monitored, and re-planned at various times, certain elements of long-term projects seem rather insurmountable. Break them down into bite-size tasks.

The Least You Need to Know

♦ Too many projects run over time and budget because the manager was over-confident and didn't feel compelled to monitor progress.

♦ It is too easy to fall in love with technical tools while missing fundamental project issues.

♦ Proceeding as scheduled and on budget represents the basic indicators of project success.

♦ Establishing project metrics helps you to know how things are progressing at various stages.

♦ If you have to endure a project audit, cooperate fully; anything else works against you.

♦ Monitor some aspect of the project every day, even if it's the smallest of tasks.

Part 5

Efficiency Hazards and Sand Traps

A mind is a terrible thing to waste, yours in particular since it's a key asset in your quest for accomplishment. For all your planning and plotting, monitoring and mother-henning, you'll need to maintain a proper frame of mind for getting things done, especially the big things. This part contains six illuminating chapters that will guide you through the obstacles that line your path to getting more done.

THINKING ABOUT THE
BIG PICTURE...

Chapter 15

Attempting Too Many Things at Once

In This Chapter

- ◆ Multitasking isn't pretty
- ◆ Multitasking is stressful and counterproductive
- ◆ Concentration is king
- ◆ Conquering techno-stress

As we've learned, the wondrous tools of technology that surround us aid and abet the inclination to multitask. We work with a computer that can search for information, while running a print job, while backing up files.

Admiring these characteristics, we attempt to emulate the operating capabilities of our gadgetry. We resonate at a speed which, all too often, is not internally generated and predictably we experience a greater or lesser degree of technostress. Technostress is everyday stress that is exacerbated by technology, most notably present when we do not rule technology, it rules us.

This chapter focuses on the productivity disruption caused by multitasking and the misuse of technology and offers methods to minimize such disruptions.

Doomed to Multitask?

In an era of committed multitaskers, concentration and focus are underrated. A magnifying glass held up at the correct angle to the sun will quickly burn a hole through a piece of paper. At the same time, no matter how much sun shines through your office window onto your desk, none of those long and tedious memos are going to catch on fire. Drat!

> **Factoid**
>
> The term *multitasking* evolved from the computer industry—performing multiple tasks simultaneously. The early mainframe computers designed with parallel processes are perhaps the prime example of automated multitasking.

Multitasking is occasionally helpful and seemingly satisfying but, along with the shower of information and communication overload, represents a paradoxical impediment to getting things done.

We offer our attention here, there, and then somewhere else. Like a one-man band, we get our strokes from strumming the guitar, tapping our foot, and blowing on the harmonica. We equate accomplishment with flapping our wings, stirring up a lot of commotion, and making a lot of noise.

Generally, we feel guilty if we don't multitask! We contemplate our increasing workloads and responsibilities and how they are subject to continual shifts, and justify multitasking as a valid response to a world of flux.

Despite the temptation to do otherwise, focusing on the task at hand is vital to getting things done. Whether there's a handful of tasks confronting you, or ideally only one, give all your time, attention, energy, focus, concentration, effort, and all that good stuff to the task at hand, and then turn to what's next.

> **Coming Undone**
>
> Multitasking has become a norm giving rise to "continuous partial attention," where nothing gets your true and undivided focus, and everything is homogenized to the point of carrying nearly equal weight. We can barely tolerate stillness. For many, silence doesn't appear to be golden, it is merely an unwelcome phenomenon that inhibits productivity. Undivided attention is a term that has fallen out of popular use.

Multitasking: Misunderstood, Over-Employment, and Undesirable

It's likely that people have always sought to handle many things simultaneously, stretching as far back as cave dwellers. Their multitasking effort probably seemed crude by comparison. Someday, somewhere, someone may discover that we are hardwired to continuously attempt to economize our use of time.

Our age-old "flight or fight" response to perceived stressors in the environment works well, at intermittent times. The small jolts of concentrated energy and vigilance help us to safeguard ourselves, our loved ones, and our possessions. As a species, however, we are not wired to effectively handle continuous streams of two major stress hormones, adrenaline and cortisol, on a daily basis.

Bruce McEwen, Ph.D., director of the neuroendocrinology lab at Rockefeller University, observes that while we can apparently weather stresses and hormone surges in the short term, about 3 to 15 days, soon thereafter chronic stress begins to ensue. The result is a weakened immune system, aggression, anxiety, and a decrease in brain functioning, which results in burnout.

 **Factoid**

Dangerously high levels of cortisol can result in poor sleep patterns and insulin resistance, which can open the door to bad eating habits and weight gain.

As it will become clear in this book, focus and concentration will be your keys for getting things done. Multitasking, as it is popularly understood and practiced, is not your answer. It is expensive in terms of the level of stress induced and the rise in errors and, hence, can actually hamper productivity.

Stress, More Mental Effort

You don't have to be a physician to observe the entrenched levels of workplace stress, but physicians themselves are noticing it with alarming regularity. Few patients ever remark that their stress levels are low, while most confess that they're stressed to the max. As the unfortunate habit of multitasking takes hold in the workforce, stress levels are rising.

Here's the unwanted news. Next week, next month, and next year, you'll be asked to do even more without necessarily being given any greater resources. If you work in government or a nonprofit organization, you may be asked to do more with less. If your budget or your staff has been reduced or eliminated, you may be asked to do more with nothing!

Evidence is appearing that multitasking adds up to a more stressful workday and life. It dampens our experience of pleasure. It hounds us long after closing time and even renders the benefits of leisure less effective.

Marcel Just, Ph.D., co-director of Carnegie-Melon's Center for Cognitive Brain Imaging, conducted a study in which he asked participants to listen to sentences while comparing two rotating objects. These tasks draw on different areas of the brain, yet the participants' ability to engage in visual processing, comparing the two rotating objects, dropped by 29 percent.

Factoid

Research conducted at the National Institute of Mental Health confirms that when the brain has to switch back to something, it has to overcome "inhibitions" that it put in place to cease doing the task to begin with. It's as if the brain is taking its foot off the brake.

The participants' capabilities for auditory processing, listening to the sentence, dropped by 53 percent when engaged in this mild multitasking test. Dr. Just says that while we certainly can do more than one thing at a time, "we are kidding ourselves if we think we can do so without cost."

It Gets Worse: More Errors, Lingering Effects

Multitasking seemingly enables one to achieve time-saving benefits, but does it? While some people remain relatively unscathed by multitasking and can get much done in the course of the workday, most people suffer in ways they don't even understand.

Rather than increasing their productivity, multitasking diminishes it. They make more mistakes. They leave too many things undone. Their quality of work is not what it could be. And the list of potential hazards of multitasking is beginning to grow. Are you a victim to any of the following:

- Suffer gaps in short-term memory?
- Experience loss of concentration?
- Have problems communicating with co-workers?
- Suffer lapses in attentiveness?
- Experience stress symptoms such as shortness of breath?

When multitasking, sometimes your brain can go into a crash mode. This is characterized by not being able to remember what you just said or did, or what you're going to do next! This has been termed "having a senior moment," but it's no joke and it doesn't only happen to seniors.

Professor David Meyer at the University of Michigan has established a link between chronic, high-stress multitasking and the loss of short-term memory. "There is scientific evidence that multitasking is extremely hard for someone to do, and sometimes impossible," he says. Also, the time lost switching between tasks tends to increase the perceived complexity of the tasks and often results in making a person less efficient than if he had chosen to focus on one task or project at a time.

The most difficult type of multitasking occurs when you try to engage the same area of the brain. You run into this all the time, people who are on the phone who are also surfing the net, listening to the radio, or in earshot of someone in the next room. Whether you're attempting to handle conflicting visual-processing tasks or conflicting auditory-processing tasks, the net result is you're not going to handle either task as well as you would handle each individually.

Lower-Level Tasks? Well, Maybe

If the multiple tasks you're seeking to handle are lower-level, such as folding a letter to insert into an envelope while gazing at your computer screen, you'll probably be okay. Both are easy enough to do, and one requires no heavy mental output (folding a sheet of paper). The more important the activities you try to do simultaneously, especially if they are of equal weight, the more likely you are to run aground.

Longitudinal studies on the effects of multitasking are still in progress, but this we know: you waste so much time backtracking, correcting, or redoing what you've done as a result of multitasking that you're better off staying focused on one task at a time. That's the key to productivity.

CAUTION   **Coming Undone** _____

> If you must know, there are indications that one can somewhat improve multitasking capabilities. Being well-rested helps, as does eliminating distractions. Yoga, meditation, and visualization each help in certain ways to improve your mental focus.
>
> Even if you could master the beast, however, you have to wonder, is it worth it? This author says *no*, multitasking is not worth it, however temporarily satisfying or momentarily gratifying.

The Pleasure of One Task at a Time

The quickest and easiest way you can diminish the unhealthy chain of events that occur with multitasking is to learn to renouce it, like a smoker who gives up smoking.

Concentrate on the task at hand. For example, read this sentence without sounds in the room, without snacking on something, and without otherwise diverting your attention. Give yourself the benefit—the pleasure—of doing one thing at a time.

◆ Your attention span will improve.

◆ Your cortisol and adrenaline levels will be more likely to stay in check.

◆ Your immune system will benefit.

◆ Your overall health and peace of mind will likely improve.

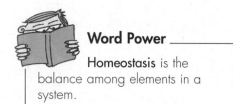

Word Power

Homeostasis is the balance among elements in a system.

When you focus on the matter at hand, achieving a form of *homeostasis*, the psychological and physiological stability engendered may enable you to become more industrious and more creative.

Think of the times when you were humming along, on a roll as they say, and while you weren't even trying apparently, new insights, new perspectives, and new ways of accomplishment came to you just like that! Only one task at a time can command our sharp attention, and more often than not, those are the times when it seems like you're on a roll.

Researchers tell us that the human brain is unable to process two or more unrelated tasks at the same time. It seems like we are able to do this, but what actually occurs is high-speed task switching.

The Rise of Technostress

In their book, *Technostress*, spouses Larry Rosen, Ph.D., and Michelle Weil, Ph.D., observe that technology can help place innovative workers in the driver's seat. It also can create such dependency that you end up questioning your own creativity and capabilities.

Multitasking at work feeds technostress. Many managers are concerned that the increasing level of work-related technology will lead to a loss of privacy, information inundation, erosion of face-to-face contact, having to continually learn new skills, and being passed over for promotion because others coming up the ladder are more technologically savvy. Larry Rosen and Michelle Weil observe that "technostress is worse on the executive suits."

To keep technology in the proper perspective, the authors advise, declare your independence, offering a "Technology Bill of Rights" as follows:

1. I am the boss, not my technology.

2. Technology is available to help me express my creativity.

3. I decide when to use the tools technology provides.

4. I have the right to choose what technology to use and what to put aside.

5. I can use technology to stay connected, informed, and productive—my way.

6. Technology offers a world of information. I get to choose what information is important to me.

7. Technology will have problems, but I will be prepared to handle them.

8. Technology can work 24-hour days, but I can choose when to begin and when to stop working.

9. Technology never needs to rest, but I do.

10. I can work successfully by enforcing my boundary needs.

Some of the "articles" to this bill of rights are particularly apropos in the context of getting things done.

You're In Control

Article #3 for example, "I decide when to use the tools technology provides," is worth its weight in microchips. Some people are ruled by their e-mail, having to check it upon arising, throughout the morning, at lunch, throughout the afternoon, as they leave the office, and then even at home a few more times. Worse, they check in the middle of doing some other task that requires steadfast concentration.

Hey, it's okay to use checking one's e-mail, or any other brief activity, as a mental break from a rigorous task. The problem with checking e-mail or a cell phone for break time is that you're likely to be exposed or introduced to more tasks at an inopportune juncture, when you are not prepared to address them.

Coming Undone

Constantly checking for messages in the middle of working on something is akin to multitasking, and you don't have to head down this path.

One executive from an Inc. 500 Company (the fastest growing entrepreneurial companies in America) revealed that he only permits himself to check e-mail three times daily: at 10 A.M, 2 P.M., and 4 P.M.

At those intervals, he remarks, he can stay on top of the e-mail communications coming his way, not miss anything, or not have anything become too "old." Hence, he's able to have long stretches free of e-mail throughout the day.

You Do the Choosing

Article #6 bears scrutiny, particularly the sentence, "I choose what information is important to me." Consider all the times you've visited the Internet in the past six to eight years, and all the information you've gleaned. If you're like most career professionals, the sites you choose to visit on a regular basis boil down to a handful—perhaps five, perhaps six or seven.

Sure, if you're going shopping, if you want to find a particular location, if you have keywords to throw into a search engine, you'll visit other sites based on a specific need. Every now and then, you go where the web will take you. Otherwise, as a creature of habit, you fall into the same routine, visiting the same sites, gaining the same kind of news and perspectives.

You may use bots and information services to alert you to news and information based on the topics you've indicated are of interest to you. Do you, however, seek out the alternative viewpoint? For example:

◆ Do you visit the sites that explore issues in greater depth?

◆ Do you visit sites from other countries?

◆ Do you use this wondrous web to paint a fuller picture of the knowledge you're seeking to assemble on a particular topic or issue?

For many people, most of the time the answer is no. We gather what we can gather as easily as we can gather it and that becomes the extent of our perspective. Much of the time, this is quite okay—you don't need a well-rounded, in-depth answer, for now and for all time. You simply need quick information. Those times where greater depth, clarity, and focus are required call for you to invoke article #6 of the Technology Bill of Rights.

Follow the Scout's Motto

Article #7, "Technology will have problems but I will be prepared to handle them," is worth noting. Do you have resources in place if your hard drive crashes, if a virus cripples your computer, or if any component of your hardware or software seems to be malfunctioning? Conscientious motorists belong to some type of auto club, have a favorite repair shop, and know a few things about how to troubleshoot their vehicle.

Similarly, conscientious technology users take precautions, particularly when it comes to computers. The greater your reliance on technology, the more adept you need to be, and the more important it becomes to have resources and backup systems in place, should problem situations arise.

Coming Undone

You don't want to be "revving" so fast, handling this and that, that you do not take the time and make the effort to safeguard your workflow. The brief time it takes to make some backup files and hardcopies can save several hours worth of backtracking if your computer crashes.

Rest, Who Needs Rest?

Articles #9 and #10, "Technology never needs to rest, but I do" and "I can work successfully by enforcing my boundary needs," are notable as well. When I hear someone profess to be available "24/7," or when people hand me business cards that contain their work phone, cell phone, home phone, and pager number, invisibly I cringe.

Will you lose out on a business deal because you are not available at 11 P.M. or 2 A.M.? Even if you do business with people in far corners of the world, do they expect you to be available and conversant at 2 A.M. or 3 A.M? If they do, and if you are, what kind of career is that? It's one thing to get important things done; it's quite another to unwittingly perpetually juggle multiple tasks and to surrender your work life to every little intrusion.

Dyna Moe

Unless your job specifically calls for you to be available on selected days around the clock—i.e., you're in law enforcement, national security, health care, or emergency services—why would you want to make yourself available to everyone at all times?

The Least You Need to Know

- Focus and concentration are the keys to getting things done. Give all your time, attention, energy, and effort to the task at hand.

- Multitasking, while seemingly making one more productive, comes at a high price.

- Multitaskers may be efficient, effective, both, or neither, and that makes multitasking too risky to practice on vital projects at work.

- To keep technology in the proper perspective, declare your independence.

- Avoid being available "24/7" any which way you can!

Incompletions and Their Hazards

In This Chapter

- ◆ Undone is no fun
- ◆ Incompletions impact individuals
- ◆ The need for neat endings
- ◆ Self-acknowledgment is vital

A powerful way to avoid succumbing to the onslaught of too much competition for your time and attention, and a good way to stay focused, perpetually, is by seeking completions. As I have alluded to in the previous chapters, "completion thinking" is one of the most fundamental ways to continually get things done despite distractions.

Fortunately, you are already a master of many aspects of completions. When you awake each morning, you have completed sleep for the previous night. When you turn in a big report at work, and you know it's ready, that is a completion. If you get nothing else from this book but guidance on using completions, then you will have benefited greatly.

The next chapter will help you to become a master of completions. But in this chapter, it is vital and illuminating, as well as potentially revelatory, to understand the nature of what has become our culture of incompletions.

The Ill-Effects of Incompletions

To get things done, especially long-term projects, it's wise to acknowledge your completions at various milestones. Divide and conquer. Unfortunately, many people unknowingly create a series of incompletions, professionally and personally, task-wise and psychologically.

The unhappiest people among us keep re-thinking what is incomplete instead of simply acknowledging the actual situation and making new choices about what action to take. When you leave tasks or activities incomplete, you have energy vested in them. A lack of completions at work can leave you feeling exhausted and used!

The Age of Incompletions

The tendency of people to not complete things, in part, may be traceable to recent sociocultural developments. In many ways, we are living in what I call the age of incompletions. Simply being alive during this age may, in one form or another, impede your ability to get things done, particularly to get one thing done after another. This is heady and takes several pages, but if you're dedicated to becoming more adept at getting things done, you need to understand this phenomenon.

I'm not sure when this age started, but 1963 was certainly a pivotal year. This may have been before you were born, so I'll take you back to November of that year. President John F. Kennedy was shot, perhaps by a lone gunman, perhaps as a result of a conspiracy. The case was solved 30 years later in 1993 and presented in *Case Closed*, by Gerald Posner.

Factoid

Noted historian William Manchester, after reading Posner's book, said that he couldn't imagine anyone having any further doubt about the fact that Lee Harvey Oswald, on his own, shot and killed John Fitzgerald Kennedy.

Gerald Posner walks the reader through every conceivable detail of the case. He shows conclusively why, acting alone, it was Lee Harvey Oswald who fired the gun. He explains how the "magic bullets" took the angles that they were supposed to.

I read *Case Closed* cover to cover and concur. *U.S. News & World Report* concluded that Posner's work was so convincing that the magazine would never feature another "who shot JFK?" book review again. Yet, new mythology and conspiracy theories about who killed John F. Kennedy will be concocted and added to the glut of information you can't use, information which serves no one.

Currently, the "who shot JFK?" industry earns $200 million a year, with the potential to go higher, constantly fed by more TV news magazine "investigations," authors, books, and tours.

Misinformation that Won't Die

I don't regard the misinformation surrounding JFK's death lightly. The nature of society changed as nearly an entire generation suspected that a conspiracy, perhaps a government-led conspiracy, may have brought down the leader of the free world in broad daylight. Who knew what cynicism about government, the press, truth itself, would ensue? And, finally, 30 years later, when Posner assembled the irrefutable evidence about the only assassin it could have been, hardly anyone knows, or worse, actually cares.

As late as 2003, 80 percent of the U.S. population surveyed still believed that President Kennedy's assassination was the result of some type of conspiracy. The case has long been solved, but there is no sense of national closure.

I submit to you, gentle reader, that the nature of your life changed as a result of the misinformation, unreality, and cultural incompletion that has glutted society's receptors.

This situation represents more than simply a mystery for the uninformed. This potentially signals the start of Baby Boomers and Gen Xers unwittingly entering the era of incompletions.

How has that impacted our psyches? Aren't we supposed to be able to get to the root of such events, especially those that shook a generation, a nation, and the world?

What heretofore recognized psychological scars has the incompletion of the JFK assassination mystery stamped into the cerebrum of an otherwise free-thinking, progressive, optimistic generation? When major cases aren't closed, everyone suffers, even if in small and undistinguishable ways.

From Intelligent Inquiry to Media-Induced Untruthfulness

Fast-forward 15 years to the death of Elvis Presley of Memphis, Tennessee. Unquestionably he died as a result of a self-induced pharmaceutical drug overdose, which resulted in heart failure. The coroner's report reveals this as do reputable follow-up inquiries and analysis. Still, many people from that era, and many who come later, think Elvis died as a result of a conspiracy.

Some people believe that Elvis never really died, that he's alive and well, and showing up in random locations captured by the ever-present photographers of the *Enquirer*, *Globe*, or *Star*.

Regardless of what you think about Elvis and his death, even amidst the jokes, and everything that's been made about it since then, the culturally pervasive message to all is that no case is ever really solved.

Everything lingers on and on and on. The results of the 2000 presidential election in Florida, with its endless motions filed, court appeals, and legal procedures, has spawned debates, arguments, and accusations that exist to this day and no doubt will linger on for years.

Some people see parallels between Ohio in the 2004 election and Florida in 2000, even though those in the upper echelons of the Democratic Party will not champion this cause. Nevertheless, the political arguments fly to and fro on both sides. No conclusions, no consensus, no closure. Just additional coverage. The media wins, the pundits win, one candidate or another wins, but everyone else loses.

All of History Up for Grabs

The contemporary turf wars fought in the age of incompletions, particularly in the political arena, now retroactively extend to virtually everything that has ever happened, whether you're assessing U.S. history, the formation of our nation, world history, the origins of Islam, the origins of Christianity, and so forth.

At one time, it was widely held that dropping the atomic bomb on Japan hastened the end of WWII, saved a minimum of 60,000 U.S. troops who would have been needed to fight a ground war in Japan, and provided the world with the closure it so sorely needed after six years of global destruction.

Since that time, the arguments about the United States being the over-aggressor, the only nation to ever drop an atomic bomb on another, and the inhumanity of it all, have risen to the forefront of many people's consciousness.

Some people pick up scraps of evidence that point to there having been no need for the United States to have dropped the bomb, as if the casualty rate of invading mainland Japan would have been minimal. Some say Japan was on its last legs (although even after one atom bomb was dropped it still would not surrender!), U.S. intentions were racially motivated (although the bomb was originally designed to use on the now-surrendered Germans), the hawks had their way, and so forth.

What had been regarded by many people as closure to the most terrible event the earth had ever encountered in which 44,500,000 perished, is now the subject of endless debate in some circles. Not that such debate isn't healthy; quite the contrary, especially for an action of such magnitude.

When every inch of political terrain is contested everywhere around the clock, and when all public discourse is subject to interpretation, reinterpretation, and revision, and essentially nothing is final, it begins to wear on humanity and notably trickles down to the level of the individual.

All this occurs on a macro level, but the age of incompletions leaves its mark on the individual. You, an otherwise confident professional seeking to get things done, have reached adulthood in an era and in a culture where incompletion more often than not is the norm.

When I worked for a consulting firm in Washington, D.C. in the mid 1980s, one of my co-workers was ex-military. He told me that often, when he received complicated directives, he didn't get shook up about it. If he just bided his time, something else would replace them. In the workaday world, this mentality shows up all the time, but in different forms.

Don't like your boss? Sweat it out for a little while; he or she will be transferred anyway. Prefer to not use the new software routine? If there are several others who feel the same way, it will be abandoned soon enough. The danger to the otherwise competent individual is the daily, pervasive notion that some goals and objectives, entirely worth pursing, on second thought, can be put off, circumvented, or modified so as to make their accomplishment far easier.

Incompletions in the Air

The socially pervasive de facto acceptance of incompletions, which is in the air and swirls around all around us, has a distinct impact.

Factoid _____

Think about how you feel when you go to a health club to have a vigorous workout but are surrounded by people who are taking it easy. They engage in long conversations. They halfheartedly step onto the stair climber. They seemingly are content to burn however few calories they will as they while away the 45 minutes they had initially earmarked for working out. They spend more time at the drink machines than on the treadmill.

Days Without End

The neat beginning and closing to the day that was once plainly evident in everyone's lives has dissipated. Television programming is on all hours of the day and night, and there are hundreds of shows, anytime you want. Add in radio, the Internet, headline news, and there simply is no end. Stores are open 24/7. Traffic is always on the road.

For some, there is simply no day and no night, just dimly lit fluorescent lighting bathing otherwise grey mundane offices. These same offices with indoor temperature control, as well as our homes, diminish the effect of the seasons. Some people even regard heat or cold upon going outside as a bother, as if nature is supposed to conform with the turn of a thermostat dial.

Breakfast, lunch, and dinner have given way to this era of no designated meal times. We eat what we want, when we want. Actually, food of all types is available at all times. It's not just the mixing of breakfast, lunch, and dinner foods with one another; there's no sense of seasonal foods. Summer squash, winter tomatoes—we want everything available all the time.

An Undeniable Impact

We _are_ impacted by our surroundings, peers, cultural norms, and that which we readily observe. If you're seeking to lose weight and you live in a culture in which being overweight and obesity have become a norm, how much easier is it for you to simply stay where you are or, at best, lose a few pounds, but not nearly what you had originally intended?

The "broken window" phenomenon in sociology holds that if an abandoned building in a neighborhood has a broken window that remains unrepaired, in time, more windows will be broken, until finally all windows will be broken. What's more, the windows of adjoining buildings will be broken. Then, it's not long before the whole neighborhood runs down.

In communities where abandoned buildings are fenced off or, miraculously, re-modeled for new industry, street cleaners keep curbs clean, and abandoned vehicles are not permitted on front lawns, everyone in that community tends to conform to the standard.

What Surrounds Us Prevails

We are impacted by our environment to a degree that we are not always aware of on a conscious level. I was waiting in the airport lounge at LaGuardia Airport in New York to board a plane to Los Angeles. You know this scene, right? Bedazzled, razzled, frazzled.

This particular section of the airport was under construction. The passengers waited in a make-shift lounge. I found the atmosphere to be unduly noisy. People looked upset, anxious, and not the type of group I wanted to fly with.

A miraculous thing happened when we boarded the plane. It was apparently a newer jet. The seat cushions were firm and soft. The rug was clean. The place seemed light and airy, and even cheery! Everything in the interior of the plane helped to muffle noise. As the passengers filed in and took their seats, an unmistakable change came over the entire group.

No longer the unruly, boisterous crowd waiting in the airport lounge, these were people heading to California. They seemed serene. They were certainly less anxious. They even looked better. There and then, I understood the supreme importance of one's environment.

Surround Yourself to Succeed

As a dedicated career professional who seeks to get things done, to become known for one's accomplishments, and perhaps be regarded as a high achiever, it is vitally important to take control of your environment, associate with other get-it-done types, and embrace the notion of "completion thinking." As you look around your office, what strikes you as having been left incomplete? Are piles building up in corners around the room? Are Post-it pads serving as proxy to-do list items adorning your desk and PC monitor? Do you have stacks of unopened mail? Is your message light blinking?

You can extend these same types of observations to your home as well as many other aspects of your life. When you're entirely honest with yourself, chances are you will find that there are visible signs of incompletions all around you.

It's not mandatory to be in total control of your work space, but it helps. (For the nitty-gritty of making your desk work for you, see Chapter 6.)

Considering the larger picture, what is incomplete in your career? Are there key instructions, an agenda, a road map, a blueprint, or an action map of some sort that you know is valid and appropriate on which you have yet to take action? Are there vital courses that you need to be taking? Are there key contacts within your industry that you haven't made? Are there other initiatives you have in mind that you have let sit for years?

Of course there are! Each item represents an incompletion. Fortunately, the path to completions, big and small, is to keep acknowledging yourself whenever you do indeed complete something. As we'll discuss in the next chapter, your brain can't tell the difference between something as small as sending out a letter versus completing a major training session.

> **Dyna Moe**
>
> If you want to finish work each night with a valid sense of accomplishment, give yourself acknowledgment for completing what you did get done. Acknowledging yourself for all you actually finished is the surest method of leaving without feeling beaten and often proves to be uplifting.

By acknowledging yourself for the smaller completions, you actually pave the way for greater and grander completions. The brain appreciates closure.

Completions represent a nice, neat ending to what you've just accomplished and a great beginning for whatever is next. Giving yourself a completion for some minor task actually opens the door and sets the stage, if you will, for tackling something much larger. Go ahead, give yourself a completion, and make your day!

The Least You Need to Know

- To get things done, especially long-term projects, it's wise to acknowledge your completions at various milestones.
- The tendency of people to not complete things may be traceable to a contemporary interruption of a cultural predisposition to attain closure.
- We are greatly impacted by our surroundings, so choose yours carefully.
- Acknowledging yourself for what you've completed allows you to finish work in an uplifting frame of mind.
- Acknowledging yourself for small completions paves the way for greater completions.

Chapter 17

All About Completion Thinking

In This Chapter

◆ Completions all around

◆ Allowing it to happen

◆ The choice you make

◆ Breakdowns and breakthroughs

You got a good sense of the effect of incompletions from the previous chapter, so in this chapter we are going to focus on how to achieve completions, everywhere, all the time!

Silent Self-Acknowledgment

A completion is not merely the accomplishment of a task. As used here, it also means mentally citing yourself for what you've gotten done. As I describe in my book *Breathing Space: Living & Working at a Comfortable Pace in a Sped-Up Society*, those who have mastered completions give themselves quick, silent acknowledgment and then move on ... "I did a

Factoid _____

Achieving completions is not synonymous with obsessive behavior or overachieving. Completions are simply useful means for giving your mind and emotions temporary energy breaks.

particularly good job here, and it's rewarding to have it done!" They are not obsessive and do not seek completions only for completion's sake.

The happiest, most productive, most prosperous people have developed the habit of achieving one completion after another, acknowledging themselves for their efforts, the experiences, and the accomplishments. Yet, to an observer it may look as if there is barely a moment to catch a breath.

Achieving completions is energizing because it offers a clean end to activities or even thoughts, and it is a good beginning for what's next.

Score One for You

Completions can be acknowledged when finishing a minor or routine task, or even a daily event, not only for monumental efforts. For example, when you awake each morning, you have completed sleep for that night.

Completions can be achieved on multi-year projects or even on activities that last seconds. The table that follows offers a brief list of rapid completions.

Rapid Completions in Everyday Life

Completions	In Seconds
Camera shutter open and close	0.001
Rest time of human nerve cell	0.001
Blink of an eye	0.10
Short-term memory receptors	0.80
One human heart beat at rest	0.86
Michael Jordan's hang-time	0.9
Average rock video scene change	1.5
Average doorbell chime	2.0
Average television camera shot	3.5
Average embrace between spouses	7.0
Average CNN headline news story	13.0
U.S. Pledge of Allegiance	14.3

Completions	In Seconds
The 1989 San Francisco Earthquake	15.0
Phone pickup after fourth ring	18.4
Star Trek opener, "Space, the final frontier …"	22.1
Average Major League home run trot	23.8
Pro basketball shot clock	24.0
Final *Jeopardy* countdown	30.0
Average teeth-brushing time by adults	58.0
Kentucky Derby (average length)	62.3
"Star Spangled Banner" (Marine Corps Band)	101.0
Average song length on radio	190.0
World record for one-mile run	217.3
1,000-person net gain in world population	314.2
Time for a cigarette to burn to ashes	326.0

Whether your completions are large or small, they are vital to acknowledge because they provide a mental and emotional break from what you had been doing. On top of that, they make you feel good!

Achieving completions is energizing because it offers a clean end to activities or even thoughts, and a good beginning for what's next. At home, simply drying and putting away the dishes, or taking out the garbage, are completions that yield benefits. At work, making copies for the staff meeting or handling a key phone call represent completions that also yield the aforementioned benefits.

Completions are somewhat like driving along a mountain highway and stopping periodically at scenic overlooks to get a breath of fresh air, stretch out, acknowledge how far you have come, and establish where you are.

Gathering the Loose Ends

As a holiday or vacation approaches, most career professionals instinctively tie up various loose ends so that they may depart in a more restful state of mind.

When your desk is cleared, files put back in place, and other things tidied up to a respectable degree, your whole countenance brightens. It's as if a weight has been taken off of your shoulders.

Consider the case of Karla. Karla was an independent health-care consultant to several large organizations. As part of each consulting engagement, she had to prepare and deliver a final report. In previous years, Karla considered it enough to write, proof, and assemble the entire report for on-schedule delivery to the client. She would then tie up loose ends several days or weeks after delivering the report, while in the midst of other activities.

After learning about the power of completions, however, Karla included binding the report, producing an attractive cover, and making an early delivery into her schedule. She also updated her hard-copy file, completed a project-cost data sheet, and the invoice. She streamlined her working notes file and chucked anything that was no longer needed. She even called the client one day in advance to alert them that the report was coming.

By viewing all aspects of the engagement as a unit, Karla was able to complete all related activities by the day the report was delivered. Karla was clear mentally and emotionally by the end of day. She felt good about her accomplishment and was energized to start what came next the following morning.

> **Dyna Moe**
>
> The great thing about completions is that they lead to another, and another and yet another. All around you, every day, you complete things, from the mundane to the magnificent.

Karla understood that unfinished tasks with one client can mount up and perceptually loom larger than they actually are. She knew that each task in finishing an engagement, like each pile she allowed on her desk, represented unfinished business.

The great change came for Karla when she began to realize that lack of completions in one aspect of her work impacted her activities in other areas. Conversely, completing one thing after another, after another leads to yet more completions.

Frustration or Invigoration

Unfortunately, there may be several areas of your career in which you rack up a number of incompletions. This could involve everything from keeping all your receipts in your wallet to perpetually allowing piles to build up on your desk.

These types of daily tasks can either drain or energize you. Completing them can make you feel accomplished, while having to postpone them can leave you frustrated. Surprisingly, the order in which you approach tasks can have a dramatic impact on your productivity, energy, and enthusiasm.

Ebbs and Flows

Some tasks are much better handled at specific times of the day, and are best avoided at other times. Each person has his own preferences. To maintain balance, get your work done, benefit from the power of completions, and still have a life at the end of the day, you need to make sure the sequence and the timing of your projects supports, rather than impedes, the likelihood that you will accomplish everything you hoped.

If you know you are better at one type of task early in the day, schedule accordingly. If you know that on, say, Tuesday, you're usually better prepared to handle a challenging task than at the end of the week, make plans that take advantage of that knowledge. To the degree that you control the timing of activities, continually give yourself the best chance to achieve desirable completions.

One Month Campaigns

My friend Allie takes a unique approach to getting things done in his consulting firm. He creates month-long completion campaigns by focus area. During each month of the year, in addition to the normal business transactions and activities that occur, Allie focuses on one major area of the business. For example, in January the focus might be on the billing system, in February, on office equipment, in March, on insurance, and so on. In the course of a year he is adept at giving extra attention to 12 major focus areas and enjoys a great sense of completion as each month rolls by.

As a variation on Allie's theme, suppose you're a salaried employee for a large corporation. You could delegate a few weeks out of each month, or all 52 weeks during the year for that matter, to serve as time intervals in which you'll focus on one particular aspect of your career or work. For example:

- In the first week of January, you review long-term goals.

- In the second week, you review the status and value of all your memberships.

- In the third week, you consider the publications you currently receive and how that line-up may need to change.

> **Dyna Moe**
>
> Periodically carve out a 30-minute stretch where you devote your attention to how your desk is stocked, the ergonomics of your office set-up, whether your e-mail signature is appropriate, and so on. This will help you stay in control and be better prepared to meet bigger challenges.

The key in each case is comfortably and conveniently fitting such reviews and assessments into your daily or monthly cycle so that you're able to maintain your normal work pace and get other things done that you've been meaning to accomplish, while staying balanced and happy and achieving completions so that you're ready for what's next.

Allowing Completions to Occur

Sometimes all you have to do is allow a completion to occur—not get in the way. At a rental place in Virginia, I purchased a 1983 Ford Thunderbird with 35,000 miles on it. The car was in fantastic shape and, amazingly, cost only $7,000 (a sizeable sum back then, but still a bargain in this case). I had that car for 18 years because I practiced preventive maintenance.

As you might imagine, by the fifteenth and sixteenth years, the car's performance had begun to decline. About once in 25 times, the car would not start properly. I'd have to turn the key 20, sometimes 40, times to get it to start. Usually these non-starting sessions would occur right after I had picked up, say, five bags of groceries!

The nuisance of having to receive a jump-start from the AAA road service or sitting there for 30 to 40 minutes repeatedly turning the key until the car started became way too much to bear. I placed an ad on a local Internet bulletin board but expected few, if any, calls. I was pleased to receive a call within a matter of days from an elderly gentleman who said that he had worked with cars all his life and would be interested in seeing it.

When the man arrived, I prayed the car would start on the first try. Being honest, however, I told him that about one in every 25 times the car would not start. He told me that wasn't a problem! He was good at tinkering with cars, and he'd look into it. When we got into my T-Bird, the car started on the first try and performed like a new vehicle!

I was asking $900, firm, for the car. After a couple of spins around the block, we switched places and he got behind the wheel. Once again, the car performed admirably, but I figured he'd want to think about it and call me later. After a few minutes he said that he'd like to buy it. Lucky me! I figured he'd go back home and write me a check. Instead he wanted to pull up to a local branch of his bank so that he could withdraw $900 in cash, right now ….

At that point I was thinking, "He wants to pay in cash. There is a God!" As he waited in line, I was completing the paperwork that would be necessary for the transfer of the vehicle. I had no idea what to do. He had every idea and walked me through the whole procedure. The fates were smiling on me that day.

We left the bank, got back in the car, and I once again prayed that it would start perfectly. It did. We made our way to the motor vehicle office, less than a quarter mile away. There was no line and we took care of business in a matter of minutes. Then we went back to the car, which again started perfectly, and headed to my house.

I had $900 in my pocket, sold off what was increasingly an automobile nightmare, and could now enjoy the next vehicle of my life. I was happy for him, truly, for he had come out of nowhere to remove what was only a scrap of metal for me, paid me cash, and all the while was cheerful about it.

The point of all this is that some completions occur on their own and your role is to simply be supportive. This marvelous sale all took place in one day. But, I could have thwarted it. What if I wasn't ready to see him on the morning he requested? What if I had suggested to the buyer that he think about it, and let me know in the next day or two? What if I hadn't assembled my end of the paperwork? And of course, the one factor out of my control, what if the car didn't start the first time we tried?

In this instance, I arranged my affairs so as to facilitate a completion, *even if I had not formally engaged in completion thinking*. Later it occurred to me, how often do we engage in noncompletion-type thinking as well as accompanying behaviors?

Completions happen. Allow them to happen, help them along, acknowledge them, and you'll have more of them in your life, your career, your week, and your day.

Coming Undone

How often do we set ourselves up to have things linger on when a completion was completely in our grasp? It's as if we snatch defeat from the jaws of victory.

The table that follows depicts the noncompletion versus completion approach to your day. Hereafter, to the degree you can proceed more along the lines of column 2 rather than column 1, you'll be setting yourself up for one nice completion after another!

Noncompletions vs. Completions

Noncompletions	Completions
Awaking in the morning, not sure if you really want to get up. Feeling time pressure, and not looking forward to going to work. Eating in a rush, if at all, and hustling out the door.	Giving yourself a completion for finishing sleep. Eating breakfast at a leisurely pace to aid digestion. Giving yourself a completion for finishing your morning routines while you head to work, and another upon arriving at work.

continues

Noncompletions vs. Completions (continued)

Noncompletions	Completions
Copying a tape of an important meeting, but not punching out the tabs to avoid accidental overtaping/ erasing, and not labeling the tape.	Copying a tape of an important meeting, labeling and dating it, and punching out the tabs to avoid accidental overtaping or erasing.
Turning in your report without making a back-up copy on hard disk or filing the supporting materials.	Turning in your report, making a back-up copy on hard disk, filing the supporting materials, and chucking the excess. Feeling complete about your accomplishment.
Finishing a major assignment at work, then without hesitation or reflection, instantly tackling another big task.	Finishing a major assignment, giving yourself a completion for having done so, then taking a stroll or an extra minute or so before tackling what's next.
Lingering after a seminar to talk to the speaker, then rushing off and being late for the next seminar, finally finding a seat, catching your breath, and not focusing on the new session for several more minutes.	Choosing to linger after a seminar to talk with the speaker, feeling glad that you did, walking to the next seminar while acknowledging yourself for fully attending the first session, and making yourself complete before arriving at the next session. Being fully present in the new lecture hall.
Dashing off to your car after work so you can slug your way through the heavy traffic on the long commute. Arriving home feeling as if you barely have enough energy to eat dinner, watch TV, and go to bed. Being concerned that each day seems to race by and that you're not enjoying enough of what you do.	Finishing the day by acknowledging your efforts, walking purposefully to your car, and giving yourself a completion for doing so. Confronting heavy traffic, but controlling your environment by playing a tape or CD or reflecting on today or the future. Arriving home and giving yourself a completion. Opting for abundant energy this evening. Retiring pleased with your day.
Looking at your child's schoolwork or artwork in the middle of doing something else, not spending much time on it, offering faint praise, and turning back to what you were doing. All the while sending the message, "I'm busy."	Suspending what you were doing so you can look at your child's work and give him/her your complete attention. Acknowledging the child for the effort, offering some affection, and suggesting what can be done with the items. Then resuming your prior activity.

Noncompletions	Completions
Having your 32nd (or 42nd or 52nd!) birthday with little fanfare, wishing it would pass quickly so you could forget about birthdays altogether.	Approaching birthdays with anticipation. Acknowledging your age and what you've accomplished, thus giving yourself a completion. Choosing to have a productive, satisfying life for your time remaining.

More Completions Through Conscious Choice

Choices are positive affirmations that help you move closer to feeling how you want to feel and accomplishing what you want to get done. Choices are not synonymous with "positive thinking." Unlike positive thinking, you make your conscious choices on a regular basis *regardless* of how you might happen to feel at any given moment. The key is to keep making them.

Choices facilitate completions because sometimes there are components of a task or project that are out of our control. To gain a sense of satisfaction and closure, we can rely upon a completion statement such as "I choose to feel complete about this project," when no other form of closure realistically will be possible. This is particularly true in the case when:

◆ Your contribution may be one of many to some larger project, or

◆ You work with others by telephone or e-mail and are geographically dispersed.

Complete on Two Fronts

Making choices also helps you to become complete in the case of accomplishing something that has a psychological as well as physical component. Suppose you have to do something that you've been putting off. You'd prefer to get it done and at the same time, you know that when you're finished, you'll have mixed feelings about what transpired.

A prime case is if you have to terminate someone at work. You don't want to be the bad guy, but it is your responsibility, and the situation certainly merits termination.

When you've completed the task, no matter how effective you've been, you still may have psychological ramifications.

No matter how good you feel about yourself, how well the day is going, and how appropriate your actions have been, to put a capper on the deed, it may be entirely advisable and even necessary to turn to completion statements in the form of conscious choices about how you would like to feel. For example, these kinds of statements are helpful:

◆ I choose to feel complete about the task.

◆ I choose to feel complete about my performance as a manager.

◆ I choose to feel complete about the challenging aspects of my job.

Also, these may prove useful to you:

◆ I choose to maintain balance and composure in the face of job-related challenges.

◆ I choose to take appropriate action for the good of the department or company.

◆ I choose to be a confident decision maker.

Many completion statements in the form of conscious choices also are helpful if made before actually having to handle the challenging task. Also, such choices can be applied to other types of challenges that you face throughout the day and week.

The Completion that Keeps On Paying Off

One of the essential choices you can make on a continuous basis to feel worthy and complete in a variety of situations is to simply affirm to yourself, "I choose to feel worthy and complete." This can help you reduce anxiety, remain calm, and feel more relaxed throughout the day.

When you choose to feel worthy and complete, you instantly tend to redirect yourself. You recognize that virtually everything you do is based on your choice. You can continue working on a particular task, specifically those that have been assigned to you, and choose to remain productive and balanced in its completions.

You can even choose to acknowledge your completions each day.

From Breakdowns to Breakthroughs

Suppose your car breaks down; you're stranded. The tow truck finally arrives and now you're two hours behind schedule. You decide it's going to be a lousy day, and many people might agree with you. There is another way to proceed. You can then choose to be thankful that the delay was only two hours.

If you have work with you, you can stay productive. Give yourself a completion for having handled the morning's mini-ordeal. In this manner, you free up the psychic energy that might have been bottled up within your frustration. Once your car is ready, you are energized to reclaim your day.

Here are other examples on how to move from potential breakdown to breakthrough by choosing how you want to feel, acknowledging where you are, and what you want to accomplish:

Breakdown Example 1: New software comes with a thick instruction manual. You plow through the instructions. The going is slow and tedious. You'd rather do things the old way. Breakthrough: New software will be a challenge to learn. Your investment of a few days will be repaid in your long-term productivity. You attack the project with vigor.

Breakdown Example 2: So many items compete for your attention that you could scream. You can't get to them all, and you hardly know where to start. It seems to get worse daily. Breakthrough: You make tough decisions about what to drop versus what merits action. You clear out the lesser items and dive headlong into the most vital one.

Breakdown Example 3 (here's a tough one): You've just learned that you're being fired and you're devastated. Thinking back about your career, it looks like one big failure. You are immobilized. Breakthrough: You've heard the bad news and are shocked. You have wages and benefits coming and you resolve to make this a time for renewal and redirection.

When you add it all up, half of the time or more you can shift from breakdown to breakthrough by simply choosing how you want to feel, and by acknowledging where you are and what you want to get done.

The Least You Need to Know

- Happy, productive, prosperous people have developed the habit of achieving one completion after another.

- Completions, large or small, are vital to acknowledge because they provide a mental and emotional break from what you had been doing.

◆ If you know you are better at one type of task early in the day, schedule accordingly.

◆ An essential choice to make on a continuous basis is "to feel worthy and complete."

◆ To move from potential breakdown to breakthrough, choose how you want to feel, acknowledge where you are, and choose what you want to accomplish.

Chapter 18

Put the Pareto Principle to Work

In This Chapter

- Learn the 80-20 rule
- Alter your approach to getting things done
- Find your own personal leverage
- Gain leverage from your resources

Vilfredo Pareto, born in 1848, observed a relationship between effort and results in 1906 that became the basis of the Pareto Principle, or what is now called the 80-20 rule. He observed that 80 percent of the land area in his native Italy was owned by only 20 percent of the population. Later, while he was gardening he realized 20 percent of the peapods he had planted accounted for 80 percent of the harvested peas.

You've likely heard of the 80-20 rule, but in this chapter we're going to look at it in ways that may change how you approach tasks or even your career. *Pareto's* observation was so profound that it would not be an exaggeration to call him the "father of getting things done."

The Father of Getting Things Done

Pareto maintained that outputs, results, and even rewards come from a small proportion of the efforts or inputs directed toward achieving them, or what productivity experts later called the concentrating on the "vital few" and not the "trivial many."

> **Word Power**
>
> The **Pareto Principle** holds that 80 percent of your actions or efforts contribute to only 20 percent of your actual results, while 20 percent of your action or efforts yield 80 percent of your results.

Pareto's observation seemed to hold true whether applied to large institutions or organizations, businesses, or even individuals.

In an accounting firm, 20 percent of the firm's clients provided 80 percent of the firm's revenue. In a hardware store, 20 percent of the floor space allotted to certain products accounted for 80 percent of the business's profits. So, owners and managers of firms large and small found it prudent to continually identify those 20 percent of inputs, be it sales representatives, clients, floor space, and so on, which contributed to 80 percent of the business's results.

It also made great sense for firms to identify the 80 percent of sales representatives, clients, or even floor space that yielded relatively poor results: only 20 percent of revenue. In the case of the hardware store, if the manager knew which 20 percent of his goods were generating 80 percent of the revenue, he would place those goods where they were most accessible and put all else, still reachable to customers, out of prime foot-traffic areas.

The 80-20 Rule and Your Career

Often you hear people lament the lack of time available for all of the things they want to get done. For most people, the lack of time is due to their focus on minutia, the 80 percent of activities that yield 20 percent of the results. The ability to forsake dwelling on minutia, however, is no small task.

If you can identify those areas at work that help you to achieve the fastest, easiest, best results, and you have the mental and emotional fortitude to forsake those activities that are not benefiting you to a great degree, you can easily increase your ability in getting things done. Perhaps the easiest place to start is to rid yourself of the unproductive 80 percent of your activities.

Alter Your Approach

When you apply the Pareto Principle to advancing your career and getting things done, some interesting results turn up. For example, 20 percent of the items you've listed as wanting to accomplish today will likely prove to yield 80 percent of your results toward important tasks and 80 percent of your satisfaction.

As hard as it may be to fathom, 20 percent of your peers at work probably account for 80 percent of the insights, perspectives, leads, and tips that you gain while on the job. They probably also account for 80 percent of your enjoyment in terms of interactions with fellow employees.

If you manage a workflow, are 80 percent of your delays attributable to 20 percent of the possible origins of the delay? If so, can you focus on the same irritating root causes so as to improve your entire system? If you're a customer service manager, are you finding that 80 percent of complaints can be traced to 20 percent of your services? That being the case, consider this: can you improve the service delivery, or eliminate those that are too problematic and not worth the trouble?

It's likely that about 20 percent of the memos you receive account for 80 percent of what you need to pay attention to, whereas 80 percent of memos add up to a heap of garbage. Likewise, consider your own communications to others. If you're in charge of a website, consider this: do 80 percent of the site visitors view only 20 percent of your site pages? And if so, can you make the entire site more inviting?

> **CAUTION**
>
> **Coming Undone**
>
> Is 80 percent of what you write and send to others regarded as drivel? If so, prune your prose, make your messages more highly targeted, and at the same time, more captivating, so that people will begin to develop the habit of noticing, reading, and acting upon what you're sending out.

Small Shifts, Big Payoffs

In terms of your daily activities, as hard as it is to believe, probably only 20 percent or far less accounts for 80 percent of your results. This being so, you practically have to go on a witch hunt to weed out those activities that traditionally or seemingly yield so few results that you could skip them all together. Recalling Stephen Covey's distinction between important and urgent tasks (see Chapter 8), examine your to-do list in whatever form you maintain it, and whatever you may call it.

Coming Undone

Offering macro effort and achieving micro results doesn't sound like a good deal, yet some of us follow this pattern for the duration of our careers. Too many career professionals are caught up in a cycle of giving activities relatively equal weight. They continue to devote 80 percent of their efforts to that which only provides 20 percent of their results.

Dyna Moe

When you look upon even a simple to-do list that you drew up this morning, go ahead and rank the items. You can put them into numerical order, you can assign them "I"s for important and "U"s for urgent, you can circle items and highlight items: whatever floats your boat.

As a career professional with an upward career trajectory, you owe it to yourself to make a handful of small shifts in your approach to tasks, small projects, and the big things in your career that you want to get done so that you will be continually directing your efforts to high-output activities.

Be on the Lookout

Sometimes you have to deal with the 80 percent of activities that are of low yield. They may be assigned, or they may be your responsibility; they may be minor but nevertheless urgent tasks. That's okay, nothing about effectively applying the Pareto Principle implies that all of the low-yield tasks will disappear. Quite the contrary, many will be with you day in and day out for the rest of your career.

The vital notion is to spend a greater degree of your time on high-yield activities, the important stuff, so that in time it won't take a lot of time. The habit is so fully developed within you that it becomes an all-pervasive discipline and, as stated, part of your character. As part of your ascension, feel free to use all manners of personal coding to assist you.

Remember Alan Lakein's statement, "What is the best and highest use of my time?" The great thing about free will is that each minute is new. You're not an extension of what came before, you get to make new choices about where you devote your time and attention. Alfredo Pareto opened the door to higher personal productivity for each of us. It's up to each of us to make the decision to walk in.

The highly effective, get-it-done type of professional is continually on the lookout for the 20 percent of his or her activities that prove to be the most strategic and yield the greatest results. If you're in selling and there are twenty different ways to make contact with potential clients, perhaps 20 percent or four of the ways prove to be most effective. Hence, you naturally and logically gravitate to those four methods and away from the other 16.

With the information and communication bombardment that you face on a continual basis, and the array of projects and tasks that come your way, sometimes it's hard to identify the 20 percent of activities that prove to be the most effective. This is where review and reflection can be helpful. Go back through your file folders, projects, or cases, and review what worked and why. What particular strategy or technique proved to be effective and conversely, what proved to be ineffective?

What activities, rituals, and behaviors do you still engage in because you've always done so? Maybe they're pleasing or comforting, maybe you've seen others do them, but upon reflection, they yield very little in terms of actual results.

Implications for Leaders

If you're a manager within an organization or perhaps an entrepreneur running your own firm, the application of the Pareto Principle can come in quite handy. Ask yourself, what are 80-20 axioms in my industry or my line of business? Where do organizations, companies, or rival firms make better-than-average profits, or even outrageous profits.

Find Your Specializations

No matter what you have to offer, in every market there are always ways to do things in a manner superior to everyone else. The 80-20 Rule implies that specialization is more often the wiser path than generalization.

What are you good at such that if you worked at, trained, and strived, you could be among the absolute best? Stake out a leadership position by taking bold and decisive action. Make it your business to be a knowledge expert in your chosen field.

Keep It Rolling

Where are you or your organization receiving far more back than you're putting in? Identify that opportunity area, exceed it, and maybe you can have double or triple the results. When

> **Dyna Moe**
>
> By capitalizing on what you do best, you may be able to create not merely a small edge, but a spectacular edge.

> **Dyna Moe**
>
> The Pareto Principle asserts that being in the right place can be as important, if not more so, than anything else you do. Stay focused on your desired outcome and often an appropriate means will appear.

you're on a roll, stay on a roll. Grease the skids, do what you can to up your efforts because you've already identified that this is a high pay-off activity.

And if something isn't proceeding so well, take a good look at why, and move decisively. It's often better to re-plot your course early, cutting losses if you have to, than doing so far too late.

Feed Your Strengths

Those areas in which you're weak may tend to be with you for the duration of your career. You can spend a lot of time and energy trying to cover up your weaknesses. It would be better to simply get help with those areas you are weak.

Depending on where you work and where you are in your career, the chances are highly likely that you need the support of others to be successful. In terms of business relationships, be selective with whom you affiliate. Allies are fundamental, and the right allies are essential.

Realizing what you want to accomplish often requires partners or a full-fledged team. The right team on the right mission with the right resources can achieve tremendous results. These are the kinds of groups that have posters on the wall that say "Miracles happen here" (see Chapters 22 and 24).

The curious thing about developing business relationships is that at their core, people generally cooperate with one another because they're friendly with one another. In the short term, sure, you can slug it out with anybody, even someone you'd rather not ever have to encounter.

> **Coming Undone**
>
> Feed your strengths and shore up your weaknesses. Don't make the mistake that so many people do by trying to be well-rounded and balanced.

In the long run, it's best if partners actually like each other. So, cultivate the relationship, revel in your shared experiences. Find areas of common ground. When someone does a favor for you, reciprocate in kind.

Catapult Your Efforts with Leverage

The concept of leverage fits nicely here. Leveraging can be regarded as taking the smallest action that will yield the largest result. It often involves nothing more than making connections between what you've already accomplished and what else you can accomplish as a result of your earlier victory.

While the Pareto Principle compels you to seek those 20 percent of activities that yield 80 percent of the results, the concept of leveraging "ups" your efficiency to yet another level.

Implement and Re-Use

Suppose you have to make a presentation at work, telling your staff how they could do better at collecting data. The notes or outline that you prepare for that presentation can be used again, as a form of leverage, to create an article. By stripping any company-specific references, you may be able to craft your in-house presentation into a generic piece of effectively collecting data that's good enough for publication.

If you're wise enough to tape your presentation to your staff, then you could transcribe the tape and be that much closer to having a finished article. In this manner, you're making your work count more than once and that is the essence of using leverage.

Generalize Your Findings

In your career, whether or not you have writing aspirations, consider what you've done or what you want to get done and all the other places where that accomplishment applies. Actually, to not do so is a form of waste.

If you've solved some dilemma for your department, and other departments thought their organization might be facing a similar type of situation, does it not make great sense for you to find a way to make yourself available to other departments so that they can benefit from your solution?

Wouldn't helping your co-workers be a great feather in your career cap? Offering such assistance is clearly in alignment with the Pareto Principle. One action that you took that proved highly effective for your own department can now be dispensed to other departments with predictably great effect there as well.

Gain Leverage from Outside Resources

Sometimes, you can leverage whom you know and how you know them for a mutual win. Suppose someone in your office is adept at a certain software procedure that represents a stumbling block for you. Have that person advise you, and you in turn advise them in some area where you are highly adept. With the Pareto Principle in mind, if you are on relatively close terms with, say, 20 people in your office, 20 percent or 4 of them likely represent those with whom you can have a high-leverage relationship.

Recognizing Resources

What resources and assets do you have at your command now that you could use to optimal effect, but thus far have barely engaged? What new ways could you use the software that you currently employ?

◆ How about your fax machine, the phone, printer, copier, e-mail, web connections, or various equipment in your office?

> **Dyna Moe**
>
> Think of high leverage as wealth and no leverage as poverty. When you expend considerable energy with little results, you feel badly and you're no further along. When you expend minimal energy with great results, you feel wonderful, you get a lot of things done, and since you've hardly depleted your resources, you're in a position to accomplish more and more.

◆ What about your office relationships, your know-how, projects you've completed, or information resources available to you?

◆ Are there human resources within your company that you have barely tapped? An information officer? A librarian? A technical assistant? An opinion leader? A mover and shaker?

If you want to get things done and be known as a person who gets things done, sometimes you have to step out of your own way. Expand your horizons, include others. Open up your vistas. Look for how the combination of resources can add up to spectacular accomplishments.

Who Is Beneficial to You

If it helps, begin to catalogue the potential resources all around you. Can you connect with others in your same job category? Make a roster of the potential mentors, gurus, advisors, and sounding boards who are employed right in your same organization. Make a roster of those outside of your organization.

◆ What are the top information resources you have at your disposal?

◆ What does your organization already subscribe to that you could be reading?

◆ What should you be subscribing to (and alternatively, what's worth dropping)?

- Are there online sources that you're not tapping?

- Are there online subscriptions worth perusing?

- What professional trade, civic, and social organizations do you already belong to, and with your expanded awareness, what resources do they provide that you can now take advantage of, when you hadn't even considered them before?

- What personal contacts within those groups represent resources for you?

- What organizations might be worth investigating?

- What's worth joining because the knowledge, skills, contacts, and exposure that you will receive will help you become more knowledgeable, skilled, or accomplished?

As you start to perceive the world and resources around you in new ways, you begin to understand that the path to getting things done sometimes takes a different turn. Often, it's not a trail you would have encountered progressing each day as you have been doing. You have to step out and step wide sometimes.

Learn from Others

Consider what kinds of barters, trades, swaps, loans, and exchanges could greatly accelerate your progress toward some desired end. What paths have others already gone down, what lessons have they learned, and what wisdom can they impart on you to make your journey shorter and easier? This is leverage at its finest. This is making 20 percent or less of your activities yield 80 percent or more of your results.

If you figure out how to do something, can you teach or train others, film it, package it, copyright it, trademark it, patent it, otherwise get the Good Housekeeping seal of approval? Can you standardize it, modernize it, refine it, and use it again and again?

Stay Vigilant

On a continual basis, ascertain what is important versus what is important and urgent, versus what is simply urgent, versus what doesn't need to be handled at all. In this manner, you can fuse the best advice you've gleaned from this book thus far. Get everything on paper, create the super to-do list, then apply the daily or short-term to-do list, and keeping the Pareto Principle in mind, assess what is important and urgent.

In selective intervals throughout the day, undertaking this simple exercise will keep you more focused than you would be able to imagine. Remembering the work of Peter and Rosemary Grant, even small changes in your immediate environment, such as being mindful as to where to devote your time and attention, can quickly add up to a huge payoff.

Consistently dealing in this type of thinking can lead to regular, desirable action. Such action on a daily basis can add up to habits, which in time help develop your character and ultimately, your destiny.

Your assignment hereafter is to consider the 80-20 rule in regards to everything that you've accomplished, to everything that you want to get done, and to everything to which you may aspire.

> **Dyna Moe**
>
> Rather than regard the Pareto Principle as some hackneyed, oversighted business dictum, embrace it as an ever-unfolding, groundbreaking, empirical approach to getting things done. This is your route to mastery.

The Least You Need to Know

- 80 percent of your actions or efforts contribute to only 20 percent of your actual results, while 20 percent of your actions or efforts yield 80 percent of your results.

- By capitalizing on what you do best, you may be able to create not merely a small edge, but a spectacular edge.

- Make connections between what you've already accomplished and what else you can accomplish as a result of your earlier victory.

- There are resources and assets at your command that you could use to an optimal effect in getting things done.

- Continually be on the prowl as to how to apply the Pareto Principle and the concept of leveraging in all aspects of your career.

Chapter 19

Blasting Through Procrastination

In This Chapter

- ◆ You aren't the only procrastinator
- ◆ Why do we procrastinate?
- ◆ Techniques for getting started on tasks
- ◆ Sometimes it's acceptable to put off a task

Procrastination is the act of putting off something until a later time, either by not starting a task or by not finishing one you've started. This can be a major stumbling block to those who would otherwise fancy themselves adept at getting things done, and is the topic of this chapter.

Sometimes even the best-laid plans run askew. You have this grand idea of a project you want to tackle, and yet week after week, month after month, and even possibly year after year, you don't get to it. Jamie Foxx portrays this to a "T" in his sensitive performance in the otherwise lackluster movie *Collateral* with Tom Cruise.

The Best-Laid Plans

Foxx plays a long-employed taxi driver who harbors notions of starting his own limousine service. The problem is, he's been driving the cab for 12 years. As the plot unfolds, we see that he's not making any tangible progress toward his dream. Rather, he's letting the idea bounce around in his head, using it as fantasy, and otherwise barely moving in the direction of his desired end.

He keeps a catalogue of new limousine models with him in the front seat and refers to it while he waits for passengers and, specifically in this drama, during tense moments. He flips through the pages and looks at the models intently as if he's going to acquire this one or that. All the while, we can see that with his present state of mind such acquisitions are simply not going to happen.

We don't know if he saved enough of his cabby earnings, has been actively seeking sources of outside capital, or has assembled a business plan. Still, it's reasonably clear that nothing is going to take place until he overcomes some hurdles, largely mental hurdles, that he has allowed to linger in his path for far too long. Any movie fan who witnesses his situation and has fallen into a long-term rut in regards to something he wants to accomplish can feel this cabby's pain.

Everyone Procrastinates ... Especially at Work!

Procrastination plagues business executives and entrepreneurs, retirees, students, and everyone else in between. Even if you're a committed procrastinator, certainly there are some areas in which you shine. Thankfully, no one procrastinates on everything, and each of us has a bevy of work-related tasks where we practically never procrastinate.

Some people procrastinate because they are leery of the high-stake tasks they face. Too easily, these people let themselves "get down." Of course, you're not like that ….

Institutional Impediments

Unfortunately, the widespread installation of cubicles has greatly contributed to the noise and confusion that permeates the modern workplace and has made Scott Adams, the author of "Dilbert," a rich man. Working all day in an environment that is ripe with noisy distractions from co-workers does little to help the individual whose powers of concentration are already strained.

Too many office environments today greatly contribute to procrastination. With so much bombarding us all the time, you have to wonder: will attention spans, concentration, and focus ever be what they used to be? Will we be pulled in so many different directions that the ability to stick to a single task will become obsolete?

Coming Undone

Researchers have discovered that procrastinators often are those types of individuals who reflexively "give up" too easily, which is most of us on selected occasions. They may also be perfectionists, continually seeking autonomy and approval, and may have a high fear of failure.

If You're So Inclined

Certainly if you're unfocused and have a high proclivity to procrastinate, the means at your disposal is immaterial. While the web, instant messenger, and a cell phone are but a few in a long line of vehicles that procrastinators have employed, in the rice bowl of life they are but meager kernels.

In the future there will be other, even more enticing distractions on the market.

Identify the Real Issue

As you learned in Chapter 16, leaving things incomplete helps induce a climate in which other things are left incomplete. The more incompletions, big and small, all around you, the harder it is to get started on anything. Procrastination becomes the norm. Give yourself the mental edge by engaging incompletions, even on the smallest of accomplishments, and one after another, mow them down.

Dyna Moe

When you identify some of the reasons behind procrastination, you have a much better chance of getting past them and getting started than if you didn't fathom the issues.

If you're honest with yourself and acknowledge when you're procrastinating, you're that much closer to taking useful action.

Find Out Why

Sometimes the real issue why you can't get started on something is because you haven't identified some lingering issues that are impacting your feelings.

◆ Perhaps you're ambivalent about the task.

◆ Perhaps you think it's unnecessary or unworthy of you.

◆ Perhaps you resent doing it, i.e., you weren't able to say "no" in the first place, and now you have to make good on your earlier promises.

Whatever the reason, when you identify some of the reasons behind procrastination, you have a much better chance of getting past them and getting started than when you don't articulate the issues to yourself and remain in a quandary.

How Can You Solve the Problem?

If the fears you experience in certain situations are holding you back, try one or more of the following tips:

◆ Permit yourself to experience the fear of whatever task you've been delaying, and you actually set yourself up to more readily initiate the task at hand. So, delve into the fear, don't mask it!

◆ Use empowering language when you find yourself reticent to begin a task that needs to be completed. Use phrases such as "I will," "I choose," "I want," and "I'll be happy to." Say them aloud to yourself.

Another option when you can't get started: identify a wise, trusted guide or mentor who can give you a jump-start—often simply an encouraging word where it's seldom heard. This kind of assistance can make all the difference in the world to you.

On other tasks, find a reliable partner who can both help you get started and remain on course.

Lead Thyself

When starting a task or project, people will often procrastinate if they don't have a clear starting point or a logical sequence of steps to take. Don't get all flustered about how or where you start. It's often more important to simply start. Identify a starting point, even if it's not the perfect starting point. For example, if you have a large job, break it down into individual tasks, each regarded as a distinct entity.

If it helps, seek an early, easy win—for whatever you're seeking to accomplish, pick some aspect of it that you can complete quickly and easily. Take the easy "win," which is an exceedingly easier approach to getting started than to tackle some difficult portion of it first.

> **Coming Undone**
>
> Some people think that if they can initiate tasks at just the "right time," won't that be grand? For most tasks, objectively speaking, there is no "perfect" time, so get over it.

Facing Challenges

What if you're up against a project where everything about it is difficult for you? It happens. How could you get an easy win right off the bat? Open the file folder, review the contents, and seek something, anything, that's familiar to you. Often, that represents a fairly easy entry point. Sometimes merely organizing materials, allocating them to smaller file folders, paper clipping items, or shuffling their order serves a suitable early win. Now at least you've gained a better idea of the project.

Suppose you're experiencing an unusually difficult time initiating a project. In that case, promise yourself that you will delve into it for only a grand total of four minutes. By the fourth minute, often you won't want to stop! Strange how that works.

When you tackle a 5-minute job, and gain the completion for having it all done, you have more energy, focus, and direction for, say, another 5-minute job. Likewise, if you do five 5-minute jobs, and with each job feeling a sense of victory, however minor, you're spurred on by the next and the next. In this manner, five 5-minute jobs can actually be easier than one 25-minute job.

Give Yourself the Edge

Toiling each day in a work setting overripe with unwelcome distractions does little to aid the person whose ability to concentrate is already strained. In far too many office environments today the noise and "hub-bub" directly contribute to procrastination. For virtually any task or project you're working on, less distraction adds up to less procrastination!

CAUTION

Coming Undone

If you find yourself in a work setting where you're hit by all manner of distractions and interruptions, even tiny tasks combined with others can seemingly loom far larger than they actually are.

Suppose you have many tasks to handle, each of which would only require about 5 to 10 minutes to complete. Singularly, none of these tasks would be that difficult to tackle. The thought of grappling with all of them, however, becomes discouraging.

As the roster of things you need to take care of grows, and you feel yourself slipping behind, they all seem to grow in complexity. Even the smallest step in pursuit of a desired goal is better than nothing.

Who Can Help

Action-oriented role models, fortunately, may be nearby. Is there someone in your office who is a take-charge go-getter? Consider the value of closely observing the behaviors of the action-takers around you. Alternatively, is there someone in reach who is seeking to finish the same sort of task? If so, you may have the ideal partner to join you.

Whenever you can identify someone who's facing the same challenge as you are, you have a good potential for getting things done faster and easier.

Bust Ruts with Regularity

When you're well-rested and well-nourished you have the best chance of doing your best work. Conversely, when you don't have enough sleep and haven't eaten well, even the simplest of tasks can loom much larger than they really are. Half the time you can't get started on something, it is due to fatigue.

Approaching the Ruts

Here is a variety of rut-busting approaches, one or more of which may prove to be effective for you on any given day and in any given situation:

◆ If you face many things competing for your attention—and these days, who doesn't—trade one project off against another. Suppose you have to do project A, and you've been putting it off. Along comes project B. It's more difficult, more involved, much scarier. So, all of a sudden, A doesn't look so bad. Now, tackle A headlong. You'll still have B to worry about and that may just keep you humming along on A.

◆ If you have somebody waiting for your results, or at least waiting to hear about your progress, you significantly increase your ability to get started and stay on the task at hand. One reason that you don't procrastinate at work as often as you might at home is that at work you generally report to a boss who is waiting for the results of your efforts and who pays you based on your efforts. If you don't complete your work, there are identifiable penalties.

◆ Often, simply having too much in your visual field is an impediment to getting started on something. When you have one project or one task at hand, your odds of maintaining clarity and focus increase dramatically. This works even better if you're not in your own office but at a conference table or at some other post where you only have the project materials at hand.

◆ Suppose you know you have to tackle a project on Monday, and you're dreading it. How can you make the project more palatable days beforehand? A very effective maneuver is to review the project contents on, say, the Friday before. Over the weekend, you don't have to do anything.

Unbeknownst to you, by reviewing project contents on a Friday, you're already in the germination state. When it's time to start the project on Monday, you find that you can actually get started with greater ease than you anticipated. The early preview you gave yourself on Friday was the key.

◆ Suppose your car conks out on the side of the road, and your battery gets a jump-start. All of a sudden, the engine is revving and this is certainly not a time to turn the car off. You want to keep it on for a good twenty minutes. Sometimes the mere gesture of turning on your computer, popping a video into the VCR, or flipping on your pocket dictator is enough to get started on a task that you have been putting off. In essence, flipping on the switch to your PC, having it boot up, and perhaps taking it to the appropriate folder and file, is analogous to jump-starting your car.

◆ Pain is a great motivator, perhaps the greatest of all. What are the consequences of not getting started? If you can identify the pain—what you will experience as a result of not doing the task or not starting the project—and if the pain is great enough, that may be an incentive for you to get started.

◆ Sometimes the only way to get started on a task is to dive into it headlong, cold turkey, not allowing yourself the opportunity to stray. Surprisingly, when you practice the cold turkey approach to procrastination, it's not nearly as upsetting as it sounds. In fact, it can be a great relief.

For any given task, at any given time, if you have difficulty starting, you now have many techniques to draw upon. Not all techniques work for everyone all the time. Still, employ one or another, or another, until you get rolling.

Capitalize on Your Progress

COO or newly hired, the more items that vie for your time and attention, the larger or even smaller projects can loom perceptually. Who among us does not feel the crush of what he needs to get done, even when the accomplishments may be nothing but the mundane? In perspective, much of what you face requires only a few minutes to complete.

If you still have trouble getting started, think about all the times you had trouble getting started in the past. What happened once you finally got started, and how good did you feel once you accomplished what you set out to accomplish? If you can evoke those same feelings of satisfaction, happiness, and the sheer joy of accomplishment, you may just have the winning formula for getting started right here.

Does This Have to Be Done at All?

Every now and then you procrastinate because the issue at hand does not need to be handled. I'm not introducing this as an easy way for you to duck out of tasks and responsibilities. Rather, you recognize that there are occasions when the root of your procrastination is based upon sound reasoning. The task you have been putting off either doesn't need to be done, done by you, done in this way, or doesn't need to be done now. It's worth taking a look.

Factoid

Some people will never be good at playing the piano, some will never be good at programming, and some people will never be good at creative writing. This is simply human nature.

Delegate Challenging Tasks

Consider as well if there is a portion of the task that you can delegate (see Chapter 21). Particularly the part you don't like to do, or are not good at doing. Let's face it, there are some tasks that no matter how hard you try, how many lessons you take, and how long you practice, you're not going to be good at them.

If you want to "nurture your nature," as author Jim Cathcart says in his book *The Acorn Principle*, capitalize on your strengths and shore up your weaknesses by getting help.

When Procrastination Is Merited

There are a handful of situations where it makes sense not to proceed. Here are just a few:

◆ The benefits of proceeding are not abundantly clear to you—sometimes a great notion that seems worth embarking upon is just that, a notion, and upon further reflection, is not something to which you're willing to commit time, energy, and effort.

◆ By postponing action, there is a clear strategic advantage—this could happen in the case where, say, by beginning three weeks from now, you'll be better prepared, stronger, smarter, or have greater resources.

◆ You haven't made the internal commitment—there are times when it makes sense to begin half-heartedly on an otherwise worthwhile project. The momentum of your start often will carry you to a full gallop. If you recognize that your underlying commitment to the project is woefully inadequate, then you have as good a reason as any to not start tasks that are at your discretion.

Don't in any way take this as Jeff Davidson's all-purpose excuses for procrastinating. Rather, these are examples of why more groundwork or reflection might be necessary before proceeding, or why now may not be a good time to proceed.

The Least You Need to Know

◆ No one procrastinates on everything, and each of us has a bevy of work-related tasks where we practically never procrastinate.

◆ The more incompletions you allow, big and small, all around you, the harder it is to get started on anything.

◆ When you don't have enough sleep and haven't eaten well, even the simplest of tasks can loom much larger than they really are.

◆ Sometimes the mere gesture of turning on your computer is enough to get started on a task that you have been putting off.

◆ When you have one project or one task at hand, your odds of maintaining clarity and focus increase dramatically.

Chapter 20

Key Queries to Keep on Course

In This Chapter

- ◆ The magic of questions

- ◆ What you've created

- ◆ Lessons from an unlikely source

- ◆ On not beating yourself up

One of the strangest secrets on the high road to getting things done is that you can devise simple questions that you ask of yourself, to great effect. In short, questions can keep you productive. Sounds too simple, right? "You want me to ask questions of myself, and that is somehow going to help me get things done?" Precisely!

Taking the time to ask yourself key questions helps you become more honest with yourself and give you a more objective view on the accomplishments you wish to achieve. And that's the subject of this chapter.

What Is the Most Effective Use of My Time?

This insightful question helps you to automatically re-direct yourself when you feel as if you're not being as productive as you could be, or somehow have strayed from the path that you originally intended to follow. The question, "What is the most effective use of my time?" is something you want to ask of yourself *anytime* you feel the need.

> **Dyna Moe**
>
> Not to get too Zen-like, at any given moment you have the opportunity to make a choice. Even if a task or project has been going particularly well, you get to make the choice as to how to use your time starting at that moment.

Suppose you face a variety of unrelated tasks (and what day does that not happen?). Or, you face a variety of related tasks on the same project. Asking yourself, "What is the most effective use of my time?" invariably helps direct you to that task that, at present, merits your attention.

Imprisoned by the Past?

In a study published in the 1996 Annual Review of Psychology, researchers Rachel Karniol, Ph.D., at Tel Aviv University in Israel and Michael Ross, Ph.D., at the University of Waterloo in Ontario, found that "people less able to relate the person of the past to the person they are now may be at greater psychological risk because they are thinking only in the present and their view of the future may not be developed."

"Individuals often react to the present as if they were living in the past," say the researchers. To make free and clear choices about what we want in the future, it behooves each of us to draw accurately upon our pasts, but also note what's different about today. This means that you do not have to proceed as an extension of what came before.

> **Dyna Moe**
>
> When the question, "What is the most effective use of my time?" comes up, it's usually a good indication that you're facing some sort of quandary, and hence probably need to re-direct your efforts.

If you're unable to recognize how you've changed, you're likely to allow your past to over-influence your decisions.

Take a New Direction

Rather than living life by looking through a rearview mirror, boldly go where you've never gone before, and you'll accomplish achievements that may have once seemed beyond your grasp. You can proceed in a totally new direction if that is what makes sense at this moment. You can make a slight twist or turn. Or, you can continue as you have been doing.

Will It Be Any Easier Later?

When faced with a situation I would prefer to put off, I ask myself: "Will it be any easier later?" If the task will be easier later, then I have rational justification for not proceeding on that particular task. For example, if I have to organize all the receipts related to a certain project that will be in progress for another week, I can easily put off this task for another week. Then, with all the receipts collected, I can organize them accordingly, knowing I can do the job until its ultimate completion.

If the task won't be any easier later, then it largely makes sense to proceed now, particularly if it may be more difficult later.

If you have the option of taking work home with you, will you still be as prepared for the task at home in a different, potentially more distracting environment as you would be in the work-related atmosphere of your office? If you will be as capable, okay, take the work home. More often, the task will not be easier later, so look for ways to handle it right where you are.

Who Created That?

Years ago, I took a course based on the work of Robert Fritz, a musician turned accomplishment guru. In his book, *The Path of Least Resistance*, he discussed how to employ self-imposed questions to move from where you are to where you want to be. One of the questions that he advised people ask of themselves is: "Who created that?"

Any time of day, for any situation you face, if you ask yourself who created that, invariably the answer comes back that you did. Allow me to explain. You are experiencing a stringent deadline and are working diligently, but feel intense pressure. Who created that situation? You did for many reasons. You applied for a job with your present employer. You assumed the post, took on the assignment, allocated available resources in some manner, and now find yourself at 10 A.M. with five hours to go before a vital project is due.

Sure, you can blame your parents for not passing on the proper genes to you. You can blame your previous employer for having a less-than-palatable work environment, allowing you to seek your present position with a new employer. You could blame your boss for not introducing the assignment hours or days earlier, and you could come up with at least a dozen other factors as to why you are a victim as opposed to a perpetrator.

<table>
<tr><td>

Dyna Moe

When you clear away the rubble, get brutally honest with yourself, and face the music; most of the situations you face are, a majority of the time, of your own doing. This is true for nearly everyone.

</td></tr>
</table>

We play in the sandbox and claim we didn't step into it, we didn't pick up the shovel, and we didn't cause that spec of sand to fly into our eye. If you milk it for all its worth, you can labor under this delusion all your life. You can credit your current situation to your boss.

Over the course of your 20,000 to 28,000 days, most of what transpires in your life is the result of choices you make. Yes, occasionally stuff happens from out of left field. Mostly, you make the choices that impact your life. When you accept responsibility for the situation, you put the *locus of control* back where it belongs, in your own head. From there, miraculous things can happen. You created the situation, and sure as heck, you're going to resolve it. No more second guessing, no more recriminations, no more lost time on the path. Take responsibility, take charge, and get it done.

<table>
<tr><td>

Word Power

Locus of control refers to the pivotal point at which action can be taken, as in "calling your own shots" or "being your own person."

</td></tr>
</table>

What Is this Problem Teaching Me?

In his book, *Love Medicine and Miracles*, Dr. Bernie Siegel discusses how one's illness can actually be a path to greater health, understanding one's self, and greater humanity. Siegel suggests to his patients that they ask themselves: what is this illness forcing me to learn? Some patients are stunned. Others understand what he is driving at immediately.

It is Siegel's belief, and that of many others in the medical community, that illnesses don't simply arrive in people's lives. They are there for a reason. Most of the time, people "invite" the illness as a result of how they live, which could mean what they eat, how they treat themselves, or even how they think.

Once cancer or heart disease has been diagnosed, Siegel maintains that a patient has much to learn from the illness in terms of how to treat one's self, how to conduct one's life hereafter, how to treat others, and even how to embrace a higher level of spirituality.

As a variation on a theme, Robert Fritz suggests a different kind of question: what is the problem forcing me to do or to learn? Suppose there is something you need to get done, but you keep coming up against stumbling blocks. Fritz suggests that to achieve breakthrough solutions, particularly in the face of recurring problems, you need to sincerely embrace each problem you have as a best friend.

Regarding a problem as a best friend enables you to benefit from what Fritz calls the "Law of Reversal." This means you're using the negative energy surrounding the problem to propel you forward—to tap into the positive forces available and achieve a solution.

Is the Answer Right Alongside the Problem?

Thomas Kettering, a founder of the Sloan-Kettering Institute, was among the most brilliant inventors in the last century, perhaps on a par with Thomas Edison, but rarely known today. Kettering perfected the diesel engine, automobile ignition systems, chrome painting procedures, and a host of other innovations that transformed the auto industry in the 1920s and 1930s.

As I discussed in *The Complete Idiot's Guide to Managing Stress*, Kettering's approach to problem solving was unsurpassed. He believed that the major difference between a problem and a solution was that people more readily understood a solution.

Kettering felt that solutions involved a strategic shift in perception, since the solution to the problem must have existed all along within the problem itself. A problem-solver's role was not to master a problem, but to make it generate its solution.

> **Factoid**
>
> In perfecting the diesel locomotive, Kettering commented that his team had little part in it. Instead, the team "offered" the engine six different types of pistons and, in essence, let the engine "choose" the one "it" liked best.

When it comes to problems that you experience as a result of stress, perhaps long-standing problems, there simply has to be a solution. And, as with Kettering's insight, the solution has existed all along in tandem with the problem itself.

The Bigger the Problem ...

In Fritz's view, since we generally help initiate most of our problems, our wisest path to resolving this situation and accomplishing that which we choose to accomplish is to cooperate with the forces at play and treat obstacles as your best friends, rather than resist them. You might even say, the bigger the problem, the greater your creative potential.

> **Dyna Moe**
>
> If you find yourself getting shot down time after time in pursuit of a specific goal, your quest is to use the energy of your plight to leap on to higher ground.

The problem you're facing is your best friend because it will help to bring out the best in you. The key is to keep asking yourself: what is the problem forcing me to learn or to do? For some people, it is learning to trust themselves more completely; for others it's involving others in the solution. It could also mean approaching the problem in a totally different way.

By regarding problems as a stepping stone for opportunity and not a roadblock, you can begin to view the problem as beneficial. The problem actually starts to lose power. And as answers emerge, you're more than willing to keep asking questions when you face other types of problems in getting other things done.

Try This at Home

As a simple exercise, think about three things right now that you want to get done that, for whatever reason, have remained undone for quite a while.

Now, identify the major problem involved in completing each of these three tasks. For each situation, ask yourself what is the problem forcing me to learn or do? Have pen and paper ready as the answers start to come forth.

1. _____
2. _____
3. _____

What Would a Paid Consultant Say?

Suppose you face a challenging work-related situation and are not sure which way to turn. Now, suppose someone hired you to be a consultant to yourself no less, and that your job is to advise this person as to which way to turn. As a paid consultant to yourself, what advice would you render? A silly exercise you think? Actually, just the opposite.

Surmising what another party would suggest to you gives you an added measure of objectivity.

By taking on the posture of a consultant, you gain a measure of objectivity that may not otherwise be available to yourself. After all, a paid consultant, ideally, is impartial. He or she is brought in to render an opinion based on a diagnosis of the issue at hand. Undoubtedly you've already had a lot of experience as a consultant, except you didn't regard yourself as a primary consultant.

When a friend asks you for advice and you offer your opinion, it's a form of consulting. Giving your child or your spouse guidance is a form of consulting, although they don't always appreciate the advice. In a manner of speaking, when you're asked to render an opinion, you're acting as a consultant of sorts. Now, you're simply going to apply the process to your own work to derive answers from yourself that may not otherwise have been forthcoming.

> **Factoid**
>
> President Richard Nixon often referred to himself in the third person. He'd ask himself, "Now, what should Nixon do next?" This generated a measure of objectivity for him that he wouldn't have otherwise had, and he often found that he came up with different answers than he would have if faced with the question, "What should I do next?"

What Else Can I Handle?

Any time you've completed a task or project of significance is a good time to contemplate what else you are able to address. Likewise, when you recognize that you have 6 or 8 minutes before a meeting, the end of the day, or at the end of the work week, independent of how you've laid out the tasks on your master to-do list, keep a keen eye out for anything you can "knock out"—take care of—right now. The key factors will be the actual time available, your frame of mind, your location, and if you're armed with the requisite tools.

Stay on a Roll

You've probably heard the expression "If you want to get something done, give it to a busy person." We're all so busy today, I question the value of that once-sage advice.

Dyna Moe

You can plot and plan all you want, but sometimes a small task emerges that begs for immediate action. In tending to that matter on the spot, you'll feel more in control, more productive, and even more creative. Getting things done during these small pockets of time also can help to alleviate stress.

On the other hand, the best time to get something done is when you're already on a roll. Fresh from the accomplishment of one task, and the resulting confidence and good feeling that imbues within you, you're prime to take on something else.

When a small pocket of time emerges, use it to "short-circuit" the to-do list, or as I often do, simply peruse your master to-do list, looking for everything and anything that might be handled during this opportune moment.

Personal Business

What about handling personal affairs at these emerging moments? The boundaries of our professional and personal lives frequently intersect. It would be unrealistic, and even draconian, to suggest that an unrelenting, 100 percent focus on professional tasks will keep you productive, focused, balanced, and happy.

One of the most pleasing tasks I encounter during these opportune moments is clearing "in-bins," either the physical in-bin on my desk or more likely an e-mail in-bin. Other worthwhile tasks include breaking down the mail, or straightening up some aspect of your office—not obsessively—to enhance your productivity for subsequent projects.

When you take on that extra something else and complete it, go a step further. Ask yourself, again, what else can I handle? Go for as long as you can with this procedure.

Soon enough, the answer that will come back to you will be "nothing else." Or more likely, you'll stop asking yourself. That's a good indication that you've run the rack. Thereafter, you can ask yourself questions such as what do I want for dinner tonight or what movie do I want to see?

What Would it Take to Feel Good about Departing on Time?

Hey, what's this business about feeling good about departing on time? Why bring up the words "feeling good"? Because any given day is significant and how you feel about your accomplishments are equally as significant.

If you get many things done that you set out to get done, day after day, but don't feel good about your productivity, then what is your life, your career, and each day all about?

When you ask this question of yourself, automatically a handful of things surface that you eagerly wish to accomplish by the end of the day.

Cut Yourself a Deal

A wonderful strategy for getting things done is to continually "cut a deal" with yourself. It's a self-reinforcing tool for achieving a desired outcome that you've identified within a certain time frame, as in the end of the day.

Suppose you want to get out of the office by 5:00 today. You ponder, "What would it take for me to feel good about ending work on time today?" Next suppose that today your answer to the question is to finish three particular items on your desk. If the boss drops a bomb on your desk late in the day, you automatically get to cut a new deal with yourself, given the prevailing circumstances.

Your new deal may include merely making an initial foray on the project that's been dropped in your lap. You could also accomplish two of your previous three tasks and some fraction of this new project.

By cutting a deal with yourself, you avoid what too many people still confront all the time: leaving, on most workdays, not feeling good about what they've accomplished, not having a sense of completion, and bringing work home. Hey, you want to get raises and promotions, but you don't want to have a lousy life in the process!

> **CAUTION**
>
> **Coming Undone**
>
> Anyone can throw his time or energy into a task with brut force and gnashing of teeth in completing a task. But at what cost? Your energy? Spirit? Peace of mind? Quality of life?

And Keep Dealin'

Most people have several things they wanted to accomplish and actually manage to accomplish some of them, crossing them off the list. Rather than feeling good about their accomplishments and accepting the reward of the freedom to leave on time, they add several more items to the list—a great way to guarantee that they'll still leave their offices feeling beleaguered.

Here you have the perfect prescription for leaving work every day not feeling good about what you've accomplished: If you always have a lengthy, running list of "stuff" you have to do, you'll never have a sense of getting things done. Regardless of projects, e-mail, faxes, phone calls, or other intrusions into your perfect world, continually cut a deal with yourself so you leave the workplace on time and feeling good about what you accomplished!

The Least You Need to Know

- Asking yourself key questions gives you a more objective view of and a good starting point for the accomplishments you wish to achieve.

- Most of the time, most of the situations you face are of your own doing.

- As true as ever: the best time to get something done is when you're already on a roll.

- Sometimes a small task emerges that begs for immediate action: handle it.

- Keep cutting deals with yourself so you leave the workplace on time and feeling good about what you accomplished.

Part 6

Becoming More Effective at Work

This part is designed to help you become more effective at work. We start off with giving you the highs and lows of dealing with the people all around you in the workplace. Then we're on to the nitty-gritty of what it takes to plan, preside over, and follow up on a successful meeting. Next you get the lowdown on how to influence others and how to assemble, manage, and motivate a cohesive, winning team. And finally, we will discuss the array of partners, mentors, coaches, and empowering people you can recruit to keep your career moving forward.

Chapter 21

Working With Peers, Subordinates, and Bosses

In This Chapter

- ◆ Working effectively with others is everything
- ◆ Fair and square managers finish first
- ◆ Become a delegation sensation
- ◆ The care and feeding of bosses

Having to work with peers, subordinates, and bosses can be as challenging in getting things done as any other situation in which you may find yourself. Because you may have little leeway as to with whom you work, in this chapter we'll have a look at what it takes to function effectively with others. Let's start with the scenario that you're the new kid on the block.

The New Guy or Gal

When you're hired for a new position, specifically one where you supervise others, you are given an unofficial 100-day window of opportunity. During this time, which stretches for 4 to 5 months, you can plead ignorance on key issues, ask questions that you wouldn't dare to ask if you had been with the company for years, and generally expect to receive gracious treatment!

This 100-day grace period represents the best time to achieve some early wins. In seeking to get things done, concentrate on projects that represent sorely needed improvements that others would like to see resolved. Establish a clear vision of what you want to get done and let others in on your plan.

Take advantage of this one-time window of opportunity to set the tone and you may achieve an operating advantage in the months and years to follow.

Supervise Successfully, Lead to Succeed

In many ways, your effectiveness on the job, new or old, is largely defined by how adept you are at working with others. Above all, the key element to working with peers, subordinates, and bosses, has to be interpersonal skills. If you have the ability to communicate effectively, offer clear and precise directions, elicit feedback, and listen well, you're going to go to the head of the class when it comes to managerial effectiveness.

> **Dyna Moe**
>
> The effective manager seeks to achieve powerful results, while recognizing that sometimes, if not often, progress is uneven, endures twists and turns, starts and stops, and reformulations and reconfigurations.

Now is a good time to recall an observation made in Chapter 2 about effective managers. This is the person who is keenly focused on how his staff proceeds throughout the day and how well they harness ideas and insights, knowledge and wisdom, and energy and enthusiasm to accomplish the tasks at hand.

Throughout business and industry, workers everywhere hunger for leadership. In today's business world, CEOs and top executives come and go, some days scandal seems to be the norm, and people are likely to pass the buck as quickly as they receive it. The manager or supervisor who is willing to step up to the plate and take a vested interest in the division, department team, or staff, and the well-being of each participant, while staying focused on the work to be done, can actually win over hearts and minds.

While scads of books and articles have been written on being an effective manager, supervisor, or staff worker, paying homage to the traits and characteristics in the following sections will serve you well.

The Few, the Proud, the Three

The Marine Corps has long used a method of command called the "Rule of Three." A corporal is in charge of managing three privates. A sergeant manages three corporals. A lieutenant manages three sergeants and so on. The underlying concept is that each officer in the chain of command needs to stay focused on three other people.

The workaday world operates, obviously, quite differently. Still, there is a management lesson or two we could learn from the Marines about staying focused and not over-reaching. On this day, what if you focused on the three most significant tasks or projects confronting you? What if you completely focused your attention and poured your concentrated effort into making progress on the first of these tasks?

If you're managing others, what if you were able to clearly and precisely direct your troops so that they were ably prepared to tackle the task at hand? In our quest to get so many things done, too often we fritter our attention in too many different directions. If we're managing others, we might convey this sense of frenzy to them.

By limiting the scope of what we wish to achieve in any given unit of time, such as an eight-hour workday, we give ourselves a strategic operating advantage that we are rarely able to enjoy. Or, if we manage others, we enable them to have a greater degree of focus and clarity that perhaps they sorely desire but have heretofore never articulated.

Being Fair and Consistent with All

Clearly, the people with whom you work are not alike in terms of their skills and background, competence and dedication, or even outlook and enthusiasm. It's easy to play favorites. Who wouldn't be more likely to act favorably toward consistent performers, or those with a winning personality, or simply those whom you seem to get along with easily?

Being unfair or inconsistent with even one other staff person has ramifications that can undermine your effectiveness as a manager. People see and hear and know when someone else in your department is being treated unfairly. If it can happen to one person, then why not again and again? What's more challenging and mandatory is to be fair and consistent with everyone.

Dyna Moe

Your quest is to fight for objectivity in dealing with staff so that your emotions don't take over.

When someone with whom you're not necessarily favorably disposed messes up in some way, can you approach the situation in the same way you would if one of your favorite people messed up in exactly the same way? Can you give equal time, equal attention, and equal caring to each staff member? If you can, be prepared for the pleasant experience of working with a staff that, overall, may prove to be a bit more productive than you would have supposed.

Use Language Accepted by All

Have you ever worked for someone who tossed about corporate buzz words or terminology that he or she apparently didn't believe in, but was trying to foist upon you? You know, the type of person who would win a Razzy for bad acting? Who wants to work around people like that? It makes you feel like they are insincere and fake.

If you're supervising younger staff, you don't necessarily need to know all of their lingo. Indeed, you'll come across as a poser if you attempt to talk their talk while not truly being in their world. Nevertheless, forsaking the platitudes and pat phrases can work wonders. You don't need to enroll in "Communication 101," simply be yourself, keep it real, and speak to a staff person as you would a good friend.

You wouldn't use jargon with a friend, would you? You wouldn't submit your friends to organizational psychobabble would you? Then don't do it among your charges. Be real with the people with whom you work or supervise. Use terminology or phrases to which they can relate.

Your Words, Your Actions

For reasons that probably only cultural anthropologists can describe, people tend to get more upset about promises that were made to them and broken than almost anything else that transpires between individuals.

If you say it, mean it. If you promise it, work like a trucker on a deadline to ensure you deliver. If you can't make good on your progress, explain why and explain what you will do to rectify the situation, either this time or next time. Then, make sure as heck that you deliver on the next promise, because the people with whom you work, and especially whom you manage or supervise, will more often and more easily recall the promises you've made than you will. So, write them down.

Delivering on your promises is an effective way to ensure that your staff delivers the type of performance you seek. After all, if they're rewarded accordingly, time after time, then they know that you'll deliver.

At all costs avoid offering a continuing promise. That means that you delay that which you said you would. Worse, you might up the ante, suggesting that ultimately the reward will be even bigger than you first introduced, and that can backfire on you as well. Keep things simple, keep things above board, and keep your word. When in doubt, tell the truth, accept responsibility, and be a stand-up kind of manager.

Factoid

Remember the Tylenol scare, in which several people died because someone had poisoned a few bottles? As soon as it became apparent that the deaths were due to poisoned Tylenol, McNeil Consumer Healthcare, the distributor of Tylenol for Johnson & Johnson leapt into action with a full-disclosure public relations campaign.

McNeil Consumer Healthcare's campaign candidly revealed the entire situation related to the Tylenol scare of the 1980s with little or no spin on the facts and not a trace of defensiveness. This unorthodox approach maintained the public trust during the company's darkest hour. The result? McNeil became the leading manufacturer of over-the-counter cold medicines in the United States. Its public relations campaign is still being studied in business schools as a perfect example of being straight with people.

Instill a Grouplike Atmosphere

We'll cover the issue of assembling a winning team in Chapter 24. Here, focusing on working with an intact team, what can you do to ensure that each member of the team feels that he or she plays a vital part? Whenever possible and practical, involve the team in decision making. Get everyone involved in the discussion. Depending on the issue at hand, encourage a wide variety of ideas in brainstorming sessions.

When you include people in this manner, they have a more vested interest in ensuring that the task or project is completed on time and within the budget. If decisions are always made by you, you and only you, that can work in the short term, but after a while it can be kind of grating. People feel stifled; they want to be able to express themselves and they want to know that their ideas matter.

Dyna Moe

When you include the group in the decision-making process, you also generate new ideas that you may never have come across by yourself.

Successful corporations continue to pay employee bonuses for ideas put into the proverbial "suggestion box" because these organizations recognize the value and power of fresh perspectives, innovative ideas, and cost-saving solutions. Not everyone has a great idea all the time, but it only takes a few ideas here and there that squarely hit the mark to realize that soliciting feedback from knowledgeable others makes great sense.

When it's obvious that the path described or solution proposed by one of your staff offers great potential, you may need the mental and emotional fortitude to proceed in a new direction. But hey, effective leaders produce results and your role is not one of manipulation; it is one of increasing participation and cooperation, while offering guidance.

Provide Challenges

Working with others would be a piece of cake if the only tasks you ever requested of them were simple to tackle, easy to complete, and well within their capabilities. In today's workplace, this is a fairy tale. Increasingly, you may find yourself having to make what seems to be an unreasonable request. The individual(s) assigned such a task may, at first, squawk. Anticipating such resistance will serve you well.

Your role is to offer staff guidance on how to get started, generate momentum, avoid pitfalls, and proceed to completion. The more challenging the task, the more often you likely need to stay in touch. In the early stages of the project, you may be putting in ten "units" of energy for every one "unit" of output you receive. That's okay. You and your staff are in a concentration mode.

Later, as the project gets rolling, you may be putting in ten units and receiving a commensurate return. Ideally, when the project is humming along, one unit of energy then offers ten units of output. Now you've achieved momentum! And when the people you supervise experience the exquisite experience of momentum, your odds of succeeding on the next challenging project increase markedly.

Secrets of Effective Delegators

For most of your career, you've read or heard that one of the key approaches to getting things done is to delegate effectively. This presumes that you have others to whom you can delegate. In my work with more than 750 organizations over the last two decades, I've found increasingly that people have fewer resources, a lower budget, and fewer staff people. If they want to get something done, often they have to do it themselves!

Assuming you have others to whom you can delegate, the first or second time you personally tackle a particular task yields valuable information. You learn more about the nature of the task, perhaps how long it takes, whether you enjoy doing it or not, and so on. By the third time, a task of the same ilk as those you've handled before often becomes best handled by someone reporting to you. Such tasks could involve entering names into a database, completing an interim report, or assembling meeting notes.

On the path to getting things done, your quest is to identify all those things that you can possibly delegate to others and then prepare those others so that they have a high probability of succeeding.

Many managers and supervisors fail to delegate effectively because either they don't fully trust the people with whom they're working, or they've always been get-it-all-done-by-myself types. Some managers feel they have to take care of everything themselves and to this day haven't been able to break the habit of "doing it all." If this someone is in your seat right now, recognize once and for all that as a category of one, you must realize that you can only get so much done.

> **Dyna Moe**
>
> In the course of your workday there may be only a handful of things that you and you alone need to do because of your experience, insight, or specialized knowledge. Everything else that can be delegated should be delegated.

Media mogul and influential editor H. L. Mencken once said, "For it is mutual trust, more than it is mutual interest, that holds human associations together." If you want to rise in your career, to assume increasing responsibility, or if you look forward to raises and all that good stuff, you're going to have to master the art of delegating at one time or another and trust that others can do the job. It might as well be now.

Delegation Starting from Zero

Sometimes your delegating task poses no mystery. It's part of your job description. Or, based on the type of organization where you work and the job roles assumed by you and your staff, areas for delegation are obvious. Short of all that, here are some general guidelines for being an effective delegator.

Prior to delegating anything to anyone, take the time to actually prepare your staff for delegation. This would involve assessing an employee's skills, interests, and needs. You could even ask people what new tasks and responsibilities they would like to assume. You might be surprised at the wide variety of responses you receive.

While you want to delegate to staff people who show enthusiasm, initiative, and interest, or have otherwise previously demonstrated the ability to handle and balance several tasks at once, sometimes you have to delegate to someone who has not exhibited any of the above. In that case, delegate on a piecemeal basis. Ensure that the staff person is able to effectively handle the small task or tasks he's been assigned and does not feel swamped or overloaded. When the staff person demonstrates competence, you can increase the complexity of assignments and even the frequency with which you delegate.

> **Dyna Moe**
>
> There may be people on your staff right now who can help you with tasks you've been dying to hand off to someone but didn't see how or when you could put them into play.

Walk Through It

The first time you delegate anything to anyone, painstakingly walk them through exactly what you want them to achieve. Paint a vivid portrait of what things will look like once the task or project is completed. You may have some instructions to provide or training to offer, but otherwise don't necessarily be concerned with how the staff person will proceed. He or she may have a notion or two completely out of your realm that prove to be suitable and even appropriate for the task.

Match up the tasks you wish to delegate with those staff people who have the requisite skills and background. However, don't be afraid to assign someone a task that represents a stretch. This is the way people learn and grow, and is a method for developing an increasingly competent staff.

Look to empower that person by offering guidance at critical junctures. Be available as much as practical, although be careful not to encourage an environment of constant interruptions in which you cannot get anything done. If it helps, plot regular intervals at which time you two will get together to compare notes. Monitor project progress, offer additional guidance, and continue on.

As staff members begin to demonstrate their capabilities on the projects you've delegated, give them even more slack in terms of how they'll approach and complete the assignments. Forsake any over-controlling predisposition. Ideally, you've delegated enough authority for your staff to successfully complete the tasks by allowing them to make their own decisions and take initiative. You know you've delegated effectively when they're able to operate even in your absence.

Your Toughest Customer: Your Boss

Unless you run your own organization, undoubtedly you report to someone else, a boss. Your boss is your toughest customer, the person whom you have to impress day in and day out. For however long it lasts, your career is linked to this individual regardless of his or her level of competence, personality type, or daily disposition.

Fortunately, your boss is human, just as you are. That being the case, it's possible to diagnose your boss to determine how he or she operates and expects others to operate, what makes their day and what ruins their day. This clearly is not rocket science.

Make Your Boss Look Good

In observing and understanding your boss, you're drawing upon the same skills that you've tapped your whole life. You've done this with your parents, your friends, lovers, teachers, professors, co-workers, and everyone in between.

As cited in Chapter 3, practice Mark McCormack's notion of "aggressive observation." Specifically, you "read" others by paying attention to their needs. Anyone can do it and hence get better at working with others. Without even knowing your boss, I'll bet the farm that he seeks praise for the work he does. Yet how often do you praise your boss? If your boss has been extra supportive of you, tell him or her you appreciate it. And make sure to be honest in your praise … sycophants can be easily spotted.

> **Dyna Moe**
>
> A great way to make your boss look good is no secret at all—handle your work efficiently and effectively.

Offer Solutions

Regardless of your boss's operating style, take it as a given that he or she will be most appreciative when you are able to both succinctly identify a problem and have some viable solutions to that problem in mind.

By having solutions ready to propose, you avoid a classic dilemma faced by too many otherwise competent staff people. They are bright, alert, and ever eager to point out ways in which the company might be losing customers, market share, revenue, and so on. However, if they don't have solutions in mind, they are simply sirens ever-sounding warnings—which do have value—but which mark the individual as rather one-dimensional.

By having solutions in mind, you do both your boss and yourself a huge favor. Your boss has lots of other issues to handle and is grateful to have some ideas about addressing a problem that, practically speaking, was not likely in her mind moments before. Concurrently, your solution-oriented style conveys the message that you have solid promotion potential. You demonstrate that you are thinking ahead, going the extra mile, and considering what's best for all.

What If Your Boss Is a Career Roadblock?

What if your boss is a terrible taskmaster, a tyrant of the office, insensitive to individual needs, or merely callous? There are ways to turn a bleak situation to your advantage.

Working for a boss whom you don't like may strengthen your ability to deal with people—including good and bad future bosses—and it may help you hone your diplomatic skills as well. If you can peacefully coexist with people whom you don't like or respect, your chances of successfully dealing with all others will improve.

When your supervisor is an incompetent boss who lacks creativity and has trouble making decisions, turn the situation to your advantage by taking on more responsibilities.

> **Dyna Moe**
>
> Keep doing a good job and uphold the name of your organization. Be professional and take your experiences in stride. Learn and benefit from them, but don't waste energy resurrecting the past.

Perhaps you're working for an insensitive boss who, intentionally or otherwise, bawls you out for minor mistakes or takes credit for your achievements while neglecting to praise your efforts. It might seem like nothing positive can come from this experience, but don't despair. You're learning one of the most valuable of business lessons—"don't take it personally." Nothing stops a career achiever in his tracks faster than the tendency to take every callous remark or each instance of a lack of recognition as a personal affront. Don't dwell on these things, move on.

You're not the only one who notices if your manager's behavior is volatile. Your ability to stay cool and perform well, contrasted with your boss's temper tantrums, may eventually win you kudos from colleagues and from top management. Sometimes you can learn as much from a negative example as from a positive one. Instead of wasting mental energy on the things your boss is doing wrong, contemplate how they could be done right in the future.

The Least You Need to Know

- Your effectiveness on the job, new or old, will be largely defined by how adept you are at working with others.

- Be real with the people with whom you work or supervise and use terminology to which they can relate.

- Whenever possible and practical, involve the team in decision making.

- Identify all those things that you can possibly delegate to others and then prepare those others so that they have a high probability of succeeding.

- In observing and understanding your boss, simply draw upon the same skills that you've tapped your whole life.

Chapter 22

Meetings, Meetings, and More Meetings

In This Chapter

◆ Pre-interviewing participants

◆ Circulating an agenda at the outset

◆ Encouraging promptness

◆ Conditioning your meeting environment

If you regard meetings as a massively unproductive way to pass the time and a major intrusion to your day, this chapter is for you!

Some people have such a great dislike for meetings that they feel stressed and anxious the moment they learn they have to attend one, let alone conduct one. Despite the fact that many managers dislike calling meetings, and staff often dread attending them, studies show that more people today are spending more time in meetings on a variety of topics with a variety of objectives than ever before.

Meetings: Now More Than Ever

The number of meetings being held is on the rise and this is borne out in recent years by workers who report attending an increasing number of meetings—not fewer meetings as one might have expected in this age of audio and video conferencing technology.

It seems that John Naisbitt had it right 25 years ago in his book *MegaTrends* when he said that as the business world develops more sophisticated technology, the need for face-to-face interaction will increase. He called this phenomenon "high-tech, high-touch."

Factoid

Based on data from the National Statistics Council, the typical U.S. employee spends 37 percent of his time, or nearly 15 hours a week, in meetings. On any given day in the United States, about 11 million business meetings are held.

In a 20- to 21-day work month, a typical career professional is likely to attend about 60 meetings of various lengths. Some will be impromptu small meetings, others will be longer, more formal, and more difficult to endure.

Meetings: The Potential Versus the Reality

Meetings are designed to inform, update, strategize, negotiate, sell, and/or review. The typical meeting is arranged by one person to convey information to many people. Ideally, the attendees will reflect upon what they heard, generate wonderful ideas, and take bold, decisive action to the delight of the meeting chair. Well, I did say ideally.

Factoid

Nearly all meeting participants say that they daydream sometimes during meetings and 73 percent of meeting participants admit to doing other work during meetings. Presumably this includes sneaking peeks at palm tops and cell phones. Thirty-nine percent admit to dozing off at some time during a meeting, hopefully without anyone else noticing.

The realities of the meeting room are people shuffling in and hardly listening to some new stuff that they have to do or learn, or take back to others. They also doodle, guzzle coffee, clean their fingernails, and still manage to fail in these efforts to stay awake. Most of what they hear is quickly forgotten.

Senior executives who arrange meetings are more likely to deem them effective than those who were summoned to the meeting. Meeting chairs seem to be more optimistic in their assessment of both the value and results of the meetings they conduct, compared to others attending the meeting. Too often, however, whatever the meeting participants are supposed to do is rarely done on time or in the fashion that the meeting manager had hoped for.

Despite your feelings toward or experience in meetings, they can serve as an effective and efficient way to aid you and your staff in getting things done.

Let the trumpets sound: there is a better way to get through these meetings and encourage staff to get things done.

Get Involved with Participants

The key to conducting a successful meeting is preparation. I know, you probably didn't want to hear that. In a study conducted by MCI Conferencing, it was determined that "the amount of time spent on preparation for a meeting characterized as highly productive" was nearly twice as long as "the preparation time for a meeting described as not very or not at all productive." So, let's talk about preparation ….

In successful meetings, the person conducting the meeting typically spends one unit of time for every two units of meeting time, and one unit of follow-up time. In other words, for a two-hour meeting, about one hour of preparation time is expended, matched by about one hour of follow-up time.

Rope 'em In Before It Starts

An effective and organized way to conduct a meeting and a vital element of preparation is to elicit the participation of those who will be part of the meeting, long before it even starts. Yes, you read it correctly. It only takes two to four minutes per attendee for you to …

- ◆ Speak with people who will be attending the meeting.
- ◆ Prep them as to what's going to take place.
- ◆ Hear their views about what they're going to get out of the meeting.
- ◆ Make them, in general, partners as opposed to subjects.

If your groups meet on an ongoing basis, pre-ask participants questions such as:

- What's worked well for you in previous meetings?

- How can we proceed in a manner that involves everyone?

- What would you like to get out of this meeting?

Does this sound like more work than it's worth? Take into consideration that meetings aren't held for the purpose of simply gathering a bunch of people into one place; they're held presumably to accomplish some worthwhile objective.

Pre-Interviewing Boosts Results

On top of conducting the meeting itself, some managers dread the thought of having to pre-interview the participants. "Gosh, talk to each person one at a time, how progressive." Yet, the process doesn't have to be strenuous if it's conducted in an organized fashion.

If discussing meeting objectives with participants will greatly accelerate progress, why wouldn't you want to do this? The meeting is likely to take less time, which will result in greater participation and, ideally, greater advancement toward getting things done.

Pre-interviewing attendees gives you a leg up on exactly how to proceed:

1. You design a custom agenda that focuses on topics identified as vital to the entire group.

2. You arrange the topics in an order conducive to achieving the group's overall objectives.

3. You circulate the agenda in advance so that participants come armed with ideas on how and when they can best contribute.

Dyna Moe

Participants routinely report high enthusiasm for this pre-interviewing. It makes them feel valued; they feel that their input matters. They may anticipate the meeting with a new perspective, since they know that "this one" is going to be different.

When you implement pre-interviewing, your meeting is far more likely to stay on course, end on time, and encourage participants to be more enthusiastic for the next meeting.

Winning Pre-Meeting Points!

Your participants will regard you as an organized, competent manager when you pre-interview and provide them with an agenda at the outset of the meeting. As you'll see with the next meeting, when participants have a vested interest in the content of a meeting, they tend to arrive on time. When they receive an agenda in advance that specifies the precise starting time, they have yet another indicator of the importance of being there.

If you're requested to attend a meeting, ask to have the meeting agenda sent to you in advance. If the other party does not have one, ask for a brief outline that highlights the key topics or sub-topics that will be covered. Otherwise, you're going in blind.

Not a Minute Too Long

In recent years, an increasing percentage of meetings have occurred within the confines of an organization itself, i.e., there have been fewer meetings at conference centers, hotels, and outside facilities, and more meetings within the offices, boardrooms, and auditoriums of the organizations employing the meeting's participants.

When meetings are held off-site, that is away from the organization's facilities, and require business travel, a majority of professionals report that they're concerned about their work responsibilities that pile up back at the office during their absence. Yet, long meetings can prove to be satisfying to everyone.

In a study conducted by InfoCom, the longer a meeting's length, surprisingly, the more likely it is deemed to be effective, based on the responses of all those who attended meetings. For meetings one half-hour long or less, 58 percent of the respondents indicated they felt they were extremely or very productive. The number jumped to 61 percent for meetings a half-hour to one hour, 67 percent for meetings one hour to five hours, and an astounding 80 percent for meetings of 5 hours or more.

> **Factoid**
>
> Of the more than 60 meetings a month attend by today's career professional, 37.4 percent are internal or on-site; 12.2 percent are held locally, i.e., within drive time; 6.7 percent are conducted by conference call; 4.6 percent involve long-distance travel, which frequently involves air travel; and 0.9 percent were conducted via video conference.

Perhaps for meetings of five hours or more, the preparation involved and the mere fact that the group has been sequestered for more than half a business day, helps to increase everyone's focus.

Begin as Scheduled

Regardless of your meeting's length, it is necessary for you, as the meeting manager, to steadfastly start meetings on time so that stragglers will realize that they are late and that the others, indeed, arrived as scheduled. Organized managers start meetings on time!

Robert Levasseur, in his book *Breakthrough Business Meetings*, suggests that at the start of any meeting, "participants reach a common understanding of what they're going to do and how they're going to do it." Hence, everyone needs to be present at the start. Levasseur says that this normally takes 10 percent of the meeting time, so if you're going to be meeting for 30 minutes, you only need 3 minutes or so to deal with some basic issues such as the …

- Main purpose of the meeting.
- Participants' desired outcomes.
- Actual agenda itself.
- Key meeting roles, which for smaller groups is understood at the outset.

Tardy Slips

There are several techniques, which work to varying degrees of effectiveness, to encourage promptness. Here are just a few:

- Require tardy people to apologize to the group. It then becomes their responsibility afterward to catch up with the group for the parts they missed. Never backtrack for late arrivals, it will only force everyone to stop and wait while the guilty party receives a personalized briefing.
- Lock the meeting room doors (only for the bold!). Anyone who tries to enter late has to knock on the door. Depending on how charitable you're feeling, the knocks may or may not be answered on the first round. Tardy attendees then sheepishly take their seats.

◆ Hand out plum assignments in the first few minutes so that tardy people are left with the least desirable tasks. This is a great incentive for arriving early.

Even after you illustrate how necessary it is to be on time at your meetings, some individuals may still arrive late.

Coming Undone

In certain organizations, and this is not my preference, the tardy are the subject of early discussion. In other words, they are the target of gossip, innuendo, and outright jokes. So be late, and be vilified!

Devise Your Own Method

On my first job, if you were late for a meeting you had to throw a dollar into the kitty for every minute you were late. Nobody ever walked in more than five minutes late. (I have no idea what they used the money for!)

Find out what works for your participants, and what steps you are willing to take to encourage promptness. You may quickly catch on that none of these subtle coercions is as effective as pre-interviewing participants, circulating an agenda, and demonstrating on a repeated basis that the meetings start promptly as scheduled.

Agendas as Game Plans

Most participants do their best to honor time frames if they know in advance that a particular item will be allotted five or ten minutes. Realizing a strict agenda helps them to stay on track. If someone admits in advance that only three minutes are needed for a particular issue, then that individual is less likely to run on and on and on ….

Follow the agenda strictly, eliciting the input of others as needed. Encourage the attendees to participate, and as each agenda item is discussed, ask the participants to keep in mind the following questions: what is the specific issue being discussed, what does the group want to accomplish in discussing the item, and what action needs to be taken to handle the issue?

Dyna Moe

Schedule meetings around breakfast rather than lunch or dinner. Most people have to get on with their day and hence are glad to get down to business. Also, some of the topics that emerge in the meeting can be carried out during the course of the day.

Define, Resolve, and Keep it Moving

When your group identifies the needed action for a particular issue, key questions include who will act, what resources does he or she require, when will the issue be resolved, and when will the group discuss the results. Upon successful conclusion of these questions, the group then moves on to the next issue, then the next. You will find yourself progressing in a group effort to get things done.

Every question does not always need to be addressed for every issue. Sometimes an agenda item merely represents an announcement or a report to the group that doesn't require any feedback or discussion. Other times the issue at hand represents an executive briefing, because the matter has already been resolved.

On occasion, unnecessary discussion ensues, and an item ends up requiring twice as much time (if you're lucky) as originally allotted. Often you will find that participants make up for the overflow in one area by being briefer in other areas.

For those items on the agenda that have a corresponding objective, you have the responsibility to seek out progress toward the objective. What else needs to be accomplished, and by when, to meet the overall objective? As with any goal or objective, they need to be written down, quantified, and assigned specific time frames.

Don't Fall Off the Track

There are a variety of techniques you can use to keep the meeting organized and on track. Consider some of the following suggestions for your meetings:

- ◆ Require participants to keep their remarks within the allotted time frames. Some groups keep a timer in plain view of all participants to encourage them to keep their comments brief. Others meet in a room with a wall clock in plain view.

- ◆ Have the meeting manager announce who will be speaking next and how many minutes have been allocated for the topic on the agenda.

- ◆ Ask participants to circulate summaries of their comments, charts, or exhibits in advance that illustrate the points they wish to make. Then, have them offer brief commentary to highlight the information in the distributed materials.

Remember, each of these techniques will vary in effectiveness depending on the purpose of your group, how often it meets, and your group's history.

Undershoot So You Can Overshoot

As a meeting planner, you know how prudent it is to undershoot the time frames within a meeting. Then, if somebody goes over the allotted time frame, then overall the meeting still stays on track and ends on time. What a world.

For a meeting that lasts longer than 30 minutes, schedule a break some time in the middle. Otherwise you'll lose the attention of participants who are thinking about sex, getting a tissue, making a phone call, or answering nature's call. You may also lose the attention of some participants whose attention spans have simply been, shall we say, influenced heavily by MTV (see Chapter 15 on partial attention).

> **Dyna Moe**
>
> A wise meeting manager may allocate five minutes for a topic that he or she will personally be covering, knowing that it will actually require about three minutes. Hence, several minutes can be saved.

Condition Your Meeting's Environment

The quickest way to lose the participants, other than being an interminable, crushing bore, is to conduct your meeting in a room where the environment can be distracting. This could involve the temperature being too high for participants, or poor ventilation. That, coupled with a dark meeting room, encourages people to fall asleep. Snooze city. It's an anthropological phenomenon—as soon as it's dark, the brain gets the message that it's okay to doze off. A warm, stuffy room only aids the process (see Chapters 5 and 6 on environment).

Make sure your meeting room is well-lit and has excellent ventilation. If you have a choice between having a room be slightly too warm or slightly too cool, opt for cool. A cool room will keep participants fresh and alert. The discomfort may prompt attendees to complain and a little frostbite might result, but at least no one will go to sleep.

Regardless of where you're meeting, here are other room-related organizing techniques:

- Meet in a room where participants won't be disturbed by ringing phones, people knocking on the door, and other intrusions. You want to achieve a meeting of the minds and accomplish great things; distractions do not help.

- Meet where there is wall-to-wall carpeting and walls adorned with pictures, posters, curtains, and the like to help absorb sounds and offer a richer texture to the voices being heard. Contrast this environment with a meeting held on a tile floor, with cold metal chairs, and blank, thin walls. Participants can't wait for the meeting to be over when the meeting room feels like a holding cell, no matter what's being discussed.

◆ Meet where the seats are comfortable and support the lumbar region of the back. However, overly comfortable seats may have a detrimental effect and encourage people to nod off

Have Sufficient Equipment Available

If participants need to take notes or work from laptop computers, make sure there are effective flat surfaces on which they can work. Pens, pads, cold water, and possibly tea or coffee should also be available. A sound majority of meeting participants say that well-planned meetings serve as a forum for them to contribute their thoughts and ideas, and hence such meetings can make a meaningful contribution to employee job satisfaction.

> **Dyna Moe**
>
> In some groups, the secretary or transcriber takes notes of everything that is being said. Other groups use the far-more-efficient tape recorder and have the notes transcribed afterward.

Whatever your recording method, set up and check out tape recorders, pocket dictators, overhead projectors, slides, chalkboards, whiteboards, and all other equipment far before the meeting begins. Also check for replacement batteries, light bulbs, extension cords, and all supporting equipment in advance.

Conduct Becoming

Maintain a supportive atmosphere for all participants; otherwise, comments come off as edicts (i.e., "I say, you do," "I command, you obey, insect"). Edicts don't encourage people to attend meetings in the future, even when something vital and interesting is presented.

Serve as a facilitator. You elicit the best responses from participants, encouraging them to cooperate with one another and to truly function as a team (see Chapter 24 on handling conflict within teams).

Follow-Up with Your Attendees

Organized and effective meeting managers have the courage to engage in meeting follow-up. They speak with participants afterward to learn if participants thought the meeting was effective, what could be added, what could be dropped, and how it could be improved. The manager then takes these suggestions back, ruminates on them, and incorporates those that would make a significant contribution.

Too many managers, in the erroneous attempt to "save time," don't bother to gather any feedback from participants following a meeting. They figure that their own observations were plenty, so why bother taking the time to consult with others?

Software To Keep You on Track

Meeting management software has grown in popularity. Such software is designed to help manage all meeting functions, including initial planning—even helping to determine if there needs to be a meeting at all—meeting objectives, and meeting outcomes.

Meeting management software provides a web-browser interface that allows the meeting planner to disseminate the agenda and meeting materials prior to the meeting, as well as to assign tasks for before and after the meeting. Such software also helps the meeting planner make decisions, establish action steps, archive meeting notes and ideas, address follow-up issues, and identify topics and agenda items for future meetings. Examples of meeting management software can be found at www.smartworks.us, www.meetingworks.com, and www.mbaware.com/meetmansof.html. If you find yourself conducting lots of meetings, it pays to check these out.

The Least You Need to Know

- The typical meeting is arranged by one person to convey information to many people.

- Elicit the participation of those who will be part of the meeting long before it even starts.

- Your participants will regard you as an organized, competent manager when you pre-interview and provide them with an agenda at the outset of the meeting.

- Steadfastly start meetings on time so that stragglers will realize that they are late.

- The quickest way to lose the participants is to conduct your meeting in a distracting environment.

Chapter 23

Influencing With or Without Authority

In This Chapter

- They like me, they really like me
- Emotion precedes logic
- Doing everyone a favor
- Self-confidence works wonders

When working with people to get things done, it seems like half or more of the time you're not necessarily in a position of authority. The people with whom you're working may not report to you, may not be responsible to you, or actually may not give a hoot as to what you're seeking to accomplish.

In this chapter, we'll examine a variety of ways you can exert influence without necessarily having authority based on your job position. Conveniently, these methods work more than fine when you do have authority via your job position.

Being Liked Is Half the Battle

Four years and seven score ago, Abraham Lincoln said to "win a person to your cause, convince him that you are his true friend." By that did he mean you're supposed to feign friendship? Did he suggest that you can only elicit cooperation and participation when others regard you as a true and lasting friend? Did he imply that unless you were liked and or respected, you won't be able to win others to your cause?

"D," none of the above.

Inducing others to be on your side or to participate with you in some way when you can't otherwise compel them to do so, in part requires them having some degree of affinity for you, what you're seeking to accomplish, or the situation itself. Robert Cialdini, professor of psychology at Arizona State University, who has studied persuasion for more than two decades, says, "Though we don't always realize it, we're more likely to be influenced by people we like or identify with."

I Like You, Do You Like Me?

In his book, *Get Anyone to Do Anything and Never Feel Powerless Again*, author David Lieberman states that "how someone feels about you is greatly determined by how you make them feel about themselves. You can spend all day trying to get them to like you and to think well of you, but it is how you make them feel when they are around you that is the key."

Hmmm, have you given any thought lately to how peers, co-workers, or staff feel when they are around you? Or are you too concerned with how you feel when you're around them?

> **CAUTION**
>
> **Coming Undone**
>
> Hard-driving, get-it-done-at-all-cost types sometime miss the forest for the trees in terms of associating with others, particularly when they regard people as a means to an end rather than unique individuals in association with each other to realize common objectives.

Lieberman refers to a process that he calls "reciprocal affection," that essentially means that when we find out that someone else thinks well of us, we are unconsciously driven to think that person is more likeable as well. It is simply human nature to do so. When those individuals whom you want to influence are aware that you like and/or respect them, given that you truly do, you increase the probability that they will like and/or respect you as well. From there, all kinds of things are possible.

Second and Lasting Impressions

Amazingly, mercifully, you can induce people to like or respect you even when you've known them for a while and the relationship hasn't gone well. Lieberman poses the question, "Who says you can't get a second chance at a first impression?" If you did something completely inappropriate, by leveling with the other party, such as by saying "I feel so embarrassed," you open the door to future participation and cooperation.

Studies show that leaders of countries, from a U.S. president to the leader of a small and distant sovereignty, achieve higher approval ratings when they own up to their blunders, however grave they may be, as opposed to attempting to whitewash them.

At work, when you're willing to admit to a previous faux pas, you win psychological strokes that reduce people's barriers to participation and cooperation. Not that you want to go around and do this as a ploy, nevertheless it's fruitful to understand how and why people are persuaded.

> **Dyna Moe**
>
> Extending yourself after acting inappropriately demonstrates that you're aware your previous action or behavior was not acceptable. This conveys to others that you're not likely to repeat the behavior. It also shows that you have the potential to be one of the "gang," a full-fledged human being who takes responsibility for your actions.

Emotion First, Logic Second

Bert Decker, who wrote *You've Got to Be Believed to Be Heard*, says that "people buy on emotion and justify with fact." If you're old enough to remember President Jimmy Carter, you may recall that his primary approach to influencing others was to appeal to their intellect, using logical explanations and rational thought. The only problem with this approach is that people first need to be won over emotionally.

David Lieberman remarks that 90 percent of the decisions we make are based on emotion. "We use logic to justify our actions," says Lieberman. "But if you appeal to someone on a strictly logical basis, you'll have little chance of persuading them."

Carter's predecessor, Ronald Reagan, knew how to appeal to people's emotions. For openers, he smiled a lot and the smiles seemed sincere. When seeking to influence others, he told stories, relied upon many facial expressions, and injected personal warmth and magnetism.

Factoid

Speaking coach Bert Decker says, "Likeability is the shortest path to believability and trust." The fastest and easiest way to start this train in motion—to be liked—is to smile.

When people were primed and ready, Reagan then would deliver the rational portion of the argument. He'd hold up a chart or refer to some statistic. By waiting until he had first made the emotional connection, he was then able to make the logical connection.

Bert Decker succinctly observes, "If you don't believe in someone on an emotional level, little if any of what they have to say will get through."

Reagan was deemed a more effective presenter, and for that matter, a more effective president, than Carter among media pundits from all sides of the political spectrum. Today, Carter's speeches are all but forgotten and his presentation style is emulated by no one, whereas Reagan is referred to as the "Great Communicator."

Persuasion as a Science

The aforementioned Robert Cialdini is a pioneer in the study of persuasion and has made breakthrough discoveries. He poses the question, "Have you ever purchased a product or service that proved to be of little value, or have you ever voted for an issue which, upon reflection, you're not truly in favor of? Of course you have! We all have, but why?

"Even the smartest people fall prey to sophisticated persuaders," says Cialdini. He has identified several ways in which one can tap powerful instincts within others to both influence and persuade them.

Reciprocity

When another person does a favor for you, even a small one, do you feel obligated to offer some favor in return? Cialdini conducted a study where restaurant waiters delivered the bill for the meal along with two free mints for each diner. The results, all things being equal, were that tips increased by 14 percent.

At work, if you offer to help someone, say in another department, and then in two weeks, a month, or two months later you ask them to help you, their inclination rises markedly. Certainly, people are often helpful simply for the sake of being helpful and undoubtedly you have both given and received help under such circumstances. However, when you need the help of others outside of your direct authority, relying on *reciprocity* will work as well as anything.

More than 70 years ago, Dale Carnegie proclaimed that when a person does a favor for someone else, the person doing the favor tends to have positive feelings toward the person he helps. Doing favors for each other increases the likelihood that both parties will have a more favorable regard for the other.

What about those individuals within your organization, or outside of it for that matter, for whom you've already done favors? What about those people who have done favors for you within recent memory? Right now, the people in these two groups represent the universe of individuals whom you can most readily influence, even if they are not under your job-related authority.

Factoid

Reciprocity is an age-old tool of persuasion that the movers and shakers among us have used since the dawn of civilization. It will continue to be a powerful tool in the future.

To increase your circle, do more favors for others and request more favors from others. In each case, proceed with sincerity and a genuine desire to help. Thereafter, don't be surprised if your ability to get things done in participation and cooperation with others rises significantly.

Consistency

Residents of a neighborhood were asked to sign a petition supporting a charity for the disabled. Two weeks later they were asked for contributions for that charity. Double the funds were collected from that neighborhood than in previous campaigns. "Most residents dug more deeply into their pockets," says Cialdini, "because they wanted to be consistent with how they responded to the petition."

Consistency is also known as "buy-in." Induce people to commit in small ways to a product or service, a charity or cause, or even an idea, and later it will be easier to get them to commit to a greater degree. In the workplace, and specifically in your career, if you have an idea that you wish to put into action, or simply a project that you wish to complete, rather than trying in one motion to influence people to jump in wholeheartedly, instead seek their approval on some minor component of what you're attempting to accomplish. Thereafter, you'll have less resistance to their participation at a higher level.

You might divide up your appeal into steps, although apparently, inducing one or two small incidences of buy-in will be sufficient. Inducing buy-in, or applying the consistency principle, ties into another tool of influence, social validation—the "bandwagon" effect.

Social Validation

You've been exposed to *social validation* techniques since you were knee-high to a CD player. Every time you watch a television commercial, you see images of happy, smiling, satisfied people whose lives have improved dramatically as a result of using the product being advertised.

When you watch an infomercial and the voiceover says, "Our switchboard is jammed, please call back in a few minutes," this is a not-so-subtle way of conveying that the item for sale is in such demand that other viewers can't wait to make a purchase.

> **Word Power**
>
> **Social validation** means people often make choices by observing the decisions others have made before them.

Yeah, right …. Nevertheless, people are notably influenced by what other people are already doing.

Cialdini refers to a study conducted by the City University of New York which revealed that when a single person on the street stared up at the sky, only one in twenty-five passersby looked up. When several people were staring at the sky, nearly 20 of 25 passersby looked up to see what the group was looking at.

In the workplace, particularly when you are not in authority, if you have already won over others on your project, the act of inducing others can be easier. The small group of advocates you have won over—as a result of exchanging favors, or otherwise inducing them to buy—increases your odds of getting still others to jump on the "bandwagon" to wherever you are leading it. Your converts can serve as missionaries, selling others on your ideas. Actually, this is how all religions start.

Authority

When you visit the doctor's office for the first time and see a wall-full of degrees, licenses, and diplomas, even if you know nothing else about that physician, you have been fairly influenced. Similarly, when someone comes into your office to repair the copier or some large, complex piece of equipment, the fact that he or she is wearing a uniform with the manufacturer logo or insignia increases your readiness to trust that person, even if you have never worked with him or her before.

Whether or not you have a position of authority, in influencing others in the workplace you can increase your level of perceived authority by displaying appropriate symbols and trappings. What would these include? Certainly, if you have any degrees, licenses, or diplomas, put them on the wall. If you've won awards, been cited for any reason, have received plaques and such, display those as well.

The initials after your name, such as Ph.D. or MBA, or a professional certification such as CPA (certified public accountant) or CMC (certified management consultant), work well. Granted, these degrees, awards, and designations may take years to earn, unless of course you're buying them online, but some people who have them, for whatever reason, downplay them.

What academic and professional distinctions and kudos have you earned that you are not employing to optimal advantage?

> **Dyna Moe**
>
> Have you ever had your photo taken with a politician or celebrity? If so, a picture with a nice frame, positioned so that others can see it when they enter your office, consistently, if not subtly, conveys that you are someone with whom to be reckoned.

Just the Basics: Write and Speak

Beside degrees, awards, and designations, other ways to establish your "authority" quotient are to get published in magazines, journals, newspapers, and even your own organization's in-house publications.

Writing articles for publication is a proactive strategy for establishing your career. If you've ever considered writing an article but hesitated, be assured that it's not as difficult as it may seem. Most publications routinely edit your material. They're far more interested in receiving interesting themes and concepts submitted by people with the right qualifications.

Your Byline, Your Credentials

Regardless of your field, you undoubtedly have information that will be of interest to your peers or clients. Don't make the common mistake of thinking, "Who would want to read something written by me?" That's a defeatist and unrealistic attitude. With thousands of magazines, newspapers, journals, and newsletters in print, and web-related publishing opportunities, several million bylined articles appear in the United States alone each year. A significant number of those are by first-time authors.

All other things being equal, if you've had a couple of articles published, you're better positioned to influence others than someone who hasn't. In a nutshell, getting published …

◆ **Positions you as an expert.** Getting published means credentials for you in the article subject area.

◆ **Makes for attractive reprints.** You can create a favorable impression by supplying co-workers, peers, staff members, and bosses with reprints of an article you've had published. Of course, be discreet to avoid seeming egotistical.

◆ **Enhances visibility for you and your organization.** Always mention your organization in your bio when you write an article. For example, "Joe Smith is a manager of XYZ Corporation." Your article therefore will market both you and your organization.

> **CAUTION**
>
> **Coming Undone**
>
> Some organizations are sensitive about publicity and would prefer not to be mentioned in connection with an employee's activities. Check out your organization's policies before proceeding.

Thereafter, appropriately displaying or circulating reprints will further add to your air of authority. You may find that the benefits of getting published can continue for a surprisingly long time.

Lend Me Your Ears

Speaking to groups, even if they are groups outside of your organization, ultimately will enhance your status as an authority within your organization. Bruce Barton, an American congressman in the mid-twentieth century, once said, "In my library are about a thousand volumes of biography—a rough calculation indicates that more of these deal with men who have talked themselves upward than all the scientists, writers, saints, and doers combined. Talkers have always ruled. And they will continue to rule. The smart thing is to join them."

What you say may be less important than the fact that you are able to say it with confidence. Others will pick up on your knowledge and devotion to the issues at hand and regard you as an authority figure.

At the most basic level, as you improve your speaking capabilities and your level of self-confidence—the two generally go hand-in-hand—you register a notable impact among those you encounter on the job. Even if you don't actively pursue opportunities to speak to groups internal or external to your organization, increasing your level of self-confidence has a succinct and highly favorable effect on others, particularly others you wish to influence.

Self-Confidence: A Vital Aspect of Influencing Without Authority

Self-confidence and lack thereof is the difference between a chocolate cheesecake and Jell-O. Self-confidence is a prerequisite to influencing when you do not have job-related authority because you become a more appealing employee and co-worker, and hence your likeability factor rises.

One of the fastest ways to increase your level of self-confidence is to learn from and emulate those who already have it. Dr. Judy Kuriasky, a New York–based psychologist, says, "Imitation is, after all, a key to learning. If you're attracted to self-confidence in others, it's a good bet that you have the capacity for greater self-confidence in yourself. That which we like or envy in others usually reflects our own values."

Imitation is a major part of learning in our early years of life but can still work well in adulthood. Simply identify the people around you who seem to have the attention of others, and watch how they behave. Is it how they work, what they say, or how they carry themselves that attracts attention? Select one small behavior at a time and emulate it.

"I Will," Not "I Could"

Self-confidence comes from feeling that you deserve to have and be what you want. A confident person writes a project proposal that says, "My project will accomplish xyz for our organization." A less confident employee says, "My project could accomplish xyz," phrasing that potentially communicates the employee's own doubt.

Confidence means taking a positive approach that rubs off on other people, causing them to view you as more appealing, whether you work on software applications, in accounting, or with a forklift in the warehouse. Others around you will sense your confidence and buy in to what you are selling.

Whatever you do on the job or in your personal life, you are more likely to do it well if you expect to succeed than if you expect mediocrity or failure. While others are consumed by self-doubt, belief in yourself and your ability to generate workable solutions to nagging problems can be one of the strongest weapons in your arsenal.

Self-doubts compromise your appeal. Worse, it's difficult for you to effectively market yourself. It's like trying to sell a product you don't believe in. Your doubt hobbles your efforts, ultimately sabotaging your efforts.

So much of what we do, both at and away from work, is in cooperation with other people. When others sense that you are confident, they want to be around you, support you, and even be like you. Conversely, people tend to avoid someone who is continually worried, hesitant, or skeptical.

Dyna Moe
It is enticing for people to be around someone who has a positive, enthusiastic, can-do attitude. They will go to bat for you and generally assist you in being as effective as you can be.

Too often in the workplace, many co-workers know next to nothing about one another. Conversant people are more likely to be viewed and treated as confident people. Getting to know the people around you will make it easier later to approach others with a project idea or to ask for a favor. A self-confident person attracts fellow employees and creates positive partnerships within the company, thereby strengthening the overall fabric of the workplace instead of weakening it.

Accentuate the Positive

When you dwell on your mistakes, they can drag down your positive attitude. Instead, try to regard them as lessons, stepping stones to a higher vantage point from which you can obtain more knowledge and wisdom. Be glad you've learned a lesson and seek to avoid making that mistake again.

Becoming confident is not about perfection; confidence is about recognizing your ability to achieve your goals and weathering the occasional storms along the way. Consider everything you typically accomplish in a day—even the small tasks. When you add it all up, you may be surprised at the length of the list and complexity of the tasks.

Dyna Moe
Conveying your best qualities in the workplace can help you in the quest to influencing others that you normally would have no authority over.

Perhaps you have capabilities and skills you hadn't previously acknowledged or valued sufficiently. Don't think all is lost if the big victories elude you for now. The smallest achievements can provide solid building blocks for increased confidence and appeal. From there, effectively influencing others is well within your capabilities.

The Least You Need to Know

◆ We're more likely to be influenced by people we like or identify with.

◆ People buy on emotion and justify with fact.

◆ People often make choices by observing the decisions others have made before them.

◆ You can increase your level of perceived authority by displaying appropriate symbols and trappings.

◆ Self-confidence means taking a positive approach that rubs off on other people, causing them to view you as more appealing and become more likely to buy in to what you are selling.

Chapter 24

Assembling a Winning Team

In This Chapter

◆ Work with the best or suffer like the rest

◆ When teams gel

◆ Negotiation comes in handy

◆ Conflict is inevitable

Assembling a winning team means being able to lead your team through the rigors of challenging projects. It's more than scheduling meetings, speaking to your team members, and broadcasting e-mail messages. It calls for an interpersonal connection with each member of the team.

Veteran team leaders understand, however, that their overall ability to get things done is largely dependent on the quality level of the individuals added to the team. You want to start with good people—there's no substitute for this!

This chapter will talk about how each team is a unique entity in the universe, the members of which thrive on understanding, responsibility, autonomy, and most of all, supervision. And although a team is more than merely the sum of the individuals who comprise it, the more competent your staff members, the more competent your team.

Connect with the Best

Lo and behold, the organization where you're employed can propel or thwart your efforts. Nurturing-type organizations enhance your ability to succeed. Such organizations have a track record for supporting teams, reward team leaders for taking appropriate risks, and have a realistic notion of what types of resources you'll require in pursuit of your task or project. Unsupportive organizations tend to do the opposite.

When each of your team members reports to you and no one else, you have the best chance to succeed. Unfortunately, your team members may be reporting to you as well as other team leaders. You might have one staff person onboard for 60 percent of his time, another for 20 percent, and another for 100 percent.

If your staff is pulled in too many directions by responsibility for other tasks and projects and cannot offer the requisite concentration and energy that would be desirable on your project, you'll have to make the best of the situation. Your job as team leader will be more difficult, your progress slower, and your enjoyment probably less.

Teams of Different Stripes

In simplest terms, a team is an assembly of individuals who have been gathered together to accomplish a particular purpose. Presumably, these individuals working in unison will accomplish far more than any single individual could accomplish, and if the team is truly effective, will create a *synergistic* effect.

Word Power

Synergy is when one plus one equals more than two.

Two people working as a team should be able to accomplish much more than the sum of what each individual would accomplish on his own. A group of three should accomplish more than what three individuals working on their own would accomplish.

Different types of teams are more suited for different types of tasks. High performance teams, which can be anywhere from four, five, or six people up to as many as 12, are committed to achieving the team's overall objectives, as well as committed to one another's individual growth, success, and personal experience.

A real *team* has been described as a small group of people with complementary skills. While holding themselves mutually accountable, they are focused on a common goal or objective, and strive to work in ways that most effectively achieve their objective.

A *workgroup* consists of individuals who exchange information, perspectives, or procedures that help one another perform more competently in his or her area of responsibility. Members of the workgroup generally don't share a common purpose and do not participate with one another in joint projects, at least those that would otherwise require a team approach. Nevertheless, members of a workgroup can be highly supportive of one another and offer support on a continuing basis.

As you might guess, of these three types of "team" assemblies, the high performance team has the greatest potential for synergy and superior performance in pursuit of specific accomplishments.

For the discussion hereafter, the term "team" will be used to mean two or more people who have assembled to accomplish a specific task or project.

> ### Dyna Moe
>
> Depending on where you work, what you're trying to accomplish, and how large or small your team may be, there are nearly endless variations as to what form your team will take and what they're capable of accomplishing.

More Members, Greater Complexity

The larger the size of your team, the more complexity. This may seem obvious, but perhaps you have never contemplated the level of complexity as one moves from, say, three to five members. On a two-person team, there's only one connection, between you and the other person. With a three-person team, the number of connections is three, as indicated in the diagram below on the following page.

Now things start to get tricky. With a four-person team, the number of possible connections grows to six, and with five it grows to ten. And, my goodness, should you have a six-person team, the number of interpersonal connections grows to a whopping 15.

The fewer number of team members you require to accomplish what you seek to get done, the fewer connections, the less complexity, and potentially the greater harmony. Not that great things can't be accomplished with teams of six or more people. Certainly, this happens all the time. Still, you have to pay homage to the increase in geometric complexity as more people are added to a team.

As the number of team members increases, so does the complexity.

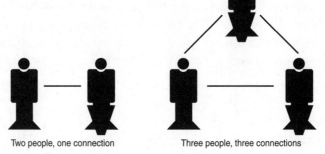

Two people, one connection

Three people, three connections

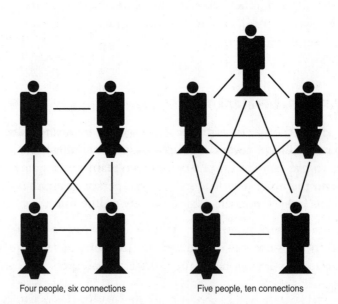

Four people, six connections

Five people, ten connections

Assembling the Highest-Quality Team Members

Starting at square one with you and no one else on the team, your goal is to attract or recruit the highest-quality team members you can, assign them roles and responsibilities commensurate with their skills and capabilities, and ensure that they work smoothly with one another.

If you're given the opportunity to be able to pick your own team members, you are fortunate. You have a fighting chance of choosing staff members who have the skills and capabilities, as well as the strengths and weaknesses, that will complement other team members.

Are There Safe Selections?

If you can choose people whom you already know, or with whom you've already worked, you're way ahead of the game. Perhaps as a result of exchanging favors with individuals throughout your organization (see Chapter 23 on influencing with or without authority), you have a reasonable idea of whom you might want to select.

> **Dyna Moe**
>
> By deploying your staff members for the highest good, in other words, in a manner that is both worthy of them and supportive of you, you increase the probability of accomplishing the desired objective.

If people who wind up on your team are complete strangers to you, fear not. You can still achieve admirable results. Many a team assembled out of the blue, never having worked with one another, find their groove and accomplish great things.

The downside of being able to choose your own team members is that your built-in biases and prejudices will prevail. You may end up choosing people who think like you, act like you, or even talk like you. As many team managers have learned, whether you get to choose staff members or have them assigned to you, you don't know how it's all going to work out until you're tested by fire.

Once you begin working on a project, put in long hours together, have numerous opportunities for cooperation or lack thereof, you then see whether or not the team has the potential to gel, meet the project challenges head on, and prevail.

> **Dyna Moe**
>
> It's entirely possible that the team members who have been assigned to you, as opposed to you picking them, can turn out to be a more cohesive and effective unit than you could have otherwise arranged on your own. For one, your bias in choosing team members has been bypassed. Also, like partners in an arranged marriage, you might grow to love them!

Building a Foundation

Whether handpicked, assigned, or some combination of the two, team members need to get to know one another. First-time team leaders can be overly eager to tackle the tasks at hand. The longer the project, the more critical it is to devote time and effort in the early stages to forming bonds between team members, defining and clarifying roles, and simply getting to know one another as individuals. From there, communication patterns emerge. You can more easily formulate a schedule that all team members understand and follow.

Getting-to-know-you sessions allow and encourage team members to speak up, share their views, and feel at ease about being on the team. Particularly for long campaigns, it makes sense to establish an orientation plan.

Orientation Sensation

The time and energy you invest in helping team members to establish bonds with one another and to feel as if they're part of a cohesive unit is seldom wasted. The payoff comes in the level of cooperation among team members.

If some or all of your team members already know each other, then obviously the time you have to invest in orientation can be shorter than if a group of complete strangers is getting together for the first time. In either case though, it behooves you to review the fundamentals, such as who reports to whom, how resources are allocated, how we order supplies, and so on.

> **Dyna Moe**
>
> The more issues you can air at the outset, the greater your probability of heading off potential problems downstream, such as individual power-plays, hidden agendas, and bottled up frustrations.

As the new team is assembled, don't be afraid to call upon each member of the group during orientation and have him or her introduce themselves. If team members already know one another, have each team member speak about what he would like to accomplish or air any concerns he may have.

Ground Rules for All

When it's your time to speak, after saying a little about yourself, focus on the team ground rules, such as how time will be allocated and money will be spent. Also talk about the internal hierarchy within the team, in the case where some team members may be reporting to others, rather than to you.

Team members may have more questions that need to be addressed, such as the following:

- Can we get in touch with you after hours?

- Will other team members be added later?

- What if we need to add outside resources?

- How do we authorize payments for needed supplies or equipment?

- Where will we store project resources?

- To what degree can we share team information with outsiders?

If it helps, establish common terminology, so that team members know the difference between, say, putting a rush on something versus handling it as soon as possible. Craft your own exhibits, such as the example that follows, and share them group-wide so that everyone is singing from the same hymnal!

A Hierarchy of Requests

1. As Soon As Possible (ASAP): Drop everything, and finish as quickly as you can.

2. High(est) Priority: Put this at the top of your to-do list.

3. Please Rush: Please complete this and report back quickly.

4. Priority: Put this task high up on your to-do list.

5. Crucial: Handle this when you can, but soon.

6. For Your Information: Look at it once, when and if you want to.

As you can begin to realize, by surfacing basic operational issues at the outset, you can alleviate burdens that you alone may have had to assume.

Head 'em Off at the Pass

You're not omniscient. You can't think of everything. It is to your extreme benefit to have team members conversing, sharing ideas, and surfacing issues early in the game. In general, issues identified at early-round meetings help to head off problems that likely would have emerged later.

Everyone wants to feel as if he or she is a valuable addition to the team. And no one wants to be completely managed. People prefer to feel as if they are in a collaborative situation. They are more than willing to acknowledge you as the team leader, but they don't want you to be autocratic in any way, shape, or form. Their highest level of contribution often directly relates to the degree to which they believe managerial-type information is shared freely with them. Especially in the case where you've assembled a number of get-it-done types on your team, you're going to find that people don't want to work in a vacuum.

For example, competent and responsible professional staff increasingly seek to gain access to the reports and management documents that you, as team leader, are privy to. If you've been a play-it-closely-to-the-chest type of manager until now, you may want to let go of the reins a little.

Charting Progress Individually and Collectively

To increase the propensity that you're all working in unison, with the same final objective in mind, each team member needs to have some access to the project management tools that you employ, such as Gantt or milestone charts, PERT charts, flowcharts, calendar tracking, and any other types of project management or schedul-ing software (see Chapter 13).

> **Dyna Moe**
>
> Project management charts offer a pictorial look at how individual team member contributions sup-port the overall project. Often, meetings, discussions, memos, and messages can't achieve the same immediate impact.

When team members have the opportunity to review Gantt or PERT charts and can observe how their current progress precisely impacts the progress of fellow team members, the probability increases that each team member will perform as required. After all, no one wants to look at a chart and discover that he or she is holding up the works!

As I stated in *The Complete Idiot's Guide to Change Management*, when all players have a vivid under-standing of their roles and how they are interrelated, then group cohesiveness, uniformity, and peer pressure can generate significant input. As much as anything, remaining on the project's schedule is fueled by each team member realizing the importance of his individual role, how responsibilities intercon-nect, and what it means to the team as a whole to stay on track. As team leader, once you're assured that each of your team members possesses this level of realization, the potential for you to complete this project on time and within budget rises markedly. Peer pressure alone can often do the trick!

Something Borrowed, Something Blue

More often than not, you will be asked to assemble a team that consists largely of individuals who are able to participate only on a part-time basis. It's not the best of all worlds, but depending on the talents and skills that team members bring to the project, it still may be more than enough to see you through to successful completion.

If you have to borrow staff from other departments and divisions within your organization, then your work is cut out for you. Getting quality people onboard in many instances means you have to dust off your negotiation skills. To recruit your staff, you may find yourself bargaining with the people in production, marketing, accounting, or finance. Even if successful, you may then have to negotiate with team members themselves as to how much energy and effort they're realistically able to expend on your project.

One Sale After Another

Here's another instance of where your skills of persuasion come into play. You'd probably prefer not to have to do this, but in some instances, you have to sell your project to others if it is going to get off the ground at all!

If there is predictable resistance from other managers to letting go of their good staff, why do they do it at all? They may be loyal and dedicated employees of the organization who recognize it's for everyone's good. Some managers realize that soon enough they're going to be making the same types of requests of you. Some are forced to at least partially let go of staff people, and some simply see it as inevitable.

Factoid

The people you would like to have on your team often are the most skilled and talented around, and those are the same people that other managers and other team leaders, heading up other projects, are least likely to want to part with.

As a team leader, don't be surprised if you find yourself in a continuing tug-of-war with other team leaders for talented staff people. This is the terrain of contemporary management and it's not likely to change in the short run.

Paint the Picture

As mentioned, even when you get clearance from other managers to recruit talented staff for your team, you then have to sell your team on what it is you're seeking to get done. Here, you draw upon every ounce of influence you can muster, all of your persuasion skills, everything you've learned about selling, whatever you know about packaging, positioning, merchandising, and successfully luring others.

You use your passion as a driving force (see Chapter 3). You paint a picture of what it would be like to realize the achievement. You convey a sense of excitement while remaining honest and above board.

You don't want to over-sell and you don't want to make promises you can't keep. It's one thing to successfully recruit people to be on your team, it's quite another when they realize that you overstated, or worse, lied about how the project would unfold and what their experiences would be.

Telling the Truth Works Wonders

Once you've successfully recruited talented staff, you maintain your passion. Until they embrace the project as their own, team members will feed off of your energy. You'll know if you've assembled a winning staff: when their energies feed off of one another, much like a baseball team proceeding toward the pennant in late September.

Just as you were truthful in recruiting skilled and talented employees to be part of your team, it pays to be truthful as you proceed along the path to getting something done.

When you leave out critical facts, or paint a rosy picture on how the team is progressing, you can actually impede performance because you're preventing your staff members from seeing reality. In other words, how can each of your team members succeed at their assigned roles if they don't know the true situation they face? So, as your project ensues, telling the truth becomes more vital than merely relating good news.

Learn to Roll with the Punches

One of the most frustrating experiences for team leaders is when they assemble the right people, establish the right action plan, and still find that progress isn't anywhere near what they envisioned. You've got to stay loose, and be willing to turn on a dime.

Flexible team leaders finish first. Inflexible team leaders are still trying to figure out what went wrong. Adopt the mindset that setbacks and mistakes that you make along the way are inevitable, and they also represent opportunities for learning, redirection, and growth.

Mistakes Happen, It's What Happens Next that Counts

Create an environment that says, "We strive to do our best, but sometimes mistakes will happen." When team members know that you won't blow your top and can handle some of the inevitable bumps in the road, they're more willing to: (1) take appropriate risks, (2) accept responsibility for any mistakes that they do make, (3) learn from them, and (4) move on.

The more challenging the project, and the tighter the time frame and more restrictive the budget, the more likely mistakes will occur. Seek to have everyone acknowledge them for what they are, and ascertain if there are any opportunities as a result of a mistake.

The knowledge and even wisdom that team members gain as a result of their mistakes, shared with the whole group, can sometimes benefit the entire project in ways that you might not have imagined.

> **Coming Undone**
>
> If you convey to team members that mistakes won't be tolerated, you'll force your staff to play it safe, proceed with caution, and not do any more than is asked of them. When fear prevails, your role becomes even more challenging.

> **Dyna Moe**
>
> When team members receive support for assuming responsibilities for the mistakes they've made, they find it far easier to critically self-assess their own performance. That tends to make them even better employees than they were before.

How Am I Doing So Far?

People at all levels of experience prefer to be held accountable for the work they do. They also want to receive regular feedback as to how they're doing. When you give them appropriate feedback, they know what they're doing right, they know what they're doing wrong, and they can learn and improve. If you go too long without giving people feedback, they begin to wonder if you're noticing at all, or if you even care.

Some team leaders make the mistake of not giving feedback, especially to highly competent staff, figuring they already know they're doing a good job, so why bother with excess verbiage? Like partners in a loving relationship, people want to know on a continuing basis that their partners still want them above all else. So too, your team members want to hear from you, even if you only offer performance feedback as little as once a day.

When Conflict Arises

Even if you have the knowledge and skills of Peter Drucker, Ph.D., the premiere management guru of the twentieth century, conflict between you and team members, or between team members themselves, often is unavoidable. Too many team leaders regard conflict as something that is to be avoided at all costs, but is that a sound approach to team leadership? Not necessarily.

When conflict is left untouched, it can fester, grow at an alarming rate, and ultimately upend a team's progress in ways you'd prefer not to experience.

The Basic Types of Conflict

It's best to identify conflict as it emerges and, generally, you'll encounter two basic types of conflict. With the first type, a single team member has problems relating to someone else on the team, or the entire team itself. Such conflict can result in jealousy, hostility, mistrust, disharmony, or withdrawal.

The other type of conflict you're likely to encounter has to do with a particular task or assignment, the appropriateness of a particular procedure, or how the group itself is managing its resources. Since this type of conflict is not based on the personalities of team members, conflict may have resulted regardless of who is on the team.

Antidotes for Each

Fortunately, with both types of conflicts, there are antidotes. By allowing underlying issues to emerge, a team can sweep away some of the barriers early in a project, while they're still relatively easy to deal with, and hence help to establish an environment that leads to project success.

In the case of conflict between individual team members, by surfacing the issues and having both parties air their grievances, the entire team can benefit. Sometimes you're able to identify and dislodge other issues that would have come up even later.

Now, in a climate of exploration and of mutual understanding, you can deal with the conflict. This opportunity wouldn't have emerged in a climate of passivity or ignorance.

In addressing the second type of conflict, recognize that it can be constructive, energizing, and even motivating. In some instances, this type of conflict actually acts to fuel progress rather than thwart it. You can help members to recognize that they share some deep-rooted values and common aspirations.

The synergy that you derive from holding such sessions often more than pays for itself in terms of team members' increased energy and renewed commitment to the project.

Dyna Moe
Sometimes it's best to take time out from the overall project, perhaps have a half-day retreat, and give team members the opportunity to join together in an atmosphere of cooperation and trust.

The Least You Need to Know

- Team members thrive on understanding, responsibility, autonomy, and most of all, supervision.

- You may have to use all your powers of persuasion to recruit staff and keep them enthusiastic.

- The insights that team members gain as a result of their mistakes can benefit the entire project in ways that you might not have imagined.

- People prefer to be held accountable for the work they do and seek regular feedback as to how they're doing.

- Don't run from team conflict, for optimal team performance identify and air out issues as early as you can.

Chapter 25

Partnering Strategies to Get Things Done

In This Chapter

- ◆ Partners are everywhere
- ◆ People respond to appeals for participation
- ◆ Empower yourself, empower others
- ◆ Coaches, mentors, and trail guides

"United we stand, divided we fall."

"Birds of a feather flock together."

"No man is an island."

"Either we all hang together, or we all hang separately."

Partnering with those around you can mean the difference as to whether or not you accomplish something big that you'd like to get done. There is something encouraging, stimulating, and even inspiring about partnering with others who are seeking to achieve the same types of goals that you are.

This chapter will show how it helps if you and your partner(s) proceed with the same intensity to get something done. It also helps if you're striving for the same goal at the same time, but it doesn't matter what you call yourselves. A classic example is two workers studying for a career-related exam, such as the CPA Exam.

Potent Professional Peers

Of all the possible others with whom you could combine forces, your professional peers are your easiest to identify and join in partnership. Your peers consist of co-workers, other people in your line of work, and others with whom you have a rather natural and easy communication channel.

Peer group partnerships tend to be more fluid, though potentially as powerful as any of the other types of groups. Undoubtedly you already belong to one or more peer groups consisting of two or more people.

What follows is a sampling of the names attributed to peer groups, although what you call your affiliation is not nearly as important as how you work together and what you're able to achieve.

Partners All

- Affiliates
- Associates
- Comrades
- Classmates
- Cohorts
- Collaborators
- Colleagues
- Contributors
- Co-venturers
- Crew members

- Friends
- Founders
- Group members
- Helpmates
- Joint venturers
- Mates
- Partners
- Principals
- Staff members
- Team members

Terms of Affiliation

- Advisory board
- Assembly
- Band
- Board
- Cabinet
- Commission
- Committee
- Conglomerate
- Congress

- Council
- Crew
- Parliament
- Party
- Skunk works
- Task force
- Team
- Union
- Unit

Managers and staff people in other departments and other divisions who have no formal role in what you're working on may serve as valuable resources. Depending on their education, background, and experiences in general, you may find selected individuals who can serve as ad hoc trail guides, at least pointing you in the right direction.

Consider this: a quick, well-delivered phone call to one of these valuable contacts, a one-line e-mail, or a brief encounter in the hallway could result in you getting the right input at just the right time to propel your project or task forward.

> **Dyna Moe**
>
> Every time you encounter another co-worker, you potentially open yourself up to a world of opportunities, knowledge, contacts, and influence that you may not realize or notice based on a brief encounter.

The Care and Feeding of Partners

In the professional services arena, accountants, attorneys, dentists, doctors, engineers, and real estate agents traditionally initiate firms as business partnerships. Changes in tax, liability, and estate planning have combined to make the corporate form of organization far more viable for many professional service firms. Still, even in the smallest of informal groups, the two-person group, it is often preferred to have one person who is in charge.

> **Coming Undone**
>
> Fifty-fifty partnerships sound fine but can lead to far more squabbles than when there is a clear leader. When parties have equal rank and no one is in command, the chance of stalemates on given issues rises.

When two friends form a partnership, trouble can loom because their friendship itself can get in the way. If they've gotten along well for years, each may assume that the same relationship is possible in a business setting; however, it's wise to be wary. Partnerships at work are a different animal.

Despite the pitfalls, there's something special about having one other person with whom you partner that can draw out the best in both of you.

As long as partners respect the capability or contributions of the other, partnerships can go on and on, independent of what type of relations the individuals have otherwise.

Partnering with Customers or Clients

Partnering with customers or clients can prove to be highly rewarding as well. From the standpoint of achieving effective solutions, how often do you consider the knowledge, operating experience, and resources of some of your organization's best customers or clients?

When it comes to getting things done, customers can offer fresh perspectives and keen insights that could mean the difference in the case of, say, developing a new product or service. Also, customers or clients may have policies and procedures in place which may be worth emulating.

Appeals for Participation

People respond to high appeals for participation. When Colin Powell assumed leadership at the U.S. Department of State in January 2001, his closed-door 90-minute session with the top agency officials reportedly was the stuff of which legends are made. Although Powell didn't allow a recording of it, allegedly lifelong State Department employees re-dedicated themselves to the agency's work in an unprecedented manner. Now that is recruitment. Likewise, you hear of coaches who give half-time pep talks that rally their teams on to victory despite the shellacking they took in the first half.

You may not possess legendary alliance-building skills, but elements of your personality and communication style undoubtedly can be harnessed to win people over, and get them to partner with you. You can start on this road, the very next time you attend a meeting or business function within your organization or outside of it. You can even start with total strangers!

Enlisting Others at Everyday Activities

Those who have achieved success at work or in life often seem to know something special about connecting with other people. They say the right things, and associate with the right people. They have a knack for keeping up with what is going on, and they find many ways to use that knowledge to form alliances.

High-octane persuaders can adapt their styles depending on degrees of formality, levels of seriousness, and the people involved. They have subconscious ideas of their desired out-comes in the back of their minds. These ideas might range from negotiating a business deal to successfully completing an involved project.

The accurate use of names is crucial in greet-ings, and alliance builders are especially adept at remembering and using them. Some natu-

> **Dyna Moe**
>
> Those with a knack for forming alliances know the importance of using a person's name. It has been said that our names are the "sweetest and most important sounds in the English language" to many of us.

rally have good memories; many others take memory-enhancement courses to learn and practice the many tricks for remembering. They know how important this skill can be. Addressing someone you have recently met with confidence, without mixing up his or her name, opens the door of opportunity.

One manager at an electronics company instructs his assistant to make calls before a meeting and create a list of the names of people who'll be in attendance. He studies the list prior to the event so that he'll be at his networking best when everyone arrives.

Exhibiting Host Behavior

At a business reception small pockets of people congregate between the bar at one end of the room and the table at the other end. The opportunity for making new business contacts here is ripe.

You'll spot at least one person, smiling and gracious, moving around the room fluidly, shaking hands and introducing himself with direct eye contact and a warm smile. This person spends some time with each individual he or she greets, listening carefully while the other talks. This person's ability to form alliances and partnerships is head and shoulders above the others in the room.

Whatever his job title, he understands a critical factor in human relations, described by Dr. Adele Scheele in *Skills for Success*—the importance of exhibiting host behavior. In other words, such people don't wait around to make connections. They know when to take the initiative to make others feel comfortable in a meeting environment.

> **Dyna Moe**
>
> It may seem elementary, but many people feel too awkward to even say who they are. State your name and position with enthusiasm. Then give enough information to lead the other person into an engaging conversation. All this takes only a matter of seconds. Practice will take away the awkwardness you may feel at first.

To make new quality contacts, you have to take advantage of the opportunities that come your way. When you have the chance to meet someone in person, first introduce yourself. Some alliance builders have a focused agenda and seek occasions for making business contacts or improving business relations.

Alliance builders seldom have the problem of having nobody to talk to; if left alone momentarily, they have a knack for acting in a commanding manner. Rather than sinking into the woodwork, they stand straight and, sipping a drink, survey the room with a look of alert interest and even slight amusement. They're never left out because they don't act left out!

Being Open to Empowering People

Some people, myself included, rely heavily on empowering people to gain the kind of insights, input, and feedback that enable us to propel ourselves forward. These people include peers, affiliates, and a wide variety of others, drawing from the best of those you might encounter at work and in life, as well as coaches.

Essential to having empowering people in your career is to be open to having them! This sounds simple enough, but many career professionals don't embrace the notion. Think about anyone from work who always:

- Looks forward to hearing from you.
- Listens to you closely.
- Heeds your advice.
- Is appreciative for having received advice.

Is this the kind of person you want to be around? Of course. That's the kind of person I am to my empowering people. They know that I want to hear from them and that I value what they tell me. I often act on what they recommend so rapidly that they're amazed how quickly their advice took effect.

You for Me, and Me for You

People who empower you are also empowered by you in some way. Otherwise the relationship would not continue. The way that you empower them often can vary. Perhaps simply valuing what they say in a way that few others do fulfills a need in them that prompts them to want to keep the relationship going. Here are other ways you may be empowering those who empower you:

◆ Perhaps few others value them the way you do.

◆ The energy, discipline, and enthusiasm you exhibit in pursuit of your projects may be inspiring to them.

◆ What you want to get done in and of itself may be of notable interest to them.

◆ The questions that you ask of them may require answers that they previously may not have articulated and they value this interaction.

◆ They value being exposed to the elements of your world and your insights.

Empowerment Is Where You Find It

You can find empowering people in your career nearly everywhere you turn. Your peers, the list of groups earlier in this chapter, the next function you attend—all represent fertile arenas. Here are some more ideas:

◆ Professional association meetings, i.e., if you're a financial planner, perhaps you meet somebody at the state chapter meeting of the Institute of Certified Financial Planners

◆ At civic, social, charitable association groups' meetings

◆ At an adult-ed course you take

◆ Through friends

◆ At conferences you attend, particularly if they're a presenter

---

Dyna Moe

The process of identifying and nurturing relationships with empowering people is a dynamic one. You're always bringing new people into the fold, while encountering yet others you suspect will become empowering people in your life.

- On airplanes, especially if you're seated in first class

- When you serve on the same task force, special committee, commission, or other elected or appointed group

Obviously you can only connect with so many people on a regular basis. The relationship with each of your empowering people requires some type of sustenance. What efforts will you undertake to maintain the relationship?

Advisory Boards: Empowerment Formalized

I have an advisory board of directors and I suggest that you devise one as well. Your initial response might be, "Okay, Jeff, you're an author and a speaker. I can see why people might want to be a member of your advisory board. Me? I simply work at XYZ organization assembling computer chips. Who would want to be on my board?" There are lots of people who would like to be on your board!

If you poll most people whom you know, you'll find that they've never been asked to be on a board in their entire lives. They've heard about people on boards, but they're never asked.

Begin to look for people in your immediate surroundings who can be members of your advisory board. These could include people in local associations, one or two people from work, perhaps somebody from your church or community group, perhaps a mentor as well.

I'll briefly describe my advisory board so that you'll have ideas as to whom you might choose to be on yours. I have two people from radio, a radio host and a radio manager. I also have a couple of people from associations, both national and local. I have a lawyer or two, a magazine editor and a newspaper editor, a professor, a high school teacher, and three entrepreneurs.

I invite the whole group to dinner twice each year. It doesn't cost as much as you might think; you can usually feed everyone for under $180.00. I let everyone know in advance what career and business challenges I'd like to tackle at the session.

First we have dinner, usually some kind of smorgasbord or a buffet. Afterward, I pass out the agenda, which is a repeat of the questions I circulated to them before that evening. One by one we discuss the things that I want to get done and they freely give me their ideas. I turn on my pocket recorder and capture it all!

I record everything and later carefully transcribe each of those gems. You might think, "Sure, people will come to my advisory board dinner once or twice, but would they come over and over again?" My board has met 14 times and I almost have to laugh because I get requests from people I've never met who have said, "So and so is on your board and suggested that you might invite me to be on it as well."

Eliciting Participation

What if assembling an advisory board is a bit much for you right now? For whatever you're trying to accomplish, when you want or need to recruit others, you can appeal to people's reasons for participating. The following list, origin unknown, frequently appears in chamber of commerce newsletters under the title "inducing people to volunteer":

1. Fill time
2. Repay a perceived indebtedness
3. Because someone they love benefits
4. To set an example for children
5. To work as a family
6. Someone they love is also involved
7. To meet people
8. To please someone else
9. To have fun
10. To gain skills
11. To gain experience
12. To be visible
13. To gain credit
14. To express their religion or belief
15. To find happiness

16. Because of tradition

17. To employ otherwise unused gifts or skills

18. As part of a group

19. To maintain health

20. To explore new learning, ideas

21. To heal

22. To avert loneliness

23. Because of interest

24. As a hobby

25. Out of concern

26. To receive a tax benefit

27. To counter-point paid work

28. As an extension of a job

29. Because they were assigned

30. To survive tragedy (cope)

31. To test leadership skills

32. To gain recognition

33. To acquire self-confidence

34. To be a change agent

35. To right a wrong

36. To work in a safe place

37. To save money

38. To have a purpose

39. To be a good neighbor

40. To get out of the house

41. To keep active

42. To experience new lifestyles

The breadth and depth of the items on this list speak for themselves. Note the linkage between many of the reasons cited and the principles of persuasion discussed in Chapter 23.

Partnerships Worth Exploring

Have you ever thought about teaming up with a coach to receive the big-picture type of guidance that you might not otherwise be getting on the job? Considering the kinds of things you want to achieve on the job and throughout your career, could a coach be helpful for you? Psychologist Harry Olson, based outside of Baltimore, Maryland, says that virtually all professional and Olympic athletes have personal coaches to help them perform to their maximum potential and deal with competition.

The better such athletes become, and the more elite their status, the more they need and rely on coaches. Why? Because the higher they rise in their fields, the more critical their moves become, and the more vital personal feedback becomes in avoiding mistakes. A personal coach offers the competitive edge!

> **Dyna Moe**
>
> Many high-achieving career professionals, with the aid of coaches, mentors, or other advisors, devise strategies to ensure success and to capitalize on new opportunities.

Olson says that a career coach can help "diagnose and sort out your situation and opportunities, offer new strategies for dealing with office politics and competition, and help you with vital stress management skills."

A good career coach helps you discover and capitalize on new opportunities, provides new tools to improve communication, and helps chart your goals and career path. A career couch can serve as your personal, behind-the-scenes counselor, confidant, and consultant.

> **Dyna Moe**
>
> Deb Giffen, based in Philadelphia, has coached many high achievers in many different professions. "The fundamentals of coaching others stay the same from person to person, almost independent of what the student is trying to achieve," says Giffen. "That's why I can help one person in one field, and another person in another, even if I personally don't have a background in those fields."

I Did It "My Way!"

"We don't question the wisdom of using tools to fix our cars or build wood projects, yet often we balk at using all the resources available to build our careers," says Olson.

> **Dyna Moe**
>
> A good coach will help you map out your goals and strategies and will monitor your progress. You will receive objective, honest feedback on an adult-to-adult basis without judgments. The coach will neither command you to do something nor let you flounder. He or she will help you sort out options clearly and objectively. The ultimate decisions and actions are always your own.

Many achievers value "doing it on my own." They see using outside help as a weakness, as if they are dependent on the helper; as if using a personal consultant or counselor somehow takes something away from them. Far from it. The career counselor simply works behind the scenes, helping you so that you do your job better.

Self-analysis is limited and faulty because of self-protective "blind spots." A coach increases your objectivity. Also, because of his or her background and training, a coach can address a broader range of issues than you'd be inclined to do. The coach's primary role is to be a trainer, a listener, an observer, a motivator, and a sounding board.

Your Ambition as the Driving Force

What you want to get done is always the foundation of your relationship with the coach. A good coach is committed to helping you succeed. Ultimately you alone decide if a coach or career counselor is for you. However, says Olson, if you encounter any of the following, the answer is probably "yes":

- ◆ Organizational changes where you work, especially if they have a direct impact on you.

- ◆ Expansion into new markets or diversification into new products or services.

- ◆ Increased competition for your company from other firms trying to take over your market share.

- ◆ Increased management or supervisory responsibility.

- ◆ Increased leadership opportunities.

- ◆ A new boss or leadership shake-up above you.

- ◆ Changes in your role or assignments within your company.

- ◆ Corporate intrigue, jockeying for position, turf protection—especially if you're on the rise.

- ◆ Blockades of your progress by internal feuds or informal political processes.

- ◆ Excess stress on the job.

- ◆ Increased production or sales quotas.

- ◆ A new project you lead or participate in developing.

If you simply have a strong desire to advance in your organization or field regardless of whether you experience any of the above, you could probably benefit by partnering with a coach.

Mentors as Partners

Having a mentor, like having a coach, can be a wonderful thing and can accelerate your path to getting things done. Many books and articles have been written on mentoring, but I can save you a ton of reading. Mentors generally emerge from those people in your career who are already among your empowering people.

Like a coach, a mentor can help to broaden your horizons. He or she might be pleased to introduce you to associates garnered over the years, key and interesting people—the people it may have taken you years to meet on your own.

You may prefer to stick with the strategy of engaging empowering people because problems often arise in the mentor-protégé relationship. One survey revealed that only about a third of mentor-protégé relationships last more than three years. And in the cases in which the mentor was the immediate supervisor to the protégé, many times the protégé ended up getting fired!

CAUTION

Coming Undone

A mentor is usually not your boss. Having a mentor outside your organization or your division is maybe better in the long run. However, always be wary of a potential problem this may cause with your own boss, especially if he or she feels threatened by someone else giving you advice.

The following issues are worth knowing about, at the least, so that you can avoid them:

- A career or business failure by one person could embarrass the other.

- Each person risks getting involved in the other's career battles (in which neither belong) because of the bond that develops.

- Confidential information exchanged can leave one or both sides vulnerable if a rift occurs later.

Some protégés develop accelerated expectations. A mentor can often make things look too easy; he or she simply calls someone on the phone and presto!, wheels are in motion. Realize that it probably took your mentor a decade or more of experience and alliance-building to be able to do that. Also, as with any partner, hold up your end of the relationship to keep it vibrant!

The Least You Need to Know

- Partnering with others seeking to achieve the same types of goals that you are can be encouraging, stimulating, and even inspiring.

- As long as partners respect the capability or contributions of the other, partnerships can continue, independent of what type of relations the individuals have otherwise.

- To make new quality contacts, take advantage of the opportunities that come your way. First, introduce yourself!

- The relationships you develop with empowering people require sustenance, so your efforts to maintain relationships is vital.

- If you have a strong desire to advance in your field you could benefit by partnering with a coach.

Part 7

Keeping Your Career in Gear

The chapters in this part of the book offer some accumulated wisdom, perspectives, and a fitting send-off as you make your way toward a career filled with accomplishments. We discuss why effectiveness starts in your mind and how to win internal battles. And then we look at the significance of taking things in stride, keeping focused on the big picture, and enjoying the ride.

Chapter 26

Reflect and Decide

In This Chapter

- ◆ The battle for your own mind
- ◆ The attachments we don't even know about
- ◆ Creativity is inexhaustible
- ◆ The science to following your gut

In a world that constantly bombards us with distractions, temptations, and all things grand as well as frivolous, the discipline of taking the time to pause and reflect, listening to your small, quiet voice, tapping your internal intelligence sources, and visualizing your desired results separates the high achievers from the rest.

When you win the battle for your mind, you can win at nearly everything. Undoubtedly, you have a fine mind, and it has brought you to where you are today. All that you've accomplished and haven't accomplished largely has been a result of your ability to tap your most vital get-it-done resource: your mind.

Leaders Win the Internal Battle

When you contemplate the challenges that you face and the things that you want to accomplish, have you considered that many other people experience the same kind of quandaries that you do? It's easy to lose sight of this perspective. The best and brightest action-types among us at work win the internal battles first and then go on to accomplish great things, at which time the results of their efforts become noticeable.

Do you remember the scientific concept of inertia from your seventh-grade Earth Science class? *The longer a body is at rest, or more specifically attached or immobile, such as a person, the harder it is to get moving.* If you're trying to break new ground, being rooted in the past is a potentially major obstacle for everyone involved.

Human beings, as creatures of habit, custom, and convenience, often become attached to the conditions around them, the equipment they use, procedures, and how things are supposed to be. This is true even when their surroundings are not pleasant.

John Kenneth Galbraith, Ph.D., a noted economist from Harvard, wrote *The Nature of Mass Poverty* in 1979. While researching his book, he visited four continents to determine why some civilizations remain poor. He wondered why some groups had stayed poor even for centuries.

Galbraith found that poor societies accommodate their poverty. As hard as it is to live in poor conditions, unfortunately people find it more difficult to accept the hardship—the challenge—involved in making a better living. Hence, they accommodate their poverty, and it lingers from year to year, decade to decade, and even century to century. Organization, departments, divisions, teams, and even small groups, if not careful, are all subject to accommodation.

Anyone Can Succumb to Attachment

On a personal level, getting stuck in a rut is no less difficult. Attachment reigns supreme to achievers of all ages. When my daughter was four years old, her mother and I bought her an old, upright piano. It was a little banged up and missing a few keys, but hey, for a four-year-old, it was fine.

To our amazement, she played well. At age six, she began piano lessons. The teacher encouraged us and said that our little girl had a special talent.

Two years later, the piano teacher told us it was time to buy a grand piano for Valerie. It would be quite expensive, but she was now winning awards, so it seemed like the right thing to do.

We went to a large piano emporium and Valerie tried all of them! Finally we came to a piano that proved to be "the one." She loved it and we bought it. We told Valerie that the piano movers were going to take the other piano in trade, but it didn't register with her. Days before the new one arrived, we cleaned up the old one, and then talked to Valerie about how that piano would be leaving and the new one would be arriving.

The old one had been her piano from the age of four and she was now eight. In other words, she had been with this piano for half of her life. She broke into a sob—not just a kid crying, but a deep mourning sob, as if she had experienced the death of a parent or a close friend.

"It's the only piano I have ever known, I have been playing with it since I was four! Why do we have to get rid of it?" Now, trying to be a good father, I started to explain to her that realistically we couldn't keep both pianos. The house was a good size, but two pianos were a bit much.

We took photos of the piano and we videotaped her playing—we made sure we had it covered. I explained to her that once the old piano departed, she would start to play on the new one and she wouldn't even think of the old one. But hey, this is not an argument for an eight-year-old. For days she lamented, "Why do we have to get rid of the old one?"

Factoid

Psychology tells us that the older you get, the harder it is to let go of attachments. The way we do things and how we think start to become embedded into the brain in the form of neural pathways. These pathways serve as the paths of least resistance that prompt us to take mental shortcuts in response to stimuli.

Finally the day arrived. The piano movers came to deliver the new piano and take away the old one. Something in me, I don't know where it came from, finally got through to her. I was able to communicate with her in a way she could understand and accept. Or, maybe she got there on her own, I don't know.

After another tearful outbreak I said, "Val, when the piano goes back to the store, then some other parents will see it and maybe they'll buy it for their little girl. She'll learn how to play, and she'll have that piano several years before she gets a bigger one."

Now, Val's expression started to change a little. She was still sobbing, but I knew that she was ready to forsake her attachment when she said to me, "Or maybe it will be a little boy."

To me Valerie's ability to adapt represented an extraordinary chain of events. Here was an eight-year-old willing to give up her attachment to something she had had for half of her life. In my own life, I have had far more difficult times with attachment. I have had attachments to objects, to people, and even to opinions, as do we all.

I once couldn't stand Elvis Presley; I thought he was a country bumpkin. One time, 25 years following his death, a TV special about him showed him discussing his acting ability and he said, "If I were as talented as James Dean …." I stopped in my tracks, I just froze, as Elvis Presley had used the past conditional, "if I were," which is correct English. Not one person out of 10 knows that this is correct grammar.

Most people would say, "If I was as talented as James Dean," but "if I were" is correct because he knew he would never be as talented an actor as James Dean.

All of a sudden I was willing to give up my attachment to having Elvis be some kind of bumpkin. A small issue you say?

Further on in the special, Elvis was shown going through 28 takes for one song. Everybody in the studio was saying, "Yeah, we got it, there is at least one take on the reel that is fabulous." Elvis says something like, "Wait, we don't have the right version yet." He went on for 35 takes in all, and later the group selected one of the takes in the 30s!

Are you so attached to the way you do things that when you're exposed to another way you fight tooth and nail? Do you resist trying another way and gravitate right back to what you've been doing, even if it doesn't best support your quest for accomplishment?

Acknowledging and Overcoming Neural Pathways

As one passes 35, 40, 45, and 50 years of age, slowly we each become familiar with certain thought and activity patterns that literally form neural pathways in the brain. All the while, we don't realize what is occurring. These patterns literally become second nature to us although they are not necessarily permanent … unless we allow them to be.

It's not that people can't change in the advancing ages, it's that their neural pathways become more firmly entrenched. Fortunately, you can change, at any age, but it requires effort.

Simply knowing that neural pathways exist and that they can be re-routed helped free me from some of my own preconceived notions regarding work, life, and what I want to get done.

Coming Undone

　If you're not careful, the neural pathways you develop will define and eventually rule the rest of your career.

Years ago I set out on a course which I think has paid off and could work for you as well. I take different paths home, hence helping to form new neural pathways. I listen to classical music occasionally, although it is not my favorite type of music. I read magazines that are otherwise outside of my immediate interest area.

I attend movies, plays, and concerts that are not necessarily my first choices. As long as I am exposed to different plots, characters, scenery, sounds, and other ways of seeing the world, I consider the experience to be beneficial. I visit websites that display viewpoints with which I don't necessarily agree. I read articles by authors whose bias is obvious. I ask young people for their opinion and I ask people older than myself for their opinion.

Flexing Your Creative Muscle

I know people who will take courses on topics completely out of their field, who try new dishes at restaurants, and who strive to keep themselves open to new ideas. The odd and wonderful thing is, you can do all kinds of new and different activities in your personal life that will serve to stimulate your creativity at work, break free of attachment, and overcome the inertia of immobility when you want to get things done.

Here are a few ideas …

At work:

◆ Take a planned 15-minute break twice daily

◆ Eat away from your desk

◆ Brainstorm with people not in your department

◆ Furnish your workspace with plants, pictures, or art that inspires you

◆ Learn some aspect of the organization that is completely foreign to you

Away from work:

♦ Change your magazine subscriptions

♦ Read a literary novel or epic

♦ Dress differently for different occasions

♦ Relax on your porch

♦ Install a hammock in your backyard

> **Dyna Moe**
>
> In a *Fast Company* article "Decisions, Decisions," Anna Muoio says, "Stripped down to essentials, business is about one thing: making decisions. We're always deciding something, from the small and daily such as which e-mails to answer, what meetings to have, to the macro and strategic, such as what product to launch and when …."

In general, to develop your awareness:

♦ Take an impromptu weekend trip to someplace you haven't visited

♦ Enroll in a course

♦ Join a book discussion group

♦ Volunteer at a charity

♦ Take up a new sport

The ultimate payoff that these types of activities generate is the ability to have a free and open mind, to make decisions on reasonably accurate observations, as well as drawing upon one's collective experience.

One Decision Leads to Another

Rebecca Merrill, in *Living in Yes*, regards effective decision-making as the quintessential skill in life and in one's career. Merrill says that we make decisions all the time, and "we never get to stop doing it." It's vital, she says, to understand that "every new decision leads to more decisions. It's just a question of how well or how poorly they set you up."

In this day and age, as discussed throughout this book, it's increasingly difficult to make effective decisions because of the surplus of information that is available. In many respects, it works against our ability to choose and creates an intelligence deficit. Choose, we must. Merrill says, "With every decision you'll experience some loss, even, and especially, if you choose to do nothing."

Since the quality of your life is directly related to the quality of your decisions, it's well worth your while to learn how to make good ones. Merrill says, "You can only make a decision you are capable of making when the decision is called for." The paradox of it all is that there are no "right" or perfect decisions. Said another way, "All decisions are a function of who you are at the time you make them." The more clear your thinking process, the greater the quality of your decisions.

Factoid

Rebecca Merrill states that although we spend a small percentage of our lives actually making decisions, they determine the course of our careers and the rest of our lives.

Thinking Is a Process that You Do All the Time!

In his book, *Thinking for a Change: 11 Ways Highly Successful People Approach Life and Work*, John Maxwell points out that since our decisions are largely based on the way we think, it's crucial to understand the nuances of the thinking process itself.

Maxwell cautions that the biggest challenges that most people face, for example, when it comes to making effective personal decisions, are their feelings. "They want to change, but they don't know how to get past their emotions," he says. Maxwell offers a syllogism that helps people readily understand that they are in control:

> Major Premise: I can control my thoughts.
>
> Minor Premise: My feelings come from my thoughts.
>
> Conclusion: I can control my feelings by controlling my thoughts.

Maxwell proclaims that if you're willing to "change your thinking, you can change your feelings. If you can change your feelings, you can change your actions."

The actions that you take based on good thinking can change your career and your life.

The Analytical, Intellectual Approach

Using one's intellect for intelligent analysis certainly has its benefits when it comes to decision making. The scientific method first introduced in 1592 by Sir Francis Bacon, an English philosopher, was improved upon a generation later by Rene Descartes, a French philosopher and mathematician, who provided the most fundamental approach to analytical thinking.

Recalling your seventh-grade science class, the scientific method consists of six steps, including observation, asking questions, formulating a hypothesis, experimentation, gathering and recording data and results, and forming a conclusion.

This stuff is pretty cut and dried, so I won't elaborate on it. However, the list that follows succinctly captures the essence of the six steps:

The Scientific Method

1. Observation. Observation involves the use of your five senses. As you observe, you begin to formulate certain questions.

2. Ask Questions. Ask questions concerning how and why certain things occur. Keep a record of your questions and take notes as you seek to answer them. Eventually, state the specific problem that you want to solve and conduct research to learn what the experts have to say about it.

3. Form a Hypothesis. Make an educated guess about the answers to your questions. One option is to keep a journal of your thoughts.

4. Experiment. Visualize experiments that could be used to test your hypothesis. After careful thought, design and perform experiments that will best serve to test this hypothesis. Repeat each test several times.

5. Gather and Record Results/Data. As you gather your data, make precise measurements. Record them carefully and accurately so that you can analyze them later and draw appropriate conclusions. This step requires unbiased observation.

6. Conclusion. Use your data to support, disprove, or leave inconclusive the original hypothesis. Report any complications that arose or possible improvements to be made in your experimental procedure. Make your findings available to others.

Remember, if your conclusion disproves your hypothesis, it is not necessarily a failure!

Shackled by the Paralysis of Analysis

Analytic and scientific approaches to decision making certainly are worth knowing and using in many instances. Many people overly rely on such analysis that takes the form of seeking reams of data before making a decision. In an overly informed society—regardless of whether you're making a purchase, hiring someone, or opening a drive-thru restaurant—you'll find enough information to persuade you to go both left and right. You'll find so much information that a clear-cut decision is nearly impossible.

A study was completed on the use of information in making decisions. Two groups of individuals had to make purchase decisions. One group was given data, analysis, and articles—everything they thought they needed. The other group made the decision based on instinct. After a few weeks, the two groups were able to see the results: the group that felt better about its decision had chosen on instinct. More data does not necessarily produce the best answer.

If you are forty years old, forty years of data is brought to bear when you make a decision. Instinct, then, is not based on a moment's whim—it's everything you've ever learned during your existence. Each of us has the ability to make intuitive choices, but for many, the words "intuition" or "instinct" are taboo. Yet the top CEOs of large companies often make decisions based on what feels right.

Find Your Own Path

When we're consumed by too many details—too much information—it makes sense to switch mental gears and employ all of our faculties, especially the power of intuition.

Intellect is certainly significant, but so are instinct, intuition, and gut feelings. In fact, recent discoveries have demonstrated that there's far more to instinct, intuition, and gut feelings than you might imagine.

Robert Cooper, Ph.D., observes, "Gut instincts are real and warrant listening to." For most things that you want to get done, even highly involved projects, you already have a strong idea as to how best to proceed.

Dyna Moe

Time and time again, astounding achievements have been realized by people who were able to look beyond what was known or accepted as true, and use their intuitive faculties as well as current observations to arrive at current decisions.

Follow that Notion

Evidence is mounting that it's okay to rely on your instincts more often! If you're figuring out how to accomplish something, it's often okay to simply start and let your intuition guide you. All the cellular intelligence throughout your body goes into a decision based on instinct or intuition. Your decision isn't whimsical, random, or foolish.

Decisions based on instinct and intuition rapidly and automatically encompass all of your life experiences and acquired knowledge.

The Least You Need to Know

- ◆ When you win the battle for your mind, you can win at nearly everything.

- ◆ The older you get, the harder it is to let go of attachments, but it is entirely attainable!

- ◆ You can change, at any age—it requires making conscious choices and sometimes intentionally taking unfamiliar paths.

- ◆ Every new decision leads to more decisions. The action that you take based on good thinking can change your career and your life.

- ◆ On the path to getting things done, it's okay to rely more on your instincts.

Chapter 27

Relax, Already: Getting Things Done in Perspective

In This Chapter

- ◆ Full bore no more
- ◆ True productivity is measured by results
- ◆ Lingering at crucial moments
- ◆ Pacing yourself

When I speak to groups or consult with individuals, I am amazed at some of the time pressure stories they tell me. The number of items competing for their time and attention and the schedules they're trying to balance and juggle would leave me in a tizzy. When I ask them how things got to be so hectic, many respond in a way that mystifies me. Their response is similar to the situation where you walk into a room and see a child and a broken toy. You ask the child what happened to the toy. He simply shrugs and says, "It broke."

Adults who are continually racing the clock to get things done are acting in ways analogous to the child who claims, "It broke." Such adults are taking little responsibility for their hectic lives. They claim that they're victims of circumstance.

Stop Creating Pressure for Yourself

Unquestionably, the world is becoming ever-more demanding. As much as anyone, I am aware of the information and communication bombardment the typical individual experiences on any given day. Nevertheless, in proceeding through work and life, presumably one begins to understand the importance of being more selective, becoming and staying organized, saying no, maintaining balance, and living in the moment.

Too many people proceed as if they've never heard of these notions or, if they have, they pay them extremely short shrift. Such people proceed at full bore. They don't seem to have established, let alone pursue, priorities; hardly ever say no; and short-change themselves of essential nutrition, relaxation, and sleep. They seem to convey the message, "The toy is breaking more each day, and I can't understand why. Soon it'll be shattered to pieces."

> **Word Power**
>
> **Living in the moment** means proceeding through your day with vibrant expression and keen perception, with an intense awareness of your surroundings. It's getting to work each day with the thought, "I'm alive, and this day is only starting."

Living in the moment remains one of the least understood, infrequently addressed, seldom used human capabilities. Too few individuals have any experience or knowledge of living in the moment; it is lost among a flurry of activity—"busy-ness."

Living in the moment means being aware of your power in the present. While it is not a recipe for getting things done per se, it helps enormously. It is being able observe the finely woven canvas of your career while you are in progress. It is giving yourself permission to be who you are. It is resting when you are tired. It is not having to constantly strive.

Freed from the preoccupation that limits your experience of the present, however, you may feel more present than you have in years, increasing your ability to focus and get things done.

Once you realize what it means to dwell in real time and how far you may have strayed from the mark, there are several things you can do to begin to catch up with today (or at least this week). Many are deceptively simple, but don't let that obscure the powerful results they offer. Foremost is giving yourself permission to take time-outs at work as you deem them to be necessary.

Who's Holding the Whip?

During my travels, I have been struck by the legions of people in my audiences who seem perpetually overwhelmed. The irony is that these people could take breaks throughout their days and weeks, but they don't. The biggest obstacle to winning back your time is the unwillingness to allow yourself a break while accomplishing your tasks.

I spoke to one group of executives and their spouses, and learned from many spouses that their executive husbands or wives simply do not allow themselves to take a break. Paradoxically, increasing evidence indicates that executives would be more effective if they paused for an extra minute a couple of times each day. This can be done every morning and afternoon, when returning from the water cooler or restroom, before leaving for lunch, or when returning from lunch. And that's only the short list.

To insist on proceeding full-speed through the day to get things done without allowing yourself moments to clear your mind all but guarantees you'll be less effective than those who do.

> **Factoid**
>
> Seven hours and 50 minutes of work plus 10 one-minute intervals of rest or reflection in a workday makes you more productive than do eight solid hours of work.

Pause to Stay Competitive

The Motorola Corporation discovered the hard way that a little instruction here and there didn't educate their employees the way they had hoped. It certainly didn't stick with their employees. So Motorola started its own university with its own staff of 300 instructors and an initial annual budget of $60 million, and developed in-house programs and long-term alliances with local colleges.

Why such elaborate procedures? They were implemented to help the organization stay competitive. Similarly, for you to stay competitive, you need to pause periodically throughout the day, every day.

Some of the most productive and energetic people in history learned how to pace themselves effectively by taking a few "time outs" each day. Thomas Edison would rest for a few minutes each day when he felt his energy level dropping. Buckminster Fuller often worked in cycles of three or four hours, slept for 30 minutes, and then repeated the process. He found that in the course of a 24-hour period, he would get far more done than if he had followed traditional waking and sleeping patterns. While this approach isn't for everyone, it worked for Bucky. By giving himself rest at shorter intervals, Fuller was able to extend his productive hours.

Remember, for most people, the time when they are least alert is between 2:00 A.M. and 5:00 A.M. Highest alertness is between 9:00 A.M. and noon, and between 4:00 P.M. and 8:00 P.M. Your alertness will vary depending on your own physiology and inclinations, as well as on the hours of consecutive duty, hours of duty in the preceding week, irregular hours, monotony on the job, timing and duration of naps, environmental lighting, sounds, aromas, temperature, cumulative sleep deprivation over the past week, and much more.

Look for the time intervals within your own workweek, and even weekends, when you are fully alert and productive in order to efficiently and effectively get things done.

Clarity in Idle Moments

Entrepreneurs, running their own businesses and managing themselves, allegedly would be more inclined to take strategic pauses throughout the day. After all, they're in charge of their own schedule. Too often, it isn't necessarily so. The temptation to overwork can be ferocious.

> ### Dyna Moe
>
> The CEOs in many top organizations routinely take naps at midday to recharge their batteries. They have executive assistants who shield them from the outside world, take their calls, and arrange their schedules while they snooze.

Conversely, if you work for others, perhaps a large organization, you may erroneously believe that pausing for the total of 10 strategic minutes throughout a workday could somehow jeopardize your standing. This misconception is unfounded.

If you are not the CEO of a large organization, the thought of being able to take a nap in the middle of the workday may seem like Nirvana to you. Yet, the 10 strategic minutes I have recommended provide a similar benefit in your quest to get things done. If you can't take a flat-out nap, 10 well-placed minutes may be your best alternative.

You can't charge through the day full throttle and expect to be at your peak level all the while. Be realistic. You need to consistently take breaks, perhaps along the lines of half a minute or so every 20 minutes, and a good three- or four-minute break at a minimum every hour, to ensure that you stay sharp, stimulate your circulation, and take care of necessities.

In general, any time you feel yourself getting bogged down with all the tasks you need to complete in the day, take a walk or switch to another task for which you have sufficient energy. Do anything else which will help to minimize tension, keep you alert, and help you to stay more productive throughout the remainder of the day. Think of it this way: execute, reflect, reevaluate, and proceed (see Chapter 5 on the energy of switching tasks). As lunch time approaches, reevaluate what you've done, and how you plan to proceed during the afternoon.

> **Dyna Moe**
>
> If you find yourself easily distracted at work, experiment with the times in which you tackle certain tasks. Maybe it makes sense for you to come in an hour earlier than everyone else, or to stay an hour later. Maybe it makes sense for you to eat lunch at a different time so that you can work during the traditional lunch hour.

Break Up Your Week

If you can work off-site one day a week, or depending on your organization, only once every two weeks, you'll be in a good position to accomplish certain types of tasks more adroitly than in the traditional office.

Also, if you're able to telecommute, using your phone, fax, and e-mail to stay in touch with your office, you've saved physical commuting time. You have also saved wear and tear on your car, prolonged the length of your wardrobe, and afforded yourself the opportunity to get an extra half-hour of sleep the night before. Furthermore, you have set up an environment in which you can work efficiently.

Taking Some Time Today and Tomorrow

The tables that follow will help you to track or, at the least, become more aware of where and when you give yourself some time-outs while getting things done. The first worksheet includes nine activities: four at work, three after work, and two during vacation time. Each of these activities has a "Lately," a "Short-Term Goal," and a "Long-Term Goal" category. In the Lately column, enter how many times in the past month you have actually engaged in some strategic time-outs and taken what I call "breathing space." In each Goal column, enter how many times you would like to, say, take a slow and leisurely lunch. In the Short-Term Goal category, for example, you could indicate two times per week.

Be realistic when recording what you have been doing. Be reflective in the short-term goal column, marking down what you can realistically get done. Be visionary in the long-term goal column, marking down what you would ideally like to achieve.

Strategic Pauses, Example

At Work:	Lately	Short-Term Goal	Long-Term Goal
Breathing Space Minutes Taken Daily	0	5	10
Breathing Space Lunches per Week	1	2	3
Breathing Space Hours per Week	1	3	5
Days per Week with No Homework	2	4	5
Full Weekends You Take off Per Month	1	2	3

After Work:	Lately	Short-Term Goal	Long-Term Goal
Days per Month Using Alternate Route Home	1	2	4
Days/Mo. You Have Fun on Way Home	0	3	6
Days per Month Telecommuting from Home	0	2	3

Vacation Time:	Last 12 Months	Next 12 Months	3 Years Hence
3- to 4-Day Vacations You Take Annually	2	3	6
Week-long Vacations You Take Annually	1	2	3

Strategic Pauses, Blank

At Work:	Lately	Short-Term Goal	Long-Term Goal
Breathing Space Minutes Taken Daily	_____	_____	_____
Breathing Space Lunches per Week	_____	_____	_____
Breathing Space Hours per Week	_____	_____	_____

At Work:	Lately	Short-Term Goal	Long-Term Goal
Days per Week with No Homework	_____	_____	_____
Full Weekends You Take off Per Month	_____	_____	_____

After Work:	Lately	Short-Term Goal	Long-Term Goal
Days per Month Using Alternate Route Home	_____	_____	_____
Days/Mo. You Have Fun on Way Home	_____	_____	_____
Days per Month Telecommuting from Home	_____	_____	_____

Vacation Time:	Last 12 Months	Next 12 Months	3 Years Hence
3- to 4-Day Vacations You Take Annually	_____	_____	_____
Week-long Vacations You Take Annually	_____	_____	_____

In the weeks and months ahead, review your chart periodically for reinforcement. The advice to take periodic breaks seems so simple, yet you may find it difficult to put into practice.

New Sources of Input

Have you ever eaten lunch with a colleague and begun discussing ways to approach your work more effectively? After a few minutes, you're both deep into the conversation, coming up with all sorts of great ideas on how to accomplish your tasks. However, when the waiter comes to take your order or bring your check, what happens? The conversation dies down.

When you both go back to work, those ideas are often forgotten or put on a back burner. Your discussion generated effective ways you can get things done that are now perhaps lost. If you consciously schedule a meeting for the sole purpose of letting the creative sparks fly, you'll grab control of your time and have some of the most productive sessions you've ever had.

Dyna Moe

When you come in contact with other people, you're exposed to whole new worlds, their worlds. When you interact with another person, you get the benefit of his/her information, in addition to your own.

I meet with a mentor once a month in his dining room. At a cleared table, we sit across from each other with a tape recorder, discussing problems and issues that face us and ways we can overcome them. Each of us keeps a copy of the tape, takes it home, and makes notes on it. We capture those ideas instead of letting them die.

Look for other ways to shake up your routine for the insights and breakthroughs that may result. Every day and every moment holds great potential for achieving your goals.

The View from Above

Think about flying on an airplane. You have a window seat, and it's a clear day. As you gaze down to the ground below, what do you see? Cars the size of ants. Miniature baseball diamonds. Hotels that look like Monopoly pieces. Life passing by.

The same effect can take place at the top of a mountain or a skyscraper. As often as possible, when things seem to be racing by too fast, get to higher ground for a clear perspective of what needs to be accomplished.

If you're among the lucky, perhaps you regularly allocate time for reflection or meditation. If you don't, no matter. There are other ways to slow it all down. After the workday, listen to relaxing music with headphones and with your eyes closed. A half hour of your favorite music with no disturbances (and your eyes closed) can seem almost endless. When you re-emerge, the rest of the day takes on a different tone and you are able to get more done than you would have at your previous level of alertness.

Laugh at Life

How many times do you actually let out a good laugh during the day, especially during the workday? Five-year-olds reportedly laugh 113 times a day, on average. However, 44-year-olds laugh only 11 times per day. Something happens between the ages of 5 and 44 to reduce the chuckle factor.

Once you reach retirement, fortunately, you tend to laugh again. The trick is to live and work at a comfortable pace and have a lot of laughs along the way, at every age.

Part of taking control of your career is being able to step back and look at the big picture, being able to see the lighter side of things. Some of your worst gaffes eventually evolve into the things you pleasantly recall, or your best ideas! Pros who survive and thrive, laugh. Enjoying moments throughout the workday can in turn motivate you to accomplish more.

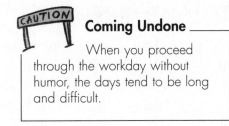

Coming Undone

When you proceed through the workday without humor, the days tend to be long and difficult.

Keep Fighting for Perspective

By altering our personal perspectives—our perceptions, our response to stimuli, even the pace at which we proceed throughout the day—we have the opportunity to engage in our careers in a manner that is more manageable, less complex, and more enjoyable. The key is to develop a mind-set that both acknowledges the multitude of items competing for one's time and attention and concurrently acknowledge that one has the capabilities and the intelligence to rise above the fray.

You possess the distinct capability to adopt seemingly minor work-style changes that result in major gains in peace of mind and getting things done, and know that:

- Much of what seems urgent and compelling is not necessarily so.

- Sometimes the single best strategy for facing challenging tasks is to slow down.

- You have the ability to pause momentarily throughout the day to mentally, emotionally, and spiritually renew yourself.

- By honing and refining your personal systems for accomplishment you will be more adept at handling crises big and small.

- You can actually have a calming effect on those all around you.

- Satisfaction with your work and your life can come in a continual, even stream.

Getting things done is more a mind-set than a set of circumstances. You have the power to alter your thinking and your surroundings so as to accomplish more and maintain a sense of work/life balance.

The Least You Need to Know

◆ Much of the pressure we face we created ourselves, and then we completely forgot that we did so.

◆ Living in the moment means being aware of your power in the present and while it is not a recipe for getting things done per se, it helps enormously.

◆ Don't charge through the day full throttle and expect to be at your peak level all the while—take breaks, to ensure that you stay sharp.

◆ As often as possible, when things seems to be racing by too fast, get to higher ground figuratively or literally for a clear perspective of what needs to be accomplished.

◆ You already possess the capability to adopt work-style changes that result in major gains in both peace of mind and getting things done.

Appendix A

Glossary

accommodation   Adapting to unfavorable circumstances.

aggressive observation   Working with people face-to-face because what you observe about a person is more revealing than what you hear or read.

attachment   Fixation on current conditions to the exclusion of new input or ideas.

benchmark   A reference point used to compare a current outcome or experience to one previously documented or noted.

codify   To organize something into a system, such as a body of laws or instructions.

communicative enslavement   The desire to stay in constant communication to the point of interfering with the activities of daily living.

concession   A form of agreement or acceptance.

de facto   Existing in fact, whether officially or lawfully sanctioned.

directives   Commands or orders.

effectiveness   Undertaking the right task, with the goal of producing a desired, worthwhile effect.

efficiency   Taking the right approach to a job, doing it quickly with few or no errors, and generating results with little or no wasted effort.

empower   To delegate power to.

fudge factor   A numerical adjustment made to an estimation.

Gantt chart   A bar chart that aids in planning and scheduling.

homeostasis   The balance among elements in a system.

immersion   Focusing exclusively on a particular task.

inertia   The scientific phenomenon whereby a body in motion tends to stay in motion unless acted upon by an outside force, and a body at rest tends to stay at rest.

leveraging   Taking the smallest action that will yield the largest result.

living in the moment   Proceeding through your day with vibrant expression and keen perception, with an intense awareness of your surroundings.

locus of control   The pivotal point at which action can be taken, as in "calling your own shots" or "being your own person."

managing the beforehand   To prepare for something in advance of a need.

marinate   Ideas lingering in one's mind so to be more fully understood.

megalomania   The over-arching desire to stay on top of things, to control, to be in the driver's seat.

mendacity   Untruthfulness.

minutia   Small or minor detail.

modus operandi   An unvarying or ritualistic method of proceeding.

over-preparation   Doing excessive groundwork instead of taking action.

Pareto Principle   A generalization that 80 percent of your actions or efforts contribute to only 20 percent of your actual results, while 20 percent of your actions or efforts yield 80 percent of your results.

patchwork efforts   Making do with available resources.

program   A set of instructions given to the computer describing the sequence of steps the computer will perform in order to accomplish a specific task.

procrastination   The act of putting off something until a later time, either by not starting a task or by not finishing one you've started.

propound   Introduce, put forward, or "lay on the table."

revelatory   Foreshadowing or prophetic.

quandary   A difficult situation with no apparent solution, or a state of uncertainty with equally unattractive options.

reciprocal affection   When two people, or groups of people, discover that they are liked, admired, or respected by one another.

resilience   Adopting behaviors to meet challenges; enduring a situation or overcoming an ordeal; having the ability to come back even stronger than before.

schlockmeister   A person who has all sorts of advice to give, some of it questionable.

singularities   One-time events in the universe.

social validation   Making choices by observing the decisions others have made before you and not necessarily based on your own independent decision-making process.

sycophant   Someone who seeks to please others in order to gain a personal advantage.

synergy   When one plus one equals more than two.

technostress   Everyday stress exacerbated by technology.

theses   Suggested reforms; situations in need of change.

transcending   Going beyond some previous standard or norm.

trepidation   A feeling of alarm or dread.

ubiquitous   Seems to be everywhere at once.

Zeigarnik Effect   The tendency for people to remember interrupted tasks better than those that have been completed.

Further Reading

Books

Adams, Scott. *Dilbert Fugitive from the Cubicle Police*. Kansas City: Andrews McMeel, 1996.

Allen, David. *Getting Things Done: The Art of Stress-Free Productivity*. New York: Penguin Books, 2003.

———. *Ready for Anything: 52 Productivity Principles for Work and Life*. New York: Penguin Group, 2003.

Bellman, Geoffrey. *Getting Things Done When You Are Not in Charge*. San Francisco: Berrett-Koehler Publishers, 2001.

Benton, Deborah. *Lions Don't Need to Roar*. New York: Warner, 1993.

Bliss, Edwin. *Getting Things Done: The ABCs of Time Management*. New York: Scribner, 1991.

———. *Guide to Getting Things Done*. New York: Bantam Books, 1977.

Bossidy, Larry, et al. *Execution: The Discipline of Getting Things Done*. New York: Crown Business, 2002.

Bradbury, Ray. *Fahrenheit 457*. New York: Ballantine Books, 1953.

Cathcart, Jim. *The Acorn Principle*. New York: St Martins, 1998.

Chang, Richard. *The Passion Plan at Work*. San Francisco: Jossey Bass, 2001.

Cialdini, Ph.D., Robert. *The Psychology of Persuasion Influence: The Psychology of Persuasion*. Chicago: Longman, 2000.

Covey, Stephen. *The 7 Habits of Highly Effective People*. New York: Fireside, 1990.

Daniels, Aubrey. *Bringing Out the Best in People*. New York: McGraw-Hill, 1994.

Davidson, Jeff. *Breathing Space: Living & Working at a Comfortable Pace in a Sped-Up Society*. New York: MasterMedia, 2000.

———. *The Complete Idiot's Guide to Managing Your Time*. New York: Alpha/Penguin, 2002.

———. *The Complete Idiot's Guide to Managing Stress*. New York: Alpha/Penguin, 2000.

———. *The Complete Idiot's Guide to Reaching Your Goals*. New York: Alpha/Penguin, 1997.

———. *Joy of Simple Living*. Emmaus, PA: Rodale, 1999.

———. *The 60-Second Organizer: Sixty Solid Techniques for Beating Chaos at Home and at Work*. Avon, MA: Adams Media, 2004.

———. *The 60-Second Procrastinator*. Avon, MA: Adams Media, 2004.

Decker, Bert. *You've Got to Be Believed to Be Heard*. New York: St. Martin's, 1993.

Emmett, Rita. *The Procrastinator's Handbook: Mastering the Art of Doing It Now*. Canada: Walker Publishing, 2000.

Fiore, Neil. *The Now Habit: A Strategic Program for Overcoming Procrastination and Enjoying Guilt-Free Play*. New York: Penguin Putnam, 1989.

Frank, Milo. *How to Get Your Point Across in 30 Seconds or Less*. New York: Pocket, 1990.

Fritz, Robert. *The Path of Least Resistance*. New York: Ballantine, 1984.

Galbraith, John Kenneth. *The Nature of Mass Poverty*. Cambridge, MA: Harvard University Press, 1979.

Glickman, Rosalene. *Optimal Thinking: How to Be Your Best Self*. New York: Wiley, 2002.

Gordon, Robert. *Macroeconomics* (9th edition). New York: Addison-Wesley, 2002.

Gottlieb, Marvin. *Getting Things Done in Today's Organizations: The Influencing Executive*. Westport, CT: Quorum Books, 1999.

Grant, Peter. *Ecology and Evolution of Darwin's Finches*. Princeton, NJ: Princeton University Press, 1986.

Hemphill, Barbara. *Taming the Paper Tiger*. Washington, DC: Kiplinger Books, 1998.

Huxley, Aldous. *Brave New World*. Garden City, NY: Doubleday, 1932.

Kolberg, Judith. *Conquering Chronic Disorganization*. Decatur, GA: Squall Press, 1999.

Kouzes, James M., et al. The *Leadership Challenge: How to Keep Getting Extraordinary Things Done in Organizations*. San Francisco: Jossey-Bass, 1996.

Labovitz, George, and Victor Rosansky. *The Power of Alignment: How Great Companies Stay Centered and Accomplish Extraordinary Things*. New York: Wiley, 1997.

Lagatree, Kirsten. *Checklists for Life: 104 Lists to Help You Get Organized, Save Time, and Unclutter Your Life*. New York: Random House, 1999.

Laird, D. A. *Technique of Getting Things Done*. New York: McGraw-Hill, 2000.

Lakein, Allen. *How to Take Control of Your Time and Your Life*. New York: Wyden, 1973.

Lauro, Cathy. *The Inside Advantage: How Ordinary People Can Accomplish Extraordinary Things*. Corte Madera, CA: Select Press, 1999.

LeBoeuf, Michael. *Working Smart: How to Accomplish More in Half the Time*. New York: Warner Books, 1988.

Levasseur, Robert. *Breakthrough Business Meetings*. Avon, MA: Adams Media, 1992.

Lieberman, David. *Get Anyone To Do Anything and Never Feel Powerless Again*. New York: St. Martin's Griffin, 2001.

Maxwell, John. *Thinking for a Change: 11 Ways Highly Successful People Approach Life and Work*. New York: Time Warner, 2003.

McCormack, Mark. *Staying Street Smart in the Internet Age*. New York: Viking, 2000.

McEwen, Bruce. *The End of Stress as We Know It*. Washington, DC: Joseph Henry Press, 2002.

McKinnon, Wayne. *The Complete Guide to E-mail*. Ontario, CN: Ryshell Books, 1998.

Merrill, Rebecca. *Living in Yes: Helping Smart People Make Good Decisions*. Philadelphia: Xlibris, 2004.

Pascale, Richard, Mark Millemann, and Linda Gioja. *Surfacing the Edge of Chaos*. New York: Three Rivers Press, 2001.

Paulson, Terry, Dr. *They Shoot Managers, Don't They?* Berkley: Ten Speed Press, 1991.

Pound, Ezra. *Confucius, The Great Digest and Unwobbling Pivot*. New York: New Directions, 1951.

Posner, Gerald. *Case Closed*. New York: Random House, 1993.

Radde, Paul. *Thrival. Superior, CO: Thrival Systems*, 2003.

Rosen, Larry, and Michelle Weil. Technostress. New York: Wiley, 1997.

Schlenger, Sunny. *How to Be Organized in Spite of Yourself: Time and Space Management That Works With Your Personal Style*. New York: New American Library, 1999.

Scholtes, Peter. *The Leader's Handbook: Making Things Happen, Getting Things Done*. New York: McGraw-Hill, 1998.

Siegel, Bernie. *Love Medicine and Miracles*. New York: Quill, 1990.

Snead, Lynne, and Joyce Wycoff. *To Do Doing Done*. New York: Fireside, 1997.

Sugarman, Joe. *Success Forces*. Chicago: Contemporary Books, 1987.

Toffler, Alvin. *Powershift*. New York: Bantam, 1991.

Waddill, Kathy. *The Organizing Sourcebook: Nine Strategies for Simplifying Your Life*. New York: McGraw-Hill, 2001.

Yanagi, Soetsu. *The Unknown Craftsman*. New York: Kodansha International, 1972.

Useful Directories

National Trade and Professional Associations. Washington, DC: Columbia Books, 2006.

Oxbridge Directory of Newsletters. New York: Oxbridge Communications, 2006.

State and Regional Associations. Washington, DC: Columbia Books, 2006.

Index

Check Out These
Best-Sellers

Read by millions!

Grammar and Style
SECOND EDITION

- Easy-to-understand instructions on writing and speaking
- Perfect punctuation, from the apostrophe to the semi-colon
- Rights and wrongs of sentence structure, word usage, spelling, and much, much more

Laurie E. Rozakis, Ph.D.

1-59257-115-8 • $16.95

Buying and Selling a Home
FOURTH EDITION

- What to expect when you buy or sell a home—with or without a broker
- Updated coverage of financing options for buyers, including mortgages and refinancing
- Idiot-proof tips on getting the best possible price when you sell

Shelley O'Hara and Nancy D. Lewis

1-59257-120-4 • $18.95

Being a Groom
SECOND EDITION

- Top 10 things to remember on the big day
- Brand-new ideas on hot honeymoon destinations
- Idiot-proof advice on breaking the ice between the in-laws

Jennifer Lata Rung and Mark Rung

0-02-864456-5 • $9.95

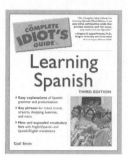

Learning Spanish
THIRD EDITION

- Easy explanations of Spanish grammar and pronunciation
- Key phrases for travel, hotels, airports, shopping, business, and more
- New and expanded vocabulary lists with English/Spanish and Spanish/English translations

Gail Stein

0-02-864451-4 • $18.95

Personal Finance in Your 20s & 30s
SECOND EDITION

- Savvy advice on getting and staying out of debt
- Idiot-proof tips on saving money for the future and still having money to spend
- Down-to-earth advice on making wise investments—especially when you're on a budget

Sarah Young Fisher and Susan Shelly

0-02-864374-7 • $19.95

Organizing Your Life
FOURTH EDITION

- Tips and tricks to getting your house in order—one room at a time
- Filing strategies to help you keep on top of everyday paperwork
- Helpful ideas for getting your kids' stuff organized—and how to get them into the habit

Georgene Lockwood

1-59257-413-0 • $16.95

Total Nutrition
FOURTH EDITION

- Food group fundamentals from the dairy, fruit, vegetable, and grain worlds
- Essential information on the good, bad, and ugly of fats, cholesterol, proteins, and carbs
- Healthy advice for people with diabetes, allergies, cancer, and other conditions

Joy Bauer, M.S., R.D., C.D.N.

1-59257-439-4 • $18.95

Positive Dog Training

- Fascinating insights into how dogs learn and communicate
- Proven pointers for training without punishment
- Expert tips for incorporating training into your daily routine

Pamela Dennison

0-02-864463-8 • $14.95

The Bible
THIRD EDITION

- Timeless stories from Genesis to Revelation and all the wondrous tales in between
- Words of wisdom from Jesus Christ's teachings and the epistles of the Apostles
- Illuminating insights into kings and prophets like David, Solomon, Moses, and Isaiah

James Stuart Bell and Stan Campbell

1-59257-389-4 • $18.95

Calculus

- Descriptive concepts that simplify the most intimidating of math subjects
- Idiot-proof solutions to difficult and confusing equations
- Practice examples that will really help you understand the problems and their solutions

W. Michael Kelley

0-02-864365-8 • $18.95

Music Theory
SECOND EDITION

- Essential information on reading and writing music—including basic notes, rhythms, and scales
- Helpful hints in valuing your own melodies, chords, and harmonies
- Aural exercises to develop your ear training skills

Michael Miller

1-59257-437-8 • $19.95

The Perfect Resume
THIRD EDITION

- Winning resume techniques that will convince an employer to call you for an interview
- Expert advice on solving tricky resume issues such as layoffs, employment gaps, and career changes
- More than 100 up-to-date samples of successful resumes and cover letters

Susan Ireland

0-02-864440-9 • $14.95

Playing the Guitar
SECOND EDITION

- Tips and tricks to get you playing your own tunes in no time
- Easy-to-follow steps for learning to read music
- Words of wisdom from a professional musician and instructor

Frederick Noad

0-02-864244-9 • $21.95

1-59257-335-5 • $19.95

Knitting and Crocheting
SECOND EDITION
Illustrated

- An all-new selection of easy-to-follow patterns with step-by-step lines and instructions
- Crafty tips on choosing the right yarn for your project
- Simple advice for going beyond the basics to create more advanced projects

Barbara Breiter and Gail Diven

1-59257-089-5 • $16.95

More than *450 titles* available at booksellers and online retailers everywhere

www.idiotsguides.com

ALPHA